Understanding the Written Translanguaging Practices of Emergent Bilinguals

Detailing qualitative research undertaken with elementary-grade children in a Korean heritage language school in the U.S., this text provides unique insight into the translanguaging practices and preferences of young, emergent bilinguals in a minority language group.

Understanding the Oral and Written Translanguaging Practices of Emergent Bilinguals examines the role of sociocultural influences on emergent bilinguals' language use and development. Particular attention is paid to the role of immigrant parental involvement and engagement in their bilingual children's language learning and academic performance. Presenting data from classroom audio-recordings, writing, and drawing samples, as well as semi-structured interviews with children and parents, this book identifies important implications for the education of emergent bilinguals to better support their overall language and literacy development.

This text will primarily be of interest to doctoral students, researchers, and scholars with an interest in bilingual education, biliteracy, and early literacy development more broadly. Those interested in applied linguistics, the Korean language, and multicultural education will also benefit from this volume.

Chaehyun Lee is assistant professor of educational instruction and leadership at Southeastern Oklahoma State University, U.S.

Routledge Research in Language Education

The *Routledge Research in Language Education* series provides a platform for established and emerging scholars to present their latest research and discuss key issues in language education. This series welcomes books on all areas of language teaching and learning, including but not limited to language education policy and politics, multilingualism, literacy, L1, L2 or foreign language acquisition, curriculum, classroom practice, pedagogy, teaching materials, and language teacher education and development. Books in the series are not limited to the discussion of the teaching and learning of English only.

Books in the series include:

TESOL Teacher Education in a Transnational World
Turning Challenges into Innovative Prospects
Edited by Osman (Othman) Barnawi and Sardar Anwaruddin

Communicating Strategically in English as a Lingua Franca
A Corpus Driven Investigation
Janin Jafari

Dual Language Education in the US
Rethinking Pedagogy, Curricula, and Teacher Education to Support
Dual Language Learning for All
Edited by Pablo C. Ramírez and Christian J. Faltis

The Influence of the Foreign Service Institute on US Language Education
Critical Analysis of Historical Documentation
Theresa Ulrich

Understanding the Oral and Written Translanguaging Practices of Emergent Bilinguals
Insights from Korean Heritage Language Classrooms in the US
Chaehyun Lee

For more information about the series, please visit www.routledge.com/ Routledge-Research-in-Language-Education/book-series/RRLE

Understanding the Oral and Written Translanguaging Practices of Emergent Bilinguals

Insights from Korean Heritage Language Classrooms in the US

Chaehyun Lee

Routledge
Taylor & Francis Group

NEW YORK AND LONDON

First published 2021
by Routledge
52 Vanderbilt Avenue, New York, NY 10017

and by Routledge
2 Park Square, Milton Park, Abingdon, Oxon, OX14 4RN

*Routledge is an imprint of the Taylor & Francis Group, an
informa business*

© 2021 Chaehyun Lee

Library of Congress Cataloging-in-Publication Data
Names: Lee, Chaehyun, author.
Title: Understanding the oral and written translanguaging
practices of emergent bilinguals : insights from Korean heritage
language classrooms in the US / Chaehyun Lee.
Description: New York, NY : Routledge, 2021. | Includes
bibliographical references and index.
Identifiers: LCCN 2020042192 | ISBN 9780367555092
(hardback) | ISBN 9781003093824 (ebook)
Subjects: LCSH: Korean language--Study and teaching
(Elementary)--United States. | Heritage language speakers--
Education--United States. | Education, Bilingual--United States. |
Bilingualism--United States.
Classification: LCC PL907.5.U6 L44 2021 |
DDC 495.7/071073--dc23
LC record available at https://lccn.loc.gov/2020042192

ISBN: 978-0-367-55509-2 (hbk)
ISBN: 978-0-367-55510-8 (pbk)
ISBN: 978-1-003-09382-4 (ebk)

Typeset in Sabon
by MPS Limited, Dehradun

*For all educators who inspire hope and instill
a love of learning to our bilingual children*

Contents

Figures

Tables

About the Author

Chaehyun Lee is assistant professor in elementary and ESL/bilingual education in educational instruction and leadership at Southeastern Oklahoma State University. She earned her doctorate in curriculum and instruction with a focus on bilingual education from the University of Illinois, Urbana-Champaign. She also works with emergent bilingual students as a Korean heritage language teacher at a local Korean heritage language school. Her research interests include bilingualism, biliteracy development, heritage language learning, multicultural education, and teacher education. Her current research examines the early bilingual and biliteracy development of English and Korean speakers in heritage language schools and the effects of curricular reform toward culturally and linguistically diverse students. Her research appears in the *Bilingual Research Journal, International Journal of Elementary Education,* and *Journal of Bilingual Education Research and Instruction.*

Acknowledgments

This monograph is based on my doctoral dissertation entitled "Korean Emergent Bilingual Students' Language Use and Translanguaging," which was conducted in a Korean heritage language school. Foremost, I would like to express my sincere gratitude to my advisor, Dr. Georgia E. García, for her caring, motivation, immense knowledge, and the continuous support of my Ph.D. study and research. Her guidance helped me through all the time of research and writing of my doctoral dissertation. I appreciate all of her contributions of time and support to make my research experience productive and stimulating. Her research was inspiring and motivational for me, even during tough times in my Ph.D. pursuit. I could not have imagined having a better advisor and a life mentor.

Besides my advisor, I would like to thank the rest of my dissertation committee. Dr. Eurydice B. Bauer continues to guide my research in the bilingual/biliteracy field, and her passion for bilingual education encourages me to be a better bilingual educator and researcher. I thank Sarah J. McCarthey for her academic support and her guidance to my work in qualitative research and writing instruction development. I thank Dr. Liv T. Dávila, whose research has contributed to global perspectives on immigration and education for multilingual learners. I thank my entire committee for their encouragement, insightful comments, and thoughtful guidance. Without them, this book would not have come to fruition.

I also would like to thank the Korean language school faculty (school principal and the third-grade teacher, Mrs. Joen) who have assisted me in this classroom research. I highly appreciate Mrs. Joen who allowed me entrance in her classroom and supported my work continuously. My sincere appreciation goes to the first- and third-grade students at the school who agreed to participate in this study. The students taught me the joy of language, the passion of learning, and the sense of their possibilities thanks to my students. I also thank the parents of the students for their participation and genuine commitments for the interviews and journal reports for this work.

My colleagues at Southeastern Oklahoma State University provided much-appreciated encouragement and genuine support. I warmly thank early childhood and elementary teacher educators in our team, Dr. Susan Morrison, Dr. Marybeth Notthingham, Dr. Barbara McClanahan, and the most encouraging department chair, Dr. Stewart Mayers, among others at Southeastern.

Nobody has been more important to me in the pursuit of this journey than the members of my family. I would like to thank my parents, whose love and guidance are with me in whatever I pursue. I would also like to thank my younger brother, who was always supporting and encouraging me with his best wishes. I would never have been able to complete this book without the support of my family.

Preface

This book is written with emergent bilingual students—children who know one language at home (heritage language) and who are acquiring English (societal language) at school (García, Kleifgen, & Falchi, 2008)—particularly in elementary grades. As there has been an increasing number of immigrant families in the U.S., research on curriculum and instruction for bilingual children from immigrant families has been investigated. However, the majority of studies have paid attention to the Spanish-English bilingual group and conducted their language use and literacy practices in dual-language programs, where academic instructions are provided in both languages. Given this consideration, this book is written to explore other language minority groups, especially those who learn non-related ancestral languages, such as Korean and English, in the heritage language (HL) classroom settings, where the language of instruction is in the target language only.

The book examines first- and third-grade Korean-English emergent bilingual students to discover their oral and written language use in the classrooms when they are allowed to utilize their full language repertoires (i.e., Korean, English, and incorporating both languages, which is known as "translanguaging"). The term "translanguaging" is an emerging theory/paradigm which describes bilingual speakers' strategy when they utilize their full language resources from their two languages, enabling them to access their *integrated* and *entire* language repertoires (Garcia, 2014). One might ask how the translanguaging practices can be activated if the instruction is delivered in the target language exclusively in the HL classroom where monoglossic language ideology is pervasive. The present book illustrates how the emergent bilingual students were able to use their entire language repertoires through translanguaging to successfully participate in verbal interactions and writing tasks within a monoglossic classroom context. The book further provides longitudinal findings for the focal third-graders' language use over the years by examining the role of sociocultural influences on their language use and development. The book also integrates parental views on their children's language education to provide insights on immigrant parents' engagement in their bilingual children's dual-language and biliteracy learning.

The purposes of this book are to add to what is known about the role of bilingual students' heritage language in their bilingual development and performance, to acknowledge the value of translanguaging in HL classroom contexts, and to extend our understanding of immigrant parents' vital roles in their children's establishment of bilingualism. Since the book specifically focuses on Korean-English emergent bilingual group, the findings of the study would fill the gaps in the bilingual/biliteracy literature, which primarily has paid attention to Spanish-English bilinguals' language use and development. The overall findings provide insights on Korean bilingual students' translanguaging practices including longitudinal language learning trajectory, which are integrated with the parents' views and practices towards their children's development of bilingualism. Hence, the book provides directions for future research and implications for scholars and researchers in the fields of bilingual/biliteracy education, early childhood and elementary literacy, and multicultural education. The findings further provide teaching implications for educators and parents of emergent bilingual learners to better support their language and literacy learning and development.

References

García, O. (2014). What is translanguaging? Expanded questions and answers for U.S. educators. In S. Hesson, K. Seltzer, & H. H. Woodley (Eds.), *Translanguaging in curriculum and instruction: A CUNY-NYSIEB guide for educators* (pp. 1–13). New York, NY: CUNY-NYSIEB.

García, O., Kleifgen, J. A., & Falchi, L. (2008). *From English language learners to emergent bilinguals* (Equity Matters: Research Review No. 1). New York, NY: Teachers College, Columbia University.

1 Introduction

Introduction to the chapter

This chapter addresses the rationale of bilingual education and research by providing an overview of the past to current research on emergent bilingual learners' language use and development. Since the book focuses on Korean-American bilingual students' language use and literacy performance, the chapter describes the historical backgrounds of Korean immigration and Korean immigrant parents' beliefs on their children's bilingual education. The chapter illustrates the phenomenon of heritage language (HL) attrition among children of immigrant families in the U.S. to understand its impact on bilingual education. Then, the chapter discusses the merits of HL learning and immigrant parents' practices and involvement in their children's HL development. By introducing a heteroglossic perspective moving away from monoglossic perspective, the chapter discusses a new research paradigm that García (2009) conceptualized with the term "translanguaging," which describes bilingual learners' strategy to utilize their *integrated* and *entire* language repertoires. The chapter ends with the aim of the current study in this book that connects the link between the studies on early bilingualism and HL education to recognize and value the sustainability of bilingual students' HL for their bilingual development.

Overview of past research on emergent bilingual students in the U.S.

In the past, researchers interested in the language development and use of emergent bilingual children in the U.S.—children who know one language at home (heritage language) and who are acquiring English (societal language) at school (García, Kleifgen, & Falchi, 2008)—paid attention to the language development of young bilingual children from a monoglossic perspective (Creese & Blackledge, 2010; Wei, 2011), in which bilinguals were viewed as developing competence in two *separate* languages since "[they] are expected to be and do with each of their languages the same thing as monolinguals" (García, 2011, p. 189). From this monoglossic point of view, researchers and educators studied bilingual learners' language uses by considering their two languages as separate rather than continuous notions (Cook, 2001; Martin-Beltran, 2010). As a result, researchers who investigated emergent bilingual children's language use often analyzed their use of each language independently of each other.

In addition, studies in bilingual and biliteracy education have focused more on the bilingual children's development and use of their second language (L2, English) than on their first language (L1) or heritage language (HL) (August & Shanahan, 2010; Goldenberg, 2011; Shanahan & Beck, 2006). For example, a number of researchers investigated how emergent bilinguals developed their English language and literacy skills (e.g., Francis, Lesaux, & August, 2006; Golberg, Paradis, & Crago, 2008; Hinton, 2015; Rodriguez-Mojica, 2017; Yang, Fox, & Jacewicz, 2015). Yet, comparatively, little attention has been given to emergent bilinguals' language and literacy development in their HLs (August & Shanahan, 2010; Goldenberg, 2011; Seals & Peyton, 2017; Szilagyi & Szecsi, 2020).

Several researchers reported that when emergent bilingual children attended U.S. schools where the instruction was delivered in English only, the children often lost or did not continue to develop their HL (Hinton, 2008; Montrul, 2018; Polinsky, 2011, 2018; Ro & Cheatham, 2009; Shin, 2005; Tse, 2001). Other researchers reported that language shift or "the replacement of one language by another as the primary means of communication and socialization within a community" (Mesthrie, Swann, Deumert, & Leap, 2001, p. 253) had largely occurred with Latinx students (Beaudrie, Ducar, & Potowski, 2014; Gandara & Hopkins, 2010; Potowski, 2016; Suarez-Orozco, Suarez-Orozco, & Todorova, 2008) as well as Korean immigrant children in the U.S. (Chung, 2008; Lee & Wright, 2014; Shin & Lee, 2013).

Understanding the phenomenon of HL attrition in the U.S.

According to Montrul (2008, 2010), HL loss occurs when an individual's primary language shifts to a new language or second language (L2) when the individual lives in an L2 environment as a result of immigration (Tse, 1998, 2001; Veltman, 1983). Schmid (2010) pointed out that immigrant children are susceptible to losing the knowledge of their HLs if they have not fully mastered their HLs before being exposed to a new language. Most young immigrant children in the U.S. are identified as potential linguistic emigrants (Veltman, 1983), who could lose their HLs when they are surrounded by the English language rather than their HLs. Several researchers pointed out that when immigrant children want to be accepted into the mainstream culture (Murphy, 2014), they are more likely to engage in English practices, which consequently leads them to experience language shift from HL to English and/or language loss in their HLs (Polinsky, 2018; Polinsky & Kagan, 2007; Shin & Krashen, 1996; Valdés, 2005).

It is important to note that language shift and loss are related to power relations between two languages. When people immigrate to a new country, the language that is used in the country is regarded as a dominant language, which has privilege and supremacy, and the immigrants' HLs are often regarded as minority and less privileged languages (Schmid, 2010; Veltman, 1983). For this reason, some immigrants want to assimilate into the majority culture by actively participating in the majority language group using the majority language only (Shin, 2005). Veltman (1983) explained this phenomenon as linguistic emigration. It applies to language minority groups who immigrate to a country where the majority language is considered a high prestige language since they are more likely to assimilate to the majority culture by losing their HLs and ceasing to participate in the communities of origin.

Veltman (1983) considered language minority children in the U.S. as potential linguistic emigrants who have the potential to lose their HLs. Many of them are not only massively expose to and frequently use the societal language (English in the U.S.) but also want to be accepted into the mainstream culture to avoid alienation (Murphy, 2014; Tse, 2001). These practices are likely to lead them to shift their dominant language from HL to English and eventually experience HL attrition or loss (Polinsky, 2011; Valdés, 2001, 2005). Researchers reported that language minority students in the U.S. often undergo a language shift by mainly interacting with interlocutors of the majority language (English), which results in them failing to gain native-like proficiency in their HLs (Carreira & Kagan, 2017; Seals & Peyton, 2017; Murphy, 2014).

The context and reasons of HL loss among Korean immigrants

Since the Immigration Act of 1965, the number of Korean immigrants to the U.S. has grown rapidly; throughout the 1980s, approximately 1 million Korean immigrants resided in the U.S., and the number has continued to increase (U.S. Census Bureau, 2018). Korean immigrant parents often decline bilingual education services (Becker, 2013; Shin, 2005). Many of them believe that their children's Korean literacy skills have little direct relevance to their U.S. school performance, while the mastery of English directly impacts their children's success in school (Hinton, 2008; Lee, 2013; Shin, 2014). The parents' desire for their children to have educational success and prestigious careers in the future leads them to immerse their children in English-only instruction (Kim & Pyun, 2014; Shin, 2014; Tse, 2001).

In an earlier study, López (1996) reported that among Asian ethnic groups in the U.S., Koreans were less likely to maintain their HL at home than other Asian ethnic groups. Indeed, Shin's (2005) study that involved 251 Korean teenagers (either U.S. born or immigrated to the U.S. at young ages) found that the majority of them experienced HL shift and/or loss as they developed English by attending all-English classrooms in the U.S. Shin pointed out that "the most common outcome for Korean immigrant children in America is not bilingualism but monolingualism in English" (p. 51). Murphy (2014) correspondingly reported that Korean children's HL loss is a natural process among Korean immigrants in the U.S. because of the exposure to the English language in American schools and in the mainstream culture.

Several researchers reported the reasons for immigrant children's HL loss. One of the reasons is that many immigrant parents in the U.S. often assumed that teaching a language other than English would hinder their children's English learning and school success (McCabe, 2016; Shin, 2014; Shin & Krashen, 1996; Tse, 2001). This false assumption has resulted in the immigrant parents discouraging their children from speaking their HLs. As research has revealed, many immigrant parents often show more interest in developing their children's English proficiency than HL learning because HL development does not directly influence on their children's school performance, whereas the mastery of English is seen to exert immediate influence on their children's success in school (Caldas, 2012; Hinton, 2008; Lee, 2013; Shin, 2014; McCabe, 2016). Hence, immigrant parents' desire for their children to have educational success and prestigious careers would lead them to allow their children to speak only in English (Becker, 2013). However, a substantial amount of research revealed that children's HL use and learning did not hinder their English acquisition. Instead, children who used their HLs at home and who were supported in HL development by their parents showed success in their academic performance at school because HL attainment largely impacted their establishment of bilingualism (Fogle, 2013; Kwon, 2017; Li, 2006; Lü & Koda, 2011; Nesteruk, 2010).

Another reason for immigrant children's HL loss is that many U.S. schools do not provide sufficient instruction in language minority children's HLs. The most common type of bilingual education is a transitional early-exit bilingual program where the students' L1 is only viewed as a bridge to learning English (Baker, 2011; Crawford, 2004). Thus, instruction in L1 is minimized and eliminated when the students gain proficiency in English. Another type of bilingual education in the U.S., dual-language program, is designed to develop language minority children's L1 (HL) and L2 (English). However, according to Kondo-Brown (2011), there are not enough dual-language programs in East Asian languages in U.S. public schools; thus, school-aged children from immigrant families have to learn their HLs at community-based HL schools on the weekends only. Kondo-Brown claimed that because of the strong emphasis on English-only instruction in K–12 schools in the U.S., "the role of non-formal HL schools has become even more critical in HL maintenance" (p. 7).

Another considerable reason for HL loss might be that emergent bilingual children have negative attitudes toward using their HLs due to their limited oral proficiency. For instance, studies have found that second-generation Korean-American children's limited Korean proficiency made them feel difficult to communicate with their family members and eventually led them to use it reluctantly (e.g., Becker, 2013; Park & Kondo-Brown, 2006). This "vicious cycle" (Krashen, 1998, p. 41) that immigrant children often encounter is one of the reasons why Korean children eventually are more likely to lose their HL.

Peer influence is another factor that can impact children's HL loss (Tse, 2001). Some young immigrant children have a strong desire to belong to a dominant language group and fit into their peer group, which eventually leads them to willingly lose their HLs (Ro & Cheatham, 2009). On the other hand, if children belong to a peer group that uses and values their HLs, they are more likely to improve their HL proficiency due to the interaction with peers (Cho, 2015; Oh & Fuligni, 2010). Thus, the existence of one's peer group can possibly determine children's HL maintenance or loss. In addition, research has found that interaction with siblings can impact children's HL development and/or loss (Fogle, 2013; Shin, 2014). Because later-born children are exposed to the societal language (English) at an earlier age than first-born children, they are more likely to be *at-risk bilinguals* (Tabors, 2008). Indeed, it has been shown that first-born immigrant children tend to use more HL with their parents at home or other HL speakers compared to second- and later-born children (Lee, 2013; Shin & Lee, 2013).

The merits of heritage language learning

Although many immigrant children in the U.S. tend to experience the challenge of preserving their HL as they develop English (Lynch, 2014; Polinsky, 2011, 2018), language minority groups have emphasized the significance and value of HL learning (Budiyana, 2017; Cho, 2000; Guardado & Becker, 2015; Keh & Stoessel, 2017; King & Fogle, 2006; Nesteruk, 2010). For example, in an earlier study, Cho (2000) conducted in-depth interviews and research questionnaires with 116 Korean-American adolescents and young adults (mean age: 21) to explore the role of HL learning in their social interactions and relationships with other second-generation Korean Americans. The participants in Cho's study reported that their HL learning had played an essential role in their personal achievement, social interaction, and bicultural development. With this finding, Cho argued that encouraging students to develop their

HL is an *additive* form of bilingualism (Cummins, 1991) because the HL is added in their language repertoires without negatively impacting their English learning, and the two languages positively impact the students' bilingual and bicultural knowledge (p. 383).

Researchers reported that when emergent bilinguals maintained their HLs, many cognitive, metalinguistic, social, and cultural advantages occurred. For example, in terms of cognitive benefit, emergent bilinguals often used what they learned in their HLs to approach the same topic in their L2 (Dressler & Kamil, 2006; Lü & Koda, 2011; Siu & Ho, 2015). In terms of metalinguistic advantage, bilinguals are more likely to reflect upon their language use and manipulate their own language-processing skills than their monolingual counterparts (Bialystok, 1991, 2018). Regarding social and cultural advantages, researchers found that emergent bilingual children who developed their HLs were more likely to have positive interactions and social relationships with their family members and other HL speakers (Kwon, 2017; Li, 2006; Park & Kondo-Brown, 2006; Song, 2016) as well as a strong sense of their ethnic identity and cultural values (Chinen & Tucker, 2005; Lee, 2013; Oh & Fuligni, 2010; Sayer, 2013; You, 2005). Moreover, HL development has been shown to contribute to children's biliteracy learning (Ro & Cheatham, 2009; Kim & Pyun, 2014; Song, 2016). For instance, it has been demonstrated that Latinx bilingual children who learned to read both in Spanish and English outperformed those who only learned to read in English (Francis *et al.* 2006; Genesee, Geva, Dressler, & Kamil, 2006; Proctor, August, Snow, & Barr, 2010). Despite the benefits of HL learning, little is known about how emergent bilingual children develop their language proficiency and literacy skills in their HLs to become balanced bilingual. Therefore, we need to know more about the role of the children's HL in their bilingual development and performance.

Immigrant parents' practices and involvement in their children's HL development

Since HL education is given less attention and support outside the home than the societal language (English in the U.S.), immigrant parents' role prominently plays a pivotal role in their children's HL learning and development in the home context. A number of researchers reported that immigrant parents' practices and involvement were the most significant factor in sustaining their children's HL and that parents' support was a critical element in the children's HL development (Guardado, 2010; Kwon, 2017; Lee & Jeong, 2013; Liang, 2018; Lü & Koda, 2011; McCabe, 2016). For example, in their quantitative literacy assessment studies with 37 first- and second-grade Chinese-English bilingual children, Lü and Koda (2011) showed that Chinese immigrant parents' HL use and literacy support at home influenced their children's language and literacy skills in Chinese (i.e., oral vocabulary knowledge, phonological awareness, and decoding skill). Similarly, Guardado (2010) in his case study involving Hispanic families in Canada revealed the importance of parental involvement and encouragement of their children's HL development by showing that immigrant children who were able to sustain their HL had received positive support from their parents to advance their HL. The studies discovered that the parents' home literacy practices facilitated the children's HL development in the long term.

Other studies showed that parents' attitudes toward HL learning and their language choices at home greatly influenced their children's HL outcomes (Budiyana, 2017; Cha & Goldenberg, 2015; Shin, 2005; You, 2005). For instance, You's (2005) study involved 3rd- to 8th-grade Korean HL learners to investigate the relationship between parents' attitudes toward and use of HL at home and their children's HL learning. His study included one particular student whose father was a Vietnamese-American but seldom spoke Vietnamese to his child but whose mother from Korea often spoke Korean and had positive attitudes toward teaching HL to her child. The findings showed that the transnational child presented more positive attitudes toward learning Korean than Vietnamese. This implies that immigrant parents' attitudes toward HL and their actual use of HL to their children play a pivotal role in children's positive attitudes toward maintaining HL.

Likewise, Cha and Goldenberg's (2015) study, including 1,400 parents of Spanish-speaking kindergartners, showed that the parents who maintained high levels of Spanish at home promoted additive bilingualism for their children, whereas the parents who used high levels of English at home resulted in their children's language shift from HL to English. The findings corroborate Wong-Fillmore's (1991) earlier argument that there was a negative influence of English-only practices at home on language minority groups' use of HL. As previous research showed, young immigrant children were more likely to be vulnerable in the sense of losing their HLs, depending on the parents' language choice at home (Hinton, 2008; King & Fogle, 2006; Lee, 2013).

Multiple studies showed how "family language policy (FLP)" that forces the use of HL exclusively at home (Spolsky, 2012) played an instrumental role in children's HL learning and development in immigrant households (e.g., Caldas, 2012; Fogle & King, 2013; Guardado & Becker, 2015; Hua & Wei, 2016; Yazan & Ali, 2018). For example, in a study with an Arabic-speaking Muslim family, Yazan and Ali (2018) showed that the parents' language ideologies and policy regarding their daughter's maintenance of Arabic in the U.S. influenced the emergence and enactment of the daughter's Arabic HL development. The major findings in the above FLP studies indicate that the exclusive and consistent use of HLs by immigrant families encouraged the children to not only practice their HLs but also construct their cultural identity (Guardado & Becker, 2015; Oh

& Fuligni, 2010; Oriyama, 2010; Park & Sarkar, 2007) since heritage language-only rules at home are "tied to the families' and individuals' sense of belonging" (Hua & Wei, 2016, p. 65). It has been found that for immigrant parents, their children's HL learning is fundamental for sustaining communication with family members and maintaining strong relationships in the family (Kheirkhah & Cekaite, 2015; Melo-Pfeifer, 2015; Nesteruk, 2010; Park & Sarkar, 2007). Many immigrant parents from past studies considered HL development as a way to build family relationships and communication and preserve their cultural identity.

Although maintaining HL is exclusively regarded as immigrant parents' responsibility, other researchers further pointed out the important role of other family members in children's HL learning (Melo-Pfeifer, 2015; Park & Sarkar, 2007). For example, Park and Sarkar showed that intensive communication between Korean children in the U.S. and their relatives in Korea avoided the children's HL shift or loss because the ongoing communication with their relatives eventually assisted the children to develop their HL proficiency. In qualitative discourse analysis, Melo-Pfeifer highlighted the important role of other family members beyond that of the parents in children's HL learning. Melo-Pfeifer found that grandparents played a critical role in children's HL maintenance because "grandparents are considered the linguistic roots and the connection with the past more than the parents" (p. 28). As shown, several researchers discovered that immigrant families across various ethnic groups of origin can support their children's HL learning and ethnic identity formation in the long term.

A considerable number of studies explored the issue of HL maintenance or loss among immigrant families from the different ethnic origins. The previous studies suggested that family context including parents' attitudes, perceptions, and home practices played an instrumental role in their children's HL maintenance and fundamentally influenced the HL outcomes for their children (Liang, 2018). The findings indicate that immigrant parents should provide adequate support for their children to develop their HL in the home setting to raise them as bilingual and biliterate. Scholars additionally revealed that many immigrant parents viewed HL maintenance as a vehicle for building affirmative parent–child relationships (Fogle, 2013; Kheirkhah & Cekaite, 2015; Hua & Wei, 2016) and preserving their ethnic/cultural identity (Farruggio, 2010; Guardado, 2010; Oriyama, 2010).

Bilingual students' language and literacy development from a monoglossic perspective

The majority of past research on emergent bilingual students' language and literacy development was conducted from a monoglossic perspective by examining their use of code-switching (CS) and code-mixing behaviors. Code-switching and code-mixing are defined as the discourse between speakers who share the same languages (Cook, 2001). Code-switching is one example of translanguaging, which refers to "the mixing of words, phrases, and sentences from two distinct grammatical (sub-) systems across sentence boundaries within the same speech event" (Bokamba, 1989, p. 278). Code-mixing is another example of trans-languaging, which refers to "the embedding of various linguistic units such as affixes (bound morphemes), words (unbound morphemes), phrases and clauses from two distinct grammatical (sub-) systems within the same sentence" (Bokamba, 1989, p. 278). Hence, the practice of alternating between languages is defined as code-switching when it occurs at an intersentential level (between sentences) and as code-mixing (CM) when it occurs at an intrasentential level (within a sentence) (Genesee, Nicoladis, & Paradis, 1995; Vihman, 1998).

In the past, scholars in bilingual education insisted that young bilingual learners' languages should be kept separate in learning (August & Hakuta, 1998; Wong-Fillmore, 1991), and the mixing of languages should not be allowed in the classroom setting (Lindholm-Leary, 2001). Hence, bilingual children's use of CS and CM was regarded as their lack of linguistic competence in either language (Bernardini & Schlyter, 2004; Vihman, 1998), and their use of the two languages was viewed negatively and considered as deficient behaviors (Gravelle, 1996; Swain, 2000). Since much of the previous research on emergent bilingual students' language and literacy development was conducted from a monoglossic perspective, bilingual's use of CS was associated with language isolation and disruption of monolingual language use (García, Johnson, & Seltzer, 2017). In addition, researchers in the past tended to consider bilingual students' HL as a mere vehicle to learn English (school language) (e.g., Bernardini & Schlyter, 2004; Reyes, 2004; Vihman, 1998).

However, a considerable number of researchers (i.e., Genesee, 2008; Gort, 2008; Reyes, 2004) refuted the previous researchers' argument that children's CS/CM was due to their lack of lexical items and an indicator of language attrition or loss of proficiency. Rather, the researchers provided evidence that bilingual children switched their languages when they had different purposes of using each of their languages in different settings. Therefore, CS and CM behaviors were considered as bilinguals' intentional acts since they consciously chose their languages according to different interlocutors and contexts (Gort, 2012; Park-Johnson, 2017). The findings from later studies demonstrated that young bilinguals' use of CS/CM was their unique communicative strategy to extend their communicative competence. In other words, the later studies contradicted the previous hypotheses that CS and CM occur because of young bilinguals' inability to differentiate their two languages or their lack of linguistic competence in either or both languages. Rather, the findings from later CS and CM studies demonstrated that young bilinguals' use of CS/CM was systematic and purposeful rather than random performance (Genesee, 2008; Gort, 2012; Park-Johnson, 2017).

Moving from monoglossic to heteroglossic perspectives

Although CS was regarded as "the most distinctive behaviour of the bilingual speaker" (Wei & Wu, 2009, p. 193), bilinguals' L1 and L2 were considered as separate rather than one linguistic repertoire (Cook, 2001; Martin-Beltran, 2010). Scholars claimed that the notion of CS is associated with language separation (e.g., García, 2009; Lewis, Jones, & Baker, 2012). In contrast to the monoglossic research on bilinguals' use of CS and/or CM, a heteroglossic paradigm for viewing and conducting research on bilingualism has recently emerged (Canagarajah, 2011a, 2013). According to Bakhtin (1981, 1984), heteroglossia refers to the multiple variations of voices within those languages; thus, it describes all the different ways people speak to one another (Bailey, 2007). Current research on translanguaging from a heteroglossic perspective does not consider languages from their two *separate* registers because heteroglossia explains the existence of multiple language varieties as a unitary system, which avoids seeing languages as separate (Canagarajah, 2011a; Creese & Blackledge, 2010).

The heteroglossic perspective opened up spaces to accept and appreciate multimodal languaging practices (Blackledge & Creese, 2010; Hornberger, 2003) using multiple semiotic modes (e.g., script, voice, music, and image) (Bailey, 2007; Moro, Mortimer, & Tiberghien, 2019). From this heteroglossic perspective, García (2009) conceptualized the term *translanguaging*, which describes bilingual speakers' strategy when they utilize their full language resources from their two languages, enabling them to access their *integrated* and *entire* language repertoires. In other words, translanguaging is viewed as a bilingual strategy, which bilinguals use to communicate and learn, in contrast to a monoglossic view of communication and learning, in which bilinguals use two separate languages (García, 2009; García & Wei, 2014). Researchers who employed a heteroglossic perspective (Bakhtin, 1981; Bailey, 2007) began to study bilingual students' entire language use and literacy development through a translanguaging paradigm, which argues that bilinguals have one integrated language repertoire instead of two separate languages (García, 2014; Lewis et al., 2012). In addition, current research on translanguaging from a heteroglossic perspective does not consider the students' HL as a mere vehicle to learn English; rather, it recognizes and values the sustainability of HL (Bartlett & García, 2011; Cummins & Persad, 2014).

Indeed, recent researchers have made a connection between the studies on early bilingualism and HL learning (Aalberse & Hulk, 2018; Kupisch & Rothman, 2018; Montrul, 2018; Venturin, 2019). Montrul argued that researchers need to connect the link between the two fields of studies by investigating bilingual children's longitudinal language use and development, which can explain what is happening to their HL learning and bilingualism during their school years. Current research on translanguaging from a heteroglossic perspective indeed considers that bilinguals' HL is a linguistic resource accessible to them to extend their communicative competence that eventually leads them to become full-fledged bilinguals in a creative and meaningful way (Baker, 2011; Canagarajah, 2011b; Velasco & García, 2014). As Bartlett and García (2011) argued that translanguaging pedagogy can "sustain home language practices" (p. 4), the present study aims to recognize the value of sustaining and supporting bilingual students' HL while they are developing their bilingualism and biliteracy through translanguaging (Cenoz, 2017; Cummins & Persad, 2014).

References

Aalberse, S., & Hulk, A. (2018). *Introduction to the special issue – Heritage language studies and early child bilingualism research: Understanding the connection. International Journal of Bilingualism*, 22(5), 491–496.

August D., & Hakuta K. (1998). *Educating language-minority children.* Washington: National Research Council, Institute of Medicine, National Academy Press.

August, D., & Shanahan, T. (2010). Response to a review and update on "Developing literacy in second-language learners: Report of the National Literacy Panel on Language Minority Children and Youth." *Journal of Literacy Research*, 42(3), 341–348.

Bailey, B. (2007). Heteroglossia and boundaries. In M. Heller (Ed.), *Bilingualism: A social approach* (pp. 257–276). Basingstoke, UK: Palgrave.

Baker, C. (2011). *Foundations of bilingual education and bilingualism* (5th ed.). Clevedon, England: Multilingual Matters.

Bakhtin, M. M. (1981). *The dialogic imagination: Four essays.* (M. Holquist, Ed.; C. Emerson & M. Holquist, Trans.). Austin, TX: University of Texas Press.

Bakhtin, M. M. (1984). *Problems of Dostoevsky's poetics.* Manchester: Manchester University Press.

Bartlett, L. & García, O. (2011). *Additive schooling in subtractive times: Bilingual education and Dominican immigrant youth in the heights.* Nashville, TX: Vanderbilt University Press.

Beaudrie, S., Ducar, C., & Potowski, K. (2014). *Heritage language teaching: Research and practices.* McGraw-Hill Education Create.

Becker, D. J. (2013). *Parents' attitudes toward their children's heritage language maintenance: The case of Korean immigrant parents in West Michigan.* Master's Thesis. p. 59.

Bernardini, P., & Schlyter, S. (2004). Growing syntactic structure and code-mixing in the weaker language: The Ivy Hypothesis. *Bilingualism: Language and Cognition*, 7(1), 49–69.

Bialystok, E. (1991). Metalinguistic dimensions of bilingual language proficiency. In E. Bialystok (Ed.), *Language processing in bilingual children* (pp. 113–140). London, England: Cambridge University Press.

Bialystok, E. (2018). Bilingual education for young children: review of the effects and consequences. *International Journal of Bilingual Education and bilingualism, 21*(6), 666–679.

Blackledge, A., & Creese, A. (2010). *Multilingualism: A critical perspective.* London, UK: Continuum.

Bokamba, E. G. (1989). Are there syntactic constraints on code-mixing? *World Englishes, 8,* 277–292.

Budiyana, Y. E. (2017). Students' parents' attitude toward Chinese heritage language maintenance. *Theory and Practice in Language Studies, 7*(3), 195–200.

Busch, B. (2012). The linguistic repertoire revisited. *Applied Linguistics 33*(5), 503–523.

Caldas, S. (2012). Language policy in the family. In B. Spolsky (Ed.), *The Cambridge handbook of language policy* (pp. 351–373). Cambridge, UK: Cambridge University Press.

Canagarajah, A. S. (Ed.). (2013). *Literacy as translingual practice: Between communities and schools.* New York, NY: Routledge.

Canagarajah, S. (2011a). Translanguaging in the classroom: Emerging issues for research and pedagogy. *Applied Linguistics Review, 2,* 1–28.

Canagarajah, A. S. (2011b). Codemeshing in academic writing: Identifying teachable strategies of translanguaging. *The Modern Language Journal, 95,* 401–417.

Carreira, M., & Kagan, O. (2017). Heritage language education: A proposal for the next 50 years. *Foreign Language Annals, 51*(1), 152–168.

Cenoz, J. (2017). Translanguaging in school contexts: international perspectives. *Journal of Language, Identity and Education, 16*(4), 193–198.

Cha, K., & Goldenberg, C. (2015). The complex relationship between home language proficiency and kindergarten children's Spanish and English oral proficiencies. *Journal of Educational Psychology, 107*(4), 935–953.

Chinen, K., & Tucker, R. G. (2005). Heritage language development: Understanding the roles of ethnic identity and Saturday school participation. *Heritage Language Journal, 3*(1), 27–-59.

Cho, G. (2000). The role of heritage language in social interactions and relationships: Reflections from a language minority group. *Bilingual Research Journal, 24,* 369–384.

Cho, G. (2015). Perspectives vs. reality of heritage language development: Voices from second-generation Korean-American high school students. *Multicultural Education, 22*(2), 30–38.

Chung, K. (2008). *Korean English fever in the U.S.: Temporary migrant parents' evolving beliefs about normal parenting practices and children's natural language learning.* Unpublished doctoral dissertation, University of Illinois, Urbana-Champaign.

Cook, V. (2001). Using the first language in the classroom. *Canadian Modern Language Review, 57*(3), 402–423.

Crawford, J. (2004). *Educating English learners: Language diversity in the classroom* (Vol. 5). Los Angeles, CA: Bilingual Education Services.

Creese, A., & Blackledge, A. (2010). Translanguaging in the bilingual classroom: A pedagogy for teaching and learning. *The Modern Language Journal, 94*, 103–115.

Cummins, J. (1991). Interdependence of first- and second-language proficiency in bilingual children. In E. Bialystok (Ed.), *Language processing in bilingual children* (pp. 70–89). Cambridge, England: Cambridge University Press.

Cummins, J., & Persad, R. (2014). Teaching through a multilingual lens: The evolution of EAL Policy and Practice in Canada. *Education Matters, 2*, 3–40.

Dressler, C., & Kamil, M. L. (2006). First- and second-language literacy. In D. August & T. Shanahan (Eds.), *Developing literacy in second-language learners: Report of the National Literacy Panel on language-minority children and youth* (pp. 197–238). Mahwah, NJ: Lawrence Erlbaum Associates.

Farruggio (2010). Latino immigrant parents' views of bilingual education as a vehicle for heritage preservation. *Journal of Latinos and Education, 9*(1), 3–21.

Fogle, L. W. (2013). Parental ethnotheories and family language policy in transnational adoptive families. *Language Policy, 12*(1), 83–102.

Fogle, L. W., & King, K. A. (2013). Child agency and language policy in transnational families. *Issues in Applied Linguistics, 19*, 1–25.

Francis, D. J., Lesaux, N. K., & August, D. (2006). Language of instruction. In D. August & T. Shanahan (Eds.), *Developing literacy in second-language learners: Report of the National Literacy Panel on language minority children and youth* (pp. 365–414). Mahwah, NJ: Lawrence Erlbaum.

Gandara, P., & Hopkin, M. (2010). *Forbidden language: English learners and restrictive language policies*. New York, NY: Teachers College Press.

García, O. (2009). *Bilingual education in the 21st century*. Malden, MA: Wiley-Blackwell.

García, O. (2011). Educating New York's bilingual children: Constructing a future from the past. *International Journal of Bilingual Education and Bilingualism, 14*, 133–153.

García, O. (2014). What is translanguaging? Expanded questions and answers for U.S. educators. In S. Hesson, K. Seltzer, & H. H. Woodley (Eds.), *Translanguaging in curriculum and instruction: A CUNY-NYSIEB guide for educators* (pp. 1–13). New York, NY: CUNY- NYSIEB.

García, O., & Wei, L. (2014). *Translanguaging: Language, bilingualism and education*. Basingstoke, UK: Palgrave Macmillan.

García, O., Kleifgen, J. A., & Falchi, L. (2008). *From English language learners to emergent bilinguals* (Equity Matters: Research Review No. 1). New York, NY: Teachers College, Columbia University.

García, O., Johnson, S., & Seltzer, K. (2017). *The translanguaging classroom: Leveraging student bilingualism for learning*. Philadelphia, PA: Caslon.

Genesee, F. (2008). *Bilingual first language acquisition: Evidence from Montreal. Diversite urbaine*, 9–26.

Genesee, F., Nicoladis, E., & Paradis, J. (1995). Language differentiation in early bilingual development. *Journal of Child Language, 22*, 611–631.

U.S. Census Bureau (2018). *Selected social characteristics in the United States*. American Community Services.

Genesee, F., Geva, E., Dressler, C., & Kamil, M. L. (2006). Synthesis: Cross-linguistic relationships. In D. August & T. Shanahan (Eds.), *Developing literacy in second-language learning: Report of the National Literacy Panel on language minority children and youth*(pp. 153–174). Mahwah, NJ: Lawrence Erlbaum.

Golberg, H., Paradis, J., & Crago, M. (2008). Lexical acquisition over time in minority L1 children learning English as a L2. *Applied Psycholinguistics*, *29*, 1–25.

Goldenberg, C. (2011). Reading instruction for English language learners. In M. Kamil, P. D. Pearson, E. B. Moje, & P. Afflerbach (Eds.), *The handbook of reading research* (Vol. 4, pp. 684–710). New York, NY: Routledge.

Gort, M. (2008). "You give me idea!": Collaborative strides toward bilingualism and biliteracy in a two-way partial immersion program. *Multicultural Perspectives*, *10*(4), 192–200.

Gort, M. (2012). Evaluation and revision processes of young bilinguals in a dual language program. In E. B. Bauer & M. Gort (Eds.), *Early biliteracy development: Exploring young learners' use of their linguistic resources* (pp. 90–110). New York, NY: Routledge.

Gravelle, M. (1996). *Supporting bilingual learners in schools*. Stoke-on-Trent, UK: Trentham Books.

Guardado, M. (2010). Heritage language development: Preserving a mythic past or envisioning the future of Canadian identity? *Journal of Language, Identity, and Education*, *9*(5), 329–346.

Guardado, M., & Becker, A. (2015). 'Glued to the family': The role of familism in heritage language development. *Language, Culture and Curriculum*, *27*(2), 163–181.

Hinton, L. (2008). Trading tongues: Loss of heritage languages in the United States. In A. Reyes & A. Lo (Eds.). *Beyond Yellow English: Toward a linguistic anthropology of Asian Pacific America* (pp. 331–346). Oxford University Press.

Hinton, A. K. (2015). "We only teach in English": An examination of bilingual-in-name-only classrooms," *Research on preparing inservice teachers to work effectively with emergent bilinguals (Advances in research on teaching*, Vol. 24), Emerald Group Publishing Limited, pp. 265–289.

Hornberger, N. H. (2003). Continua of biliteracy. In N. H. Hornberger (Ed.), *Continua of biliteracy: An ecological framework for educational policy, research, and practice in multilingual settings* (pp. 3–34). Clevedon, England: Multilingual Matters.

Hua, Z., & Wei, L. (2016). Transnational experience, aspiration and family language policy. *Journal of Multilingual and Multicultural Development*, *37*(7), 655–666.

Keh, M. L., & Stoessel, S. (2017). How first is first? Revisiting language maintenance and shift and the meaning of L1/L2 in three case studies. *International Multilingual Research Journal*, *11*, 101–114.

Kheirkhah, M., & Cekaite, A. (2015). Language maintenance in a multilingual family: Informal heritage language lessons in parent–child interactions. *Journal of Cross-cultural and Interlanguage Communiciation*, *34*(3), 319–346.

Kim, C., & Pyun, D. (2014). Heritage language literacy maintenance: A study of Korean-American heritage learners. *Language, Culture, and Curriculum*, *27*(3), 294–315.

King, K. A., & Fogle, L. W. (2006). Bilingual parenting as good parenting: Parents' perspectives on family language policy for additive bilingualism, *International Journal of Bilingual Education and Bilingualism*, 9(6), 695–712.

Kondo-Brown, K. (2011). Maintaining heritage language perspectives of Korean parents, *Multicultural Education*, 19(1), 31–37.

Krashen, S. (1998). Language shyness and heritage language development. In S. Krashen, L. Tse, & J. McQuillan (Eds.), *Heritage language development* (pp. 31–39). Culver City, CA: Language Education Associates.

Kupisch, T., & Rothman, J. (2018). Terminology matters! Why difference is not incompleteness and how early child bilinguals are heritage speakers. *International Journal of Bilingualism*, 22(5), 564–582.

Kwon, J. (2017). Immigrant mothers' beliefs and transnational strategies for their children's heritage language maintenance. *Language and Education*, 31(6), 495–508.

Lee, B. Y. (2013). Heritage language maintenance and cultural identity formation: the case of Korean immigrant parents and their children in the USA. *Early Child Development and Care*, 183(11), 1576–1588.

Lee, J. S., & Jeong, E. (2013). Korean-English dual language immersion: Perspectives of students, parents, and teachers. *Language, Culture and Curriculum*, 26(1), 89–107.

Lee, J. S., & Wright, W. (2014). The rediscovery of heritage and community language education in the United States. *Review of Research in Education*, 38(1), 137–165.

Lewis, G., Jones, B., & Baker, C. (2012). Translanguaging: Developing its conceptualisation and contextualization. *Educational Research and Evaluation*, 18, 655–670.

Li, G. (2006). Biliteracy and trilingual practices in the home context: Case studies of Chinese-Canadian children. *Journal of Early Childhood Literacy*, 6(3), 355–381.

Liang, F. (2018). Parental perceptions toward and practices of heritage language maintenance: Focusing on the United States and Canada. *International Journal of Language Studies*, 12(2), 65–86.

Lindholm-Leary, K. J. (2001). *Dual language education*. Clevedon, UK: Multilingual Matters.

López, D. (1996). Language: Diversity and assimilation. In R. Waldinger & M. Bozorgmehr (Eds.), *Ethnic Los Angeles* (pp. 139–163). New York: Russell Sage Foundation.

Lü, C., & Koda, K. (2011). The impact of home language and literacy support on English-Chinese biliteracy acquisition among Chinese heritage language learners. *Heritage Language Journal*, 8, 119–231.

Lynch, A. (2014). The first decade of the Heritage Language Journal: A retrospective view of research on heritage languages. *Heritage Language Journal*, 11(3), 224–242.

Martin-Beltran, M. (2010). The two-way language bridge: Co-constructing bilingual language learning opportunities. *The Modern Language Journal*, 94(2), 254–277.

McCabe, M. (2016). Transnationalism and language maintenance: Czech and Slovak as heritage languages in the Southeastern United States. *International Journal of the Sociology of Language*, 238, 169–191.

Melo-Pfeifer, S. (2015). The role of the family in heritage language use and learning: Impact on heritage language policies. *International Journal of Bilingual Education and Bilingualism, 18*(1), 26–44.

Mesthrie, R., Swann, J., Deumert, A., & Leap, W. (2001). *Introducing sociolinguistics*. Philadelphia PA: John Benjamins Publishing Company.

Montrul, S. (2008). *Incomplete acquisition in bilingualism: Re-examining the age factor*. Amsterdam, Netherlands: John Benjamins.

Montrul, S. (2010). Current issues in heritage language acquisition. *Annual Review of Applied Linguistics, 30*, 3–23.

Montrul, S. A. (2018). Heritage language development: Connecting the dots. *International Journal of Bilingualism, 22*(5), 530–546.

Moro, L., Mortimer, E., & Tiberghien, A. (2019). The use of social semiotics multimodality and joint action theory to describe teaching practices: Two cases studies with experienced teachers. *Classroom Discourse, 11*(3), 1–23.

Murphy, V. (2014). *Second language learning in the early school years: Trends and contexts*. Oxford University Press.

Nesteruk, O. (2010). Heritage language maintenance and loss among the children of Eastern European immigrants in the USA. *Journal of Multilingual and Multicultural Development, 31*(3), 271–286.

Oh, J. S., & Fuligni, A. J. (2010). The role of heritage language development in the ethnic identity and family relationships of adolescents from immigrant backgrounds. *Social Development, 19*, 202–220.

Oriyama, K. (2010). Heritage language maintenance and Japanese identity formation: What role can schooling and ethnic community contact play? *Heritage Language Journal, 7*(2), 76–111.

Park, E. (2006). Grandparents, grandchildren, and heritage language. In K. Kondo-Brown (Ed.), *Heritage language development: Focus on East Asian immigrants* (pp. 57–86). Amsterdam, Netherlands: John Benjamins.

Park, S. M., & Sarkar, M. (2007). Parents' attitudes toward heritage language maintenance for their children and their efforts to help their children maintain the heritage language: A case study of Korean-Canadian immigrants. *Language, Culture and Curriculum, 20*(3), 223–235.

Park-Johnson, S. (2017). Code mixing as a window into language dominance: Evidence from Korean heritage speakers. *Heritage Language Journal, 14*(1), 49–69.

Polinsky, M. (2011). Reanalysis in adult heritage language. *Studies in Second Language Acquisition, 33*(2), 305–328.

Polinsky, M. (2018). Bilingual children and adult heritage speakers: The range of comparison. *International Journal of Bilingualism, 22*(5), 547–563.

Polinsky, M., & Kagan, O. (2007). Heritage languages: In the 'wild' and in the classroom. *Language and Linguistics Compass, 1*(5), 368–395.

Potowski, K. (2016). Bilingual youth: Spanish-speakers at the beginning of the 21st century. *Language and Linguistics Compass, 10*(6), 272–283.

Proctor, P., August, D., Snow, C., & Barr, C. (2010). The interdependence continuum: A perspective on the nature of Spanish–English bilingual reading. *Bilingual Research Journal, 33*(1), 5–20.

Reyes, I. (2004). Functions of code switching in schoolchildren's conversations. *Bilingual Research Journal, 28*(1), 77–98.

Ro, Y. E., & Cheatham, G. A. (2009). Biliteracy and bilingual development in a second-generation Korean child: A case study. *Journal of Research in Childhood Education, 23,* 290–308.

Rodriguez-Mojica, C. (2017). From test scores to language use: Emergent bilinguals using english to accomplish academic tasks. *International Multilingual Research Journal, 12*(1), 31–61.

Sayer, P. (2013). Translanguaging, TexMex, and bilingual pedagogy: Emergent bilinguals learning through the vernacular. *TESOL Quarterly, 47*(1), 63–88.

Schmid, M. S. (2010). Languages at play: The relevance of L1 attrition to the study of bilingualism. *Bilingualism: Language and Cognition, 13,* 1–7.

Seals, C., & Peyton, J. K. (2017). Heritage language education: Valuing the languages, literacies and cultural competencies of immigrant youth. *Current Issues of Language Planning, 18*(1), 87–101.

Shanahan, T., & Beck, I. L. (2006). Effective literacy teaching for English-language learners. In D. August & T. Shanahan (Eds.), *Developing literacy in second-language learners; Report of the National Literacy Panel on language-minority children and youth* (pp. 415–488). Mahwah, NJ: Lawrence Erlbaum.

Shin, S. J. (2005). *Developing in two languages: Korean Children in America.* Clevedon, UK: Multilingual Matters.

Shin, S. J. (2014). Language learning as culture keeping: Family language policies of transnational adoptive parents. *International Multilingual Research Journal, 8*(3), 189–207.

Shin, S. J., & Lee, J. S. (2013). Expanding capacity, opportunity, and desire to learn Korean as a heritage language. *Heritage Language Journal, 10*(3), 64–73.

Shin, F. H., & Krashen, S. (1996). Teacher attitudes toward the principles of bilingual education and toward students' participation in bilingual programs: Same or different? *Bilingual Research Journal 20,* 45–53.

Siu, C. T., & Ho, C. S. (2015). Cross-language transfer of syntactic skills and reading comprehension among young Cantonese–English bilingual students. *Reading Research Quarterly, 50*(3), 313–336.

Song, K. (2016). "Okay, I will say in Korean and then in American": Translanguaging practices in bilingual homes. *Journal of Early Childhood Literacy, 16*(1), 84–106.

Spolsky, B. (2012). Family language policy—The critical domain. *Journal of Multilingual and Multicultural Development, 33*(1), 3–11.

Suarez-Orozco, C., Suarez-Orozco, M., & Todorova, I. (2008). *Learning a new land: Immigrant students in American society.* Cambridge, MA: Harvard University Press.

Swain, M. (2000). The output hypothesis and beyond: Mediating acquisition through collaborative dialogue. In J. Lantolf (Ed.), *Sociocultural theory and second language learning* (pp. 97–114). Oxford: Oxford University Press.

Szilagyi, J., & Szecsi, T. (2020). Why and how to maintain the Hungarian language: Hungarian-American families' views on heritage language practices. *Heritage Language Journal, 17*(1), 114–139.

Tabors, P. O. (2008). *One child, two languages: A guide for early childhood educators of children learning English as a second language* (2nd ed.). Baltimore, MD: Brookes.

Tse, L. (1998). Affecting affect: The impact of heritage language programs on student attitudes. In S. Krashen, L. Tse, & J. McQuillan (Eds.), *Heritage language development* (pp. 51–72). Culver City, CA: Language Education Associates.

Tse, L. (2001). *Why don't they learn English? Separating fact from fallacy in the U.S. language debate*. New York; London: Teachers College Press.

Turnbull, B. (2018). Reframing foreign language learning as bilingual education: epistemological changes towards the emergent bilingual. *International Journal of Bilingual Education and Bilingualism*, *21*(8), 1041–1048.

Valdés, G. (2001). Heritage language students: Profiles and possibilities. In J. Peyton, J. Ranard, & S. McGinnis (Eds.), *Heritage languages in America: Preserving a national resource* (pp. 37–80). McHenry, IL: The Center for Applied Linguistics and Delta Systems.

Valdés, G. (2005). Bilingualism, heritage learners, and SLA research: Opportunities lost or seized? *Modern Language Journal*, *89*(3), 410–426.

Velasco, P., & García, O. (2014). Translanguaging and the writing of bilingual learners. *Bilingual Research Journal*, *37*, 6–23.

Veltman, C. (1983). *Language shift in the United States*. The Hague: Mouton.

Venturin, B. (2019). "I don't fit in here and I don't fit in there:" Understanding the connections between L1 attrition and feelings of identity in 1.5 generation Russian Australians. *Heritage Language Journal*, *16*(2), 238–268.

Vihman, M. (1998). A developmental perspective on code-switching: Conversations between a pair of siblings. *International Journal of Bilingualism*, *2*(1), 45–84.

Wei, L. (2011). Moment analysis and translanguaging space: Discursive construction of identities by multilingual Chinese youth in Britain. *Journal of Pragmatics*, *43*, 1222–1235.

Wei, L., & Wu, C. (2009). Polite Chinese children revisited: Creativity and the use of code-switching in the Chinese complementary school classroom. *International Journal of Bilingual Education and Bilingualism*, *12*(2), 193–211.

Wong-Fillmore, L. W. (1991). When learning a second language means losing the first. *Early Childhood Research Quarterly*, *6*(3), 323–347.

Yang, J., Fox, R., & Jacewicz, E. (2015). Vowel development in an emergent Mandarin-English bilingual child: A longitudinal study. *Journal of Child Language*, *42*, 1125–1145.

Yazan, B., & Ali, I. (2018). Family language policies in a Libyan immigrant family in the U.S.: Language and religious identity. *Heritage Language Journal*, *15*(3), 369–388.

You, B. K. (2005). Children negotiating Korean American ethnic identity through their heritage language. *Bilingual Research Journal*, *29*, 712–721.

2 The framework for the study

Introduction

The study is situated within two major theoretical frameworks: (a) a sociocultural perspective on literacy and learning (Heath, 1983; Street, 2003; Vygotsky, 1978) and (b) translanguaging theory (García, 2009) from a heteroglossic perspective (Bakhtin, 1981, 1984). The chapter first introduces the sociocultural perspective on literacy and learning informed by Street (2003) and then discusses the translanguaging theory conceptualized by García (2009). To understand how translanguaging paradigm is adopted in bilingual education and research, the chapter reviews recent translanguaging studies that investigated teachers' use of translanguaging as their pedagogical practice, emergent bilinguals' translanguaging performance in the classrooms, and everyday trans-languaging practices in homes, families, and communities. The chapter ends with a summary of literature reviews and gaps in the existing literature, followed by the purpose of the book by providing research questions of the current study.

Sociocultural perspective on literacy and learning

Many literacy scholars whose work reflects sociocultural perspectives (Gee, 2012; Lewis, Enciso, & Moje, 2007; Tracey & Morrow, 2006) were influenced by the work of Vygotsky (1962, 1978). Vygotsky, a socio-constructivist, argued that learning takes place through interaction with people and participation within the social environment; thus, for him, learning is not an individual or isolated activity but a joint activity that occurs through active and dynamic interaction. By emphasizing the social environment, Vygotsky (1962) pointed out that "the true direction of development of thinking is not from the individual to social, but from social to individual" (p. 20). That is, from the Vygotskian perspective, learning a language is a social behavior that is developed through social interactions.

Following Vygotsky, Halliday (1973) claimed that language is not independent of the social world. Rather, it occurs within a cultural context;

thus, culture is generated through language. Halliday (1973) viewed children's language development as a function of their participation in a social world. According to Halliday, language could not be separated from the culture because it reflected and generated it. Halliday considered language and communication to be social semiotics and multiple-meaning systems that involved varied modes of representation or multimodality, such as oral and written language, gestures, drawings, signs, and symbols. Researchers who studied Halliday's systemic functional linguistics reported that he was interested in the functions or purposes of humans' use of semiotic resources to interact with each other and to create oral and written texts (Moro, Mortimer, & Tiberghien, 2019).

Similarly, Gee's (1996) Discourses (with the capital "D") as an "identity kit" also illustrated how language is connected with social and cultural contexts. According to Gee's notion of language, language instantiates culture because the speaker's language use varies according to social and cultural contexts. Street (2001) pointed out that to understand literacy practices, researchers need "detailed, in-depth accounts of actual practice in different cultural settings" (p. 430). According to Street (2001), a sociocultural view of literacy emphasizes literacies that are situated in and created by participants. Street argued that literacy emerges as a result of social and cultural practices because it involves "thinking about, doing, and reading in cultural contexts" (p. 11). Heath (1983) introduced the concept of "literacy events," which describes "any occasion in which a piece of writing is integral to the nature of the participants' interactions and their interpretative processes" (p. 50). Drawing on Heath, Street (1984) employed the phrase "literacy practices" by focusing on "the social practices and conceptions of reading and writing" (p. 1) to emphasize the social models of literacy in which participants negotiate and make meanings when they read and write in specific cultural contexts.

Street (1984) made a distinction between an autonomous model and an ideological model of literacy. The autonomous model of literacy is a traditional psychological approach, which views literacy as a mental or cognitive phenomenon; thus, reading and writing are treated as things people do inside their heads as a technical skill. In opposition to the autonomous model of literacy, Street proposed an ideological model. The ideological model of literacy challenges the traditional model since it offers a more culturally sensitive view of literacy practices by insisting that people engage in literacy practices in society, not just inside their heads.

Since the present study in this book is conducted in the classroom settings, where the participants negotiate and make meanings during their literacy practices in certain cultural contexts, the study is consistent with Street's social view of literacies. Considering Street's argument that literacy should be studied in an integrated way by looking at social, cultural, and historical aspects beyond cognitive facets, I considered the cultural contexts and social practices when investigating the participating students' language use, performance, and development.

Translanguaging paradigm from a heteroglossic perspective

In the past, bilingual educators believed that bilingual students' languages should be kept separate in the classroom so that emergent bilingual learners were provided with appropriate amounts of instruction in the target languages (August & Hakuta, 1998; Wong-Fillmore, 1991). For example, the language policy in many two-way bilingual immersion programs in the U.S., where balanced numbers of native English speakers and native speakers of the partner language are integrated for instruction (Crawford, 2004), was that instruction should be delivered in one target language at a time, and the mixing of languages should not be allowed in the classroom setting (Lindholm-Leary, 2001). Baker (2011) described bilingual education as bilingualism with diglossia, which explains a situation where two languages are used under different conditions and for distinct and separate social functions. Based on this notion of bilingualism, Heller (2001) coined the term *parallel monolingualism*, in which "each [language] variety must conform to certain prescriptive norms" (p. 217). Other researchers used the phrases "separate bilingualism" (Creese & Blackledge, 2010), "two solitudes" (Cummins, 2005), and "code-segregation" (Guerra, Dunston, & Fullerton, 2012) to describe the strict separation of the languages and the boundary between the two languages.

To move away from the concept of bilingualism as parallel monolingualism, Bailey (2007) made a clear distinction between monoglossic and heteroglossic. Bakhtin (1981) initially coined the term *heteroglossia* to explain speakers' simultaneous use of a diverse range of registers, voices, languages, or codes in their daily lives. According to Bakhtin (1981, 1984), heteroglossia refers to the multiple variations of voices within speakers' languages. The Bakhtinian notion of heteroglossia replaced monolingual ideology in language education and advanced multilingual practices and polylingual pedagogy. Influenced by Bakhtin's theory, Bailey (2007) argued that heteroglossia explains the existence of different and multiple language varieties as a unitary system. The heteroglossic perspective allows speakers to utilize their collective linguistic repertoires to achieve their communicative aims in a given situation. Thus, heteroglossia opened up the spaces to accept and appreciate all kinds of multimodal languaging practices by rejecting the monolingual perspective, which viewed using two languages at the same time as a deficient behavior (Busch, 2012; Canagarajah, 2011a). This heteroglossic viewpoint, in terms of language ideologies and linguistic practices, has led to the recent theory of translanguaging (García, 2009), which is different from traditional concepts of bilingualism (Blackledge & Creese 2010; Wei 2011).

A translanguaging paradigm has recently been established and used in research on bilingualism and bilinguals (e.g., Blackledge & Creese, 2010; Canagarajah, 2011a; García, 2009, 2014). García (2009) preferred the term *translanguaging* to code-switching (CS) to describe bilinguals' normal and natural practices that are divergent from "diglossic functional separation" (Blackledge & Creese, 2010, p. 106). Lewis, Jones, and Baker (2012) also distinguished the concepts of CS and translanguaging by arguing that CS is associated with language separation, whereas translanguaging supports the use of the speaker's entire language repertoires flexibly. Likewise, García and Wei (2014) made clear distinctions between the two terms, CS and *translanguaging*. According to them, CS refers to when bilingual speakers shift from one language to the other by choosing a more applicable language from their two *separate* registers in a given context. In contrast, translanguaging practices enable bilinguals to "turn off their language switching function" (p. 23) and to access their *integrated* and *entire* language and linguistic repertoires.

By differentiating the two concepts, García (2009, 2014) critiqued the use of the term *CS* because it "put[s] to the service of the majority language ... encouraging switching towards the dominant language only, and used progressively to take space and time away from the minority language until it disappears completely" (p. 297), whereas, in translanguaging practice, "there are no clear-cut boundaries between the languages of bilinguals .... what we have is a languaging continuum that is accessed" (p. 47). Thus, García's concept of translanguaging goes beyond CS since translanguaging theorizes that bilinguals' language practices are not separated into home language and school language (García & Wei, 2014). Rather, it incorporates language flexibility through the speaker's full language repertoires (Lewis et al., 2012). In a further elaboration of differences between CS and translanguaging, García and Lin (2017) pointed out that translanguaging focuses on the *speaker's* use of languages rather than the perspective of the "named languages" (p. 120). In other words, CS views language from an "external perspective" (i.e., national or standard languages) as if bilinguals were two monolinguals in one, whereas translanguaging indicates the ways that bilinguals use their languages from their "internal perspectives" (García, Johnson, & Seltzer, 2017, p. 20).

Translanguaging was initially coined by Cen Williams to refer to "pedagogical practice where students are asked to alternate languages for the purposes of receptive or productive use" (as cited in García & Wei, 2014, p. 20). Unlike traditional bilingual classrooms, where teachers only use the target language during instruction from a monolingual instructional approach (Creese & Blackledge, 2010), translanguaging explains that bilinguals are not "two monolinguals in one body" (Gravelle, 1996, p. 11) and "reject[s] society's monoglossic view of bilinguals as two monolinguals"

(Jiang, García, & Willis, 2014, p. 314). In this regard, the term *trans-languaging* currently is being used to explain both an act of teachers' instructional strategy and/or pedagogical approach and an act of bilingual learners' language performance (García & Leiva, 2014).

The translanguaging approach contrasts with dual immersion bilingual programs because it does not advocate isolating or separating the two languages; rather, it acknowledges and values bilinguals' employment of their full language repertoires. García and Wei (2014) proposed "dynamic bilingualism" that challenges traditional notions of bilingualism, which involves two autonomous linguistic systems. In other words, translanguaging refers to flexible language practices to describe bilingual speakers' dynamic and integrated ways of communication instead of the alternation between their two separate languages (Allard, 2017). Others referenced bilingual students' employment of their entire linguistic resources while writing as "translingual" (Durán, 2017), "code-meshing" (Canagarajah, 2011b). Both terms—*translingual* and *code-meshing*—under the umbrella term of *translanguaging* characterize the unique strategies that bilingual individuals, compared to monolingual individuals, can access to problem-solve their writing and to reach readers from more than one language.

Translanguaging further implies a move away from hierarchical conceptions of language (e.g., English as a majority language vs. Korean as a minority language) as well as distinctions between home language (HL/L1) versus school language (L2; English) since speakers of more than one language do not separate their languages; instead, they translanguage strategically to attain specific purposes (García, 2011). Otheguy, García, and Reid (2015) further claimed that translanguaging can be valuable for speakers of minority languages that are often regarded as vulnerable and not always secured in the majority language context. Otheguy et al. pointed out that "translanguaging ... provides a smoother conceptual path than previous approaches to the goal of protecting minoritized communities, their languages, and their learners and schools" (p. 283). In the same sense, García and Kano (2014) regarded translanguaging as not only including bilingual speakers' all-inclusive language practices but also "sustain[ing] old ones and giv[ing] voice to new sociopolitical realities by interrogating linguistic inequality" (p. 261). In other words, translanguaging pedagogy protect and endorse minority languages as it balances the power relations among languages in the classroom (Allard, 2017; Bartlett & García, 2011; Cenoz, 2017). In contrast to the monoglossic approach to bilingualism, current research on translanguaging aims to recognize and value the sustainability of home language (Bartlett & García, 2011; Cummins & Persad, 2014). Indeed, current research on translanguaging from a heteroglossic perspective consider that bilinguals' HL is their linguistic resources available to them when they are communicating, making meaning, sharing experiences, and transmitting knowledge in a creative and meaningful way (Lewis et al., 2012; Canagarajah, 2013; Velasco & García, 2014).

As the heteroglossic perspective opened up spaces to appreciate language diversity and multilingualism (Canagarajah, 2011a), researchers began to study bilingual students' entire language use and development (HL + English) through a translanguaging paradigm (García, 2009, 2011; García & Wei, 2014). To date, multiple studies have explored translanguaging as teachers' pedagogical practices in bilingual classroom settings and as bilingual students' communicative and literacy learning strategies. Thus, the chapter continues to provide literature reviews on translanguaging studies to exemplify how it is used in the classrooms by teachers as their pedagogical practices and also by bilingual students as their learning strategies. The chapter continues to discuss translanguaging practices at homes and communities.

Translanguaging as teachers' pedagogical practices in bilingual classrooms

After García and Leiva (2014) clarified translanguaging is both an act of bilingual performance and a pedagogical approach to teaching, Cenoz (2017) distinguished between the pedagogical and spontaneous translanguaging. According to Cenoz, *spontaneous translanguaging* refers to "fluid discursive practices that can take place inside or outside the classroom" (p. 194), which is natural and instinctive use of two languages by bi/multilingual learners. Whereas, *pedagogical translanguaging* indicates instruction "planned by the teacher inside the classroom and refers to the different languages for input and output or to other planned strategies based on the use of students' resources from the whole linguistic repertoire" (p. 194), which explains the intentional practice of alternating between languages by the teacher for pedagogical purposes.

Since the term *translanguaging* was initially used to refer to the teacher's pedagogical practices to scaffold bilingual students' learning (Canagarajah, 2011a), a large number of research focused on teachers' use of translanguaging as an instructional strategy in classroom settings (e.g., Duarte, 2020; Esquinca, Araujo, & de la Piedra, 2014; García et al. 2017; Gort & Sembiante, 2015; Palmer, Martínez, Mateus, & Henderson, 2014; Worthy, Durán, Hikida, Pruitt, & Peterson, 2013). The majority of the studies dealt with preschool and elementary Spanish-English bilinguals in dual-language classrooms. In these studies, the teachers implemented diverse types of translanguaging strategies, such as code-switching (CS), code-mixing (CM), translating, and using cognates, which are words in two languages with ancestral roots that share similar meanings and spellings (Nagy, García, Durgunoglu, & Hancin-Bhatt, 1993), to scaffold the students' learning in both languages and to mediate their understanding by utilizing their complete linguistic resources.

For instance, in their year-long ethnographic study, Esquinca et al. (2014) examined a Spanish bilingual teacher in a 4th-grade two-way dual-language school. The researchers investigated how the teacher provided a space for translanguaging so that the complete repertoires of the students' languages were recognized and validated in her classroom. Although the disciplinary (science) instruction was delivered in English, the teacher guided her students to utilize their entire language resources through translanguaging to engage in the science content learning. For example, when the students used Spanish to discuss the concept of science that was delivered in English, the teacher did not interrupt the flow of conversation, but rather she continued the discussion by employing translanguaging as a tool. The teacher created spaces for bilingual students to use both languages flexibly; thus, their languages did not remain separate in class discussions. Thanks to the teacher's bilingualism, the students were able to make meaning of their science concepts and actively participated in the discourse practice through translanguaging.

Similarly, Palmer et al. (2014) in a two-year ethnographic study explored two classroom teachers' (one in 1st grade and another in kindergarten) translanguaging pedagogies in dual-language classrooms. The researchers were interested in examining how the teachers used translanguaging as their instructional strategy and whether their translanguaging worked as academic tools for students' language and literacy learning. Although there was the school's "language of the day" policy that specified one language should be used each day, the teachers employed their dual-language resources during instruction in a natural manner to ensure the students' understanding of logistics and classroom activities. The findings showed that the teachers' translanguaging provided a space for dynamic bilingualism, which supported the simultaneous coexistence of different languages for communication and making meanings in different cultural contexts (Flores & Schissel, 2014; García & Leiva, 2014). The study indicates that language minority students could benefit when bilingualism was modeled and encouraged in the classroom.

In a two-year ethnographic study, Gort and Sembiante (2015) examined teachers' translanguaging pedagogies and practices in a Spanish/English dual-language preschool classroom. The classroom was regularly scheduled show-and-tell activities with three teachers (one lead teacher and two teaching assistants, each of whom was fluent in Spanish or English). The teachers' various forms of pedagogies demonstrated that the teachers positioned translanguaging as a normal practice and important resource for their bilingual students in the classroom. The findings also revealed that although the head teacher's language designation was English on a particular week, her prevalent and intentional use of Spanish "protect[ed] the position and value of Spanish in the classroom" (p. 22). The teacher's intentional use of Spanish in the classroom challenged the hegemony of English, which was regarded as a more dominant and powerful language than Spanish. The three teachers' dynamic bilingual practices and their language use in this study suggest that when teachers challenge ideologies that deprecate students' cultural and linguistic assets, they can generate spaces for bilingualism and support bilingual students' language and identity development.

Worthy et al. (2013) conducted an ethnographic study to investigate a 5th-grade teacher's use of translanguaging during her reading instruction in a late-exit transitional bilingual program. In the latter type of bilingual education program, teachers use students' L1 to teach content and literacy but steadily reduce the amount of L1 usage over the grade levels while increasing content and literacy instruction in English (Baker, 2011). Since the research was conducted in a 5th-grade classroom, only 10% of the instruction was delivered in Spanish. By resisting the greater focus on English than Spanish, the teacher tried to provide her students with instructional experiences in both languages. For instance, the teacher used both English and Spanish flexibly when initiating literature discussion and provided a space for students to use Spanish by asking specific questions in Spanish.

Furthermore, the teacher positively valued her students' translanguaging practice by supporting the use of both Spanish and English so that the students could draw on their linguistic and cultural knowledge and resources during the class discussions. Thus, this study showed how the teacher's translanguaging supported her students' learning by helping them to negotiate the meaning of academic content as well as how teachers can ideally build rich learning spaces for their bilingual students. Although the study demonstrated that the teacher created rich learning spaces for her Spanish-speaking bilingual students by providing a bilingual pedagogical practice (e.g., translanguaging), the study was conducted in a transitional bilingual program with upper elementary grade (5th-grade) students. Thus, more research is needed to find out how teachers and students utilize their language resources when instruction is delivered more in the HL. In addition, since the study focused on upper elementary students, it is important to further examine how teachers' language use and instruction would be different in elementary transitional bilingual classrooms for younger students.

In a study that focused on a native-language Chinese teacher's instruction in a transitional program of instruction, in which students from a range of languages other than English were in ESL classrooms for almost half of the day, HL classrooms for 45 minutes daily, and all English classrooms the rest of the day, Jiang et al. (2014) reported that the teacher used translanguaging not just to promote his 4th-/5th-grade Chinese emergent bilinguals' Chinese language development and comprehension but also to promote their bicultural awareness. The researchers' discourse analysis findings showed that the teacher used CM (as an example of translanguaging) not only to enhance students' bilingual learning by crossing the boundary of L1 and L2 but also to increase the students' understanding of cross-cultural differences.

Focusing on the teachers' language use and ideologies in kindergarten/1st-grade classrooms, Martínez, Hikida, and Durán (2015) examined two bilingual teachers in an English-Spanish dual-language program. One teacher taught in kindergarten/1st grade while the other teacher taught in 2nd/3rd grade. The researchers investigated the two teachers' instruction to explore how their language ideologies were reflected in their everyday linguistic and pedagogical practices. When the teachers were asked about their beliefs, thoughts, and feelings regarding translanguaging, the kindergarten/1st-grade teacher (Ms. Birch) favored bilingualism and held an appreciative view of students' translanguaging while speaking. However, she believed that translanguaging should not be promoted during their writing because her students' (1st-graders) literacy was at an emerging stage unlike older bilingual students or adults; thus, emergent bilingual writers should be encouraged to stick to one language. Similarly, the 2nd-/3rd-grade teacher, Ms. Quixote, believed that maintaining the designated language of instruction was an ideal pedagogy for her students. She saw that her responsibility was to avoid translanguaging and indeed be attentive to her own translanguaging. The teachers' belief and ideologies were closed to language separation and language purism as they believed that language mixing was a deficient behavior.

However, it was interesting to find that there was a contrast between the teachers' language ideologies (i.e., language separation and linguistic purism for each teacher) and their actual language practices in the classrooms since both teachers engaged in translanguaging more than their stated ideologies. Considering the classroom context where English monoglot prevailed (California), the teachers privileged Spanish to confront English hegemony ideologies. In other words, the teachers cultivated the students' Spanish proficiency as a way to sustain Spanish since they believed that there was a power imbalance between the two languages. That is, their ideologies were not based on language separation; instead, they showed their efforts to support and protect the Spanish language. Unlike their ideologies, the teachers' actual practices showed that they naturally engaged in translanguaging, which embodies ideologies of linguistic hybridity and pluralism. With their findings, Martínez et al. (2015) pointed out that in order to promote and sustain students' HL (Spanish in this study), teachers did not need to exclude their use of translanguaging or discourage the students from translanguaging. They further suggested that teachers in bilingual classroom can support their students to become competent bilingual and bicultural if they engage in frequent translanguaging and encourage their students to do so.

A later study by Cenoz and Gorter (2017) agreed with Martínez et al.'s argument that translanguaging practices can contribute to the protection and promotion of minority languages because translanguaging serves as "a tool for empowering language minority students ... [as] it accepts the way bilinguals communicate" (p. 907). However, at the same time, they claimed that translanguaging has to be controlled in the context of learning regional minority language (e.g., Basque, Māori). Since regional minority languages are vulnerable and susceptible in the U.S., allowing translanguaging in a predominantly English-speaking setting might lead the learners to use more of the majority language (English). By pointing out "a difficult balance between using resources from the multilingual learner's whole repertoire and shaping contexts to use the minority languages on its own," Cenoz and Gorter argued that educators and scholars should carefully take into consideration the specific character- istics of the socio-linguistic context so that translanguaging can be sus- tainable for regional minority languages.

The studies discussed in this section illustrated how bilingual teachers implemented translanguaging as their instructional pedagogies in their classrooms. The findings suggested that when classroom teachers employed and incorporated translanguaging into their instruction, bilingual students' languages can be valued and validated in the classroom, and teachers are more likely to leverage the students' potential to develop their bilingualism.

Emergent bilingual learners' oral translanguaging practices

Although the term *translanguaging* often referred to the teacher's ped- agogical practices in bilingual classrooms to scaffold bilingual students' language and literacy development (Canagarajah, 2011a), an increasing number of researchers have examined how bilingual learners engaged in translanguaging practices in classroom settings. The majority of the translanguaging studies have dealt with bilinguals' oral translanguaging practices by examining their spoken language use (Smith & Murillo, 2015). The studies to date have shown that bilingual students utilized their full language repertoires during their oral communication in school settings. Much of the research on young bilingual students' oral trans- languaging in school settings focused on how the students benefited when their teachers created opportunities for translanguaging or facilitated its use in the classroom (e.g., Durán & Palmer, 2014; García- Mateus & Palmer, 2017; Hopewell & Abril-Gonzalez, 2019; Martin- Beltran, 2010; Martínez, Durán, & Hikida, 2017; Sayer, 2013).

For instance, Durán and Palmer (2014) used qualitative discourse analysis to investigate Spanish bilingual students' language use in two 1st-grade dual-language classrooms. The researchers reported when 1st-grade teachers provided space for Spanish when the instruction was supposed to be in English and vice versa, the students employed trans- languaging in appropriate ways to engage in classroom interactions. The students self-positioned their roles as language learners or experts during bilingual pair time by switching between the languages in a natural manner; thus, translanguaging became a normalized classroom practice. The findings displayed that the students' languages were valued and validated in the classroom, and each individual's flexible use of full language repertoires created a classroom environment where bilingualism was welcomed.

In an ethnographic study of a kindergarten/1st-grade classroom within a Spanish-English dual-language strand, Martínez et al. (2017) reported that students' translanguaging practices intersected with how they co-constructed their identities (by asserting, contesting, and negotiating) within classroom discourse. For example, during their classroom literacy event, the students alternated Spanish and English when their spoke, which signaled solidarity and approval. The findings showed that the students' translanguaging practices enabled them to position as bilingual through everyday classroom talk.

Similar to Martínez et al., the 1st-grade students in García-Mateus and Palmer's (2017) study used translanguaging in their dual-language classroom to represent their multilingual identities in relation to their peers' language use. The findings showed that the emergent bilingual students utilized their full linguistic repertoires when the teacher opened up spaces in their bilingual classroom. García-Mateus and Palmer found that translanguaging in a dual-language classroom offered empowering language and educational opportunities to minoritized bilingual students. In a study that examined young trilingual (English, Cantonese, and Mandarin) preschoolers' oral translanguaging in a Hong Kong preschool, Sanders-Smith and Dávila (2019) found that the preschoolers spontaneously translanguaged to support each other linguistically, socially, and academically. When they translanguaged, they made connections across different languages, language proficiencies, and ethnic affiliations.

Other researchers identified specific purposes that characterized bilingual students' oral translanguaging. Sayer's (2013) ethnographic study of a bilingual teacher and her Mexican-American 2nd-graders in a BE classroom illustrated how the students communicated their bilingual identities using TexMex. The students translanguaged for different functions, for example, to check comprehension and to conform to a principle of code alignment. According to Sayer (2013), bilingual speakers tended to follow the language that the more powerfully positioned speakers used (p. 81). Thus, the students in his study purposefully used translanguaging through TexMex in order to make sense of their language use and to actively participate in bilingual discourse practices. Martin-Beltran (2010) employed qualitative discourse analysis to study bilingual 5th-graders' classroom interactions in a Spanish-English BE program. The findings displayed that the bilingual students drew on their bilingual resources to understand unfamiliar concepts. The students' language use in the classroom also revealed that they used translanguaging when engaged in collaborative dialogue, which Swain (2000) defined as dialogue in which speakers are engaged in problem solving and knowledge building through social interaction. Martin-Beltrán concluded that the students' translanguaging had promoted their metalinguistic awareness because they engaged in private speech by utilizing both languages to verbally problem solve. Martínez-Roldán (2015) described how a Spanish-English bilingual student in an after-school program demonstrated metacognitive awareness when the student employed Spanish to read and discuss a book with the teacher and English to talk and make comments to himself. Jönsson (2013) reported that Swedish-English bilingual adolescents at an international school translanguaged to create jokes. Similarly, in a study on bilingual teachers' use of translanguaging practices in complementary or HL Chinese and Gujarati schools in the United Kingdom, Creese and Blackledge (2010) observed that the Gujarati students translanguaged in pairs to "joke, tease, and play around" (p. 110).

Hopewell and Abril-Gonzalez (2019) employed a multilingual translanguaging perspective to investigate how a bilingual teacher and her Spanish-speaking 2nd-graders utilized a specific translanguaging practice (code-switching) during their English instruction in a biliteracy block over the spring semester. Hopewell and Abril-Gonzalez rejected the historical definition of code-switching as the employment of two languages in the same utterance and/or the switching of languages between utterances (Genesee, Nicoladis, & Paradis, 1995; Jiang et al., 2014) because they thought the definition reinforced a monolingual perspective. Instead, they defined code-switching as a "multilingual exchange" that involved "the use of multiple languages" (p. 8). Notwithstanding, to analyze the multilingual exchanges, they utilized Baker's (2011) overlapping code-switching taxonomy, which included 13 purposes for code-switching. Their analysis showed that the teacher and students conducted multilingual exchanges for seven of Baker's code-switching purposes: to "add emphasis, ... to express a word that has no equivalent," to express a word they didn't know, "to reinforce a request, to clarify a point, ... to ease tension or interject humor," and to employ "the language of commerce" (p. 107). In addition, the teacher and/or students employed multilingual exchanges for three purposes that Baker did not identify: to express "respect or terms of endearment," to demonstrate "excitement," and to expand metalinguistic awareness (p. 114). In terms of respect and endearment, the students always employed Spanish when referring to their family members even though they knew how to refer to them in English. The authors thought that the students' use of Spanish, their home language, for family terms reflected the "intimacy ... and closeness of [the family] relationship" that would have been lost if they had used English (p. 114). Hopewell and Abril-Gonzalez concluded that the strategic integration of languages had enhanced and augmented the meanings of the teacher and students' communication.

Emergent bilingual learners' written translanguaging practices

Canagarajah (2011b) argues that translanguaging represents a move toward having students access their entire language repertoires not only for their oral communication but also for their written communication. Canagarajah (2011b) introduced the term *code-meshing* for translanguaging in texts beyond bi/multilinguals' communicative competence in oral form. Although it is still true that the majority of the translanguaging studies have paid more attention to bilinguals' spoken language than their literacy practices (Smith & Murillo, 2015), several researchers reported that young emergent bilingual writers also were engaged in written translanguaging in their biliteracy development (e.g., Bauer, Presiado, & Colomer, 2017; Velasco & García, 2014).

In earlier studies by Edelsky (1986) and Lanauze and Snow (1989), even though the researchers did not employ the term translanguaging, they showed evidence of emergent bilingual writers' use of translanguaging utilizing transliteration—in which bilingual individuals utilize the phonology from one language to write characters in the other language—during their writing process. For instance, Edelsky reported that Spanish-speakers (grades 1–3) transliterated when they utilized their Spanish linguistic knowledge to write in English by using Spanish phonology (e.g., "ai joup llu gou agien …. [I hope you go again ….])" (as cited in Velasco & García, 2014, p. 8). Edelsky found that 1st- to 3rd-grade Spanish-speaking students utilized their linguistic knowledge in Spanish when writing in English by using Spanish phonology (e.g., "ai joup llu gou agien tu scu ll [I hope you go again to school]" p. 8), but they did not directly use Spanish words or phrases in their compositions. Velasco and García (2014) argued that the traditional biliteracy studies in writing provided evidence that young bilingual writers were able to use their entire linguistic repertoires in the writing process. In a later study, Soltero-Gonzalez and Butvilofsky (2016) reported similar findings for Spanish-English preschoolers in a bilingual program. The preschoolers in their study employed transliteration when they applied their knowledge of Spanish phonetics to write English words.

Several researchers have focused on the presence of translanguaging when the students wrote or discussed their writing (Gort, 2012; Velasco & García, 2014; Bauer et al., 2017). Gort (2012) conducted a qualitative study for six months to examine the patterns of 1st-grade emergent Spanish-English bilingual students' CS, as an example of translanguaging, when they engaged in writing-related talk. Gort discovered that bilingual

(Spanish-English) 1st-graders in a dual-language classroom strategically employed their oral repertoires (i.e., code-switching) in Spanish and English to talk about their writing. Gort reported that one of the students displayed metacognitive awareness when she talked to herself in English about how to revise her Spanish writing, which Gort called bilingual metacognitive speech. Because the students used their dual-language repertoires as they engaged in bilingual interactions to carry out their writing tasks, translanguaging practices appeared during their writing process.

Velasco and García (2014) conducted a qualitative study that specifically investigated the written translanguaging practices of 24 Korean-English and Spanish-English bilingual students (K-4) enrolled in dual-language classrooms. Although only 8 of the 24 writing samples demonstrated written translanguaging, 5 samples showed that the students employed translanguaging to plan, draft, and produce final compositions. Velasco and García concluded that "bilingual writers use different problem-solving strategies and exhibit ways of expressing meaning that are not present in monolingual writing" (p. 10). However, they questioned why so few of the students had employed translanguaging while writing. They wondered if the dual-language context, in which there was adherence to monoglossic instruction for each language, might have affected the students' translanguaging.

Bauer et al. (2017) specifically focused on young bilingual students' use of oral translanguaging while writing. They employed qualitative methods to examine how two minority kindergarteners (a Spanish-speaking Latino student and an English-speaking African-American student) in a dual-language classroom worked as buddy pairs during writing activities. Bauer et al. reported that the students translanguaged during their bilingual dialogues to scaffold each other's language repertoires and writing. Because the students showed that they understood differences in the two languages, Bauer and her colleagues concluded that the students had engaged in metalinguistic talk. Their study corroborated previous findings that translanguaging encouraged students to develop their thinking, planning, and writing (Gort, 2012; Velasco & García, 2014).

Other researchers examined bilingual students' writing and drawing by conducting multimodal and social semiotic analyses to understand how bilingual children describe their personal experiences and construct their bilingual identities through their linguistic knowledge and visual drawings (e.g., Alvarez, 2018; Melo-Pfeifer, 2015). In Melo-Pfeifer's study, she investigated children from Portuguese backgrounds, who were in Portuguese HL classes in Germany. As a part of the study, she asked the students "to draw themselves while speaking the languages that they knew" (p. 202). The children employed multimodal resources, including semiotics (i.e., signs and symbols), to create visual narratives (drawings) with writing (speech bubbles). Throughout the students' writing samples, one particular student's drawing and writing included "information about his name in French, about his age in English, about his personal preferences in Portuguese, and about his plurilingual repertoire in German" (p. 205), which Melo-Pfeifer considered as a multimodal translanguaging example by the student who has been raised in a multilingual context. Melo-Pfeifer recommended that when studying multilingualism, researchers should strive to understand the social, economic, political, and ideological factors that shaped the context in which multilingualism was embedded.

Similarly, Alvarez (2018) showed how the monthly drawings and narrative writings of Mexican-American 1st-graders in a dual-language classroom represented their interpretations of the world and socio-political contexts. She conducted a multimodal analysis to show how the children employed text, space, and drawings to convey meaning and a semiotic analysis to show how they employed signs and symbols for communication purposes. Although the findings showed the students' written text in one language, their writing and drawings provided a richer understanding of how bilingual children's use of multimodality and semiotic systems can document their experiences outside school and their socialization practices including relationships with family and peers.

Additional researchers conducted investigations that did not specifically focus on young bilingual students' written translanguaging, but that provided implications for biliteracy research. For example, Nam (2017) investigated whether 6-year-old Korean students who were learning English as a foreign language in Korea did not become confused when exposed to writing in both Korean and English. Nam reported that the Korean students understood that Korean has a shallow orthography or consistent matching of phonemes and graphemes, and English has a deep orthography or inconsistent matching of phonemes and graphemes. Nam concluded that the young Korean students were becoming biliterate without any confusion. Only one of the above studies (Velasco & García, 2014) presented and analyzed students' translanguaging in their actual writing. Additional research on how bilingual writers engage in translanguaging practices during composing is needed.

Translanguaging practices in bilingual homes, families, and communities

García (2011) explained that translanguaging is a natural and inevitable practice among bilingual families and communities. Studies taking place in bilingual home and community settings have indicated that translanguaging is a necessary discursive resource for bilingual children with parents who primarily speak a minority language (Alvarez, 2014; Orellana & García, 2014; Song, 2016). Although researchers in the past documented the language use in bilingual homes, families, and communities, they did not use the term *translanguaging* because it had not been introduced. Nevertheless, earlier researchers provided evidence of how bilingual children and families engaged in translanguaging practices in home settings as part of their everyday experience (e.g., Dorner, Orellana, & Li-Grining, 2007; Donor, Orellana, & Jiménez, 2008; Li, 2006).

For example, Orellana, Reynolds, Dorner, and Meza (2003) discussed the concept of language brokering, which refers to the language process of interpreting and translating from one language to another. In their study, Orellana et al. showed that it was common practice for children to help their immigrant parents by serving as "language brokers" during inter-actions with other adults, such as teachers or institutional representatives when the parents received mail, letters, and/or advertisements in English. The children in their study used their linguistic repertoires to interpret and translate from English to Spanish the information for their parents. This particular linguistic practice in immigrant homes helped Spanish-speaking parents survive in the English-only context.

Similarly, Dorner et al. (2007) also showed how immigrant children worked as language brokers in their home in a longitudinal case study with 5th- and 6th-grade Mexican immigrant students in the U.S. by documenting their everyday language use with their family members. Their findings revealed that the immigrant children served as language brokers to provide linguistic help for their family members through translating and interpreting practices. Dorner et al. argued that the children's language practices were not solitary activities; rather, they were "social and relational events in which families engage together and in relation to society" (p. 538). The two studies corroborate García's argument that children from immigrant households serve as language brokers by drawing "from one linguistic repertoire that then is socially constructed as two autonomous language systems" (Orellana & García, 2014, p. 387). The findings imply that understanding bilingual children's language brokering practices across diverse contexts provides evidence of their potential to translanguage.

After the concept of translanguaging introduced, the study by Alvarez (2014) theorized language brokering as a translanguaging event where emergent bilingual youth use their linguistic repertoires to "translate, inter-pret, and mediate oral and written texts" (p. 327) during the communication with immigrant families. Alvarez examined translanguaging practices of bilingual children when they worked on their English homework in an after-school program with bilingual mentors and Spanish-speaking parents col-laborating in these events. For these homework experiences, the children were doing language brokering between their parents and the mentor to clarify the meaning of words or to offer alternative meanings during con-versations. Ultimately, the children's translanguaging was necessary to mediate and facilitate communication between adults and to support their own sense-making of academic homework. Since their findings further showed that the parents' involvement had been increased thanks to the culturally sensitive mentors whose pedagogical tools leveraged translanguaging practices, Alvarez claimed that educators must value multilingual families' everyday translanguaging events.

A later study by Song (2016) explored whether and how translanguaging was used among bilingual families in the home setting. In her participant observation study, Song investigated four Korean bilingual children and their family members in the U.S. during home literacy events to examine how the immigrant parents supported their children in becoming bilingual and biliterate in Korean and English. Song found that the bilingual families engaged in everyday literacy practices by using their two languages flexibly and strategically to create and negotiate meaning. Similarly, in a study with an Arabic-speaking Muslim family, Yazan and Ali (2018) showed that the parents' language ideologies and policy regarding their daughter's maintenance of Arabic in the U.S. influenced the emergence and enactment of the daughter's Arabic HL development.

Studies situated in communities and public places have additionally considered how translanguaging played in a role in supporting bi/multilingualism (Alvarez & Alvarez, 2016; Creese, Blackledge, & Hu, 2018; Hua, Wei, & Lyons, 2017). In their case study, Alvarez and Alvarez (2016) investigated the ways in which immigrant communities nurtured and sustained bilingualism outside the school context. Taking place in a public library, their findings demonstrated that the library supported the bilingual Latinx community by providing a translanguaging space, such as incorporating bilingual materials, providing mentorship, and honoring biliteracy practices for the community. With the targeted translanguaging practices the public space of the library extended the critical practices of bilingual and biliteracy learning and ultimately met the sociocultural needs of the local emergent bilingual community.

Relatedly, other researchers illuminated the role translanguaging played in other public places serving bi/multilingual communities. For instance, Hua et al. (2017) situated their ethnographic study in a Polish shop located in London to explore the dynamic practices in a *translanguaging space* (Wei, 2011). The meaning of translanguaging in this study was inclusive of language, embodied practices, and multimodal resources. They paid particular attention to the various multimodal practices and resources in communicative zones to examine how participants communicated with and involved each other in encounters. Since translanguaging space features the dynamic and fluid nature of everyday communication using the multimodal and multisensory resources (Wei, 2011), their findings revealed that the Polish shop was a translanguaging space, created by and for translanguaging to connect with multilingual customers in the local community.

Similarly, Creese et al. (2018) documented a butcher's stall in the United Kingdom as a linguistically diverse context where translanguaging was a resource to interact with multilingual customers. The butchers crossed languages among Mandarin, Cantonese, and English to meet the customers' demands and to convey their messages. During the interactions between the butchers and the customers, they often drew on translanguaging practices by translating and shuttling between languages. Their translanguaging interaction became an important linguistic tool for understanding each other's meanings and negotiating potential misunderstandings from their conversations. Overall, these studies suggest that translanguaging is a practice that occurs in multilingual communities as daily interactions to meet the everyday communicative needs of bi/multilingual communities.

Summary and gaps in the literature

This chapter discussed the theoretical framework that informed this study by focusing on a sociocultural perspective on learning and the trans-languaging paradigm as a model of dynamic bilingualism. The chapter then reviewed recent studies that were conducted from a heteroglossic perspective to examine translanguaging practices in the classrooms, homes, and communities.

Specifically, the chapter discussed research on teachers' use of trans-languaging as an instructional strategy by implementing diverse types of translanguaging strategies, such as code-switching/code-mixing, trans-lating, and using cognates (Esquinca et al., 2014; Gort & Sembiante, 2015; Jiang et al., 2014; Palmer et al., 2014). The studies reviewed in this chapter also examined how emergent bilingual learners engaged in translanguaging practices. The findings demonstrated that bilinguals were able to utilize their complete language repertoires orally (Durán & Palmer, 2014; Martin-Beltran, 2010; Sayer, 2013) and while writing (Gort, 2012; Velasco & García, 2014; Bauer et al., 2017). Although the term *translanguaging* had not been introduced, earlier researchers displayed evidence of potential translanguaging in bilingual homes and communities as part of their natural and everyday experience (Dorner et al., 2007; Li, 2006; Orellana et al., 2003). The further examinations on language practices in bi/multilingual communities displayed trans-languaging was a practice by bi/multilingual speakers as their daily interactions among them to meet their everyday communicative needs.

Although scholars in bilingual research have adopted the translanguaging paradigm from a heteroglossic perspective, there still are gaps in the literature. First, the majority of the studies paid attention to the Spanish-English bilingual group, and little is known about other language groups (such as Korean-English). Second, most of the studies were conducted in dual-language programs in the U.S.; thus, there is little research that investigated bilingual students' translanguaging practices in other types of classroom settings (such as HL classrooms). Third, the majority of the studies to date have paid attention to teachers' translanguaging pedagogies (e.g., Esquinca et al., 2014; Gort & Sembiante, 2015; Martínez, et al., 2015; Palmer et al., 2014; Worthy, et al., 2013) and older bilingual learners' translanguaging practices (e.g., Martin-Beltran, 2010; García & Godina, 2017); thus, we still have little understanding of young emergent bilingual students' translanguaging practices both in the classroom and home/community settings. Fourth, since most translanguaging research has tackled bilinguals' oral discourse (Durán & Palmer, 2014; Martin-Beltran, 2010; Sayer, 2013) rather than their writing practices (Velasco & García, 2014), there is still not enough research findings about emergent bilingual writers' translingual practices (Canagarajah, 2013, Durán, 2017). Lastly, compared to the translanguaging studies conducted in instructional settings, there is little research that investigated the trans-languaging practices among bilingual families in the home setting.

Purpose and research questions of the present study

The current study was informed by García's (2009) theoretical conceptualization of translanguaging. García (2009, 2011) argued that when examining emergent bilingual students' language use, it is important to study how they are able to utilize their linguistic repertoires across two languages to communicate orally and in writing. García and Wei (2014) warned that "bilingual students' linguistic repertoires should not be measured with a single construct in a standard language" (p. 133). Other scholars also recommended that bilingual students should be given the opportunity to use their entire linguistic repertoires to make meaning and to develop their biliteracy skills (Escamilla & Hopewell, 2010; Hopewell & Escamilla, 2014; Soltero-González, Escamilla, & Hopewell, 2012).

To fill the gaps stated above in the literature, the present study investigates *elementary grade* (1st- and 3rd-grade) *Korean-English* bilingual students' *oral and written* language use *in a HL classroom* as well as their translanguaging practices in the *home* setting. The findings can help to fill the gaps in the bilingual and biliteracy literatures, which primarily have paid attention to Spanish-English bilinguals' language use and development and that were conducted in dual-language programs. To understand the influence of sociocultural factors, the study also explores the role of the children's parents and other family members in their Korean and English language use and HL learning. Lastly, to address bilingual students' HL development over the years, the oral and written language performance of two focal 3rd-graders were compared when they were in 1st grade. The following research questions guided the inquiry:

1. What characterized the 1st-grade Korean bilingual students' oral

and written language use and their translanguaging practices at a Korean HL School?

2. What were the parents of 1st-graders' attitudes toward bilingualism and their home practices to support their children's HL learning?

3. What characterized the 3rd-grade Korean bilingual students' oral and written language use and their translanguaging practices at a Korean HL School?

4. How did the two focal 3rd-graders' oral and written language use differ compare to their earlier use as 1st-graders?

5. What were the family and sociocultural influences on the two focal 3rd-graders' longitudinal language use?

References

Allard, E. (2017). Re-examining teacher translanguaging: An ecological perspective. *Bilingual Research Journal*, 40(2), 116–130.

Alvarez, S. (2014). Translanguaging *Tareas*: Emergent bilingual youth as language brokers for homework in immigrant families. *Language Arts*, 91(5), 326–339.

Alvarez, S. (2018). Drawn and written funds of knowledge: A window into emerging bilingual children's experiences and social interpretations through their written narratives and drawings. *Journal of Early Childhood Literacy*, 18(1), 97–128.

Alvarez, S., & Alvarez, S. P. (2016). "La Biblioteca es Importante": A case study of an emergent bilingual public library in the Nuevo U.S. South. *Equity and Excellence in Education*, 49(4), 403–413.

August D., & Hakuta K. (1998). *Educating language-minority children*. Washington: National Research Council, Institute of Medicine, National Academy Press.

Bailey, B. (2007). Heteroglossia and boundaries. In M. Heller (Ed.), *Bilingualism: A social approach* (pp. 257–276). Basingstoke, UK: Palgrave.

Baker, C. (2011). *Foundations of bilingual education and bilingualism* (5th ed.). Clevedon, England: Multilingual Matters.

Bakhtin, M. M. (1981). *The dialogic imagination: Four essays* (M. Holquist, Ed.; C. Emerson & M. Holquist, Trans.). Austin: University of Texas Press.

Bakhtin, M. M. (1984). *Problems of Dostoevsky's poetics*. Manchester: Manchester University Press.

Bartlett, L., & García, O. (2011). *Additive schooling in subtractive times: Bilingual education and Dominican immigrant youth in the heights*. Vanderbilt University Press.

Bauer, E. B., Presiado, V., & Colomer, S. (2017). Writing through partnership: Fostering trans- languaging in children who are emergent bilinguals. *Journal of Literacy Research*, 49(1), 10–37.

Bernardini, P., & Schlyter, S. (2004). Growing syntactic structure and code-mixing in the weaker language: The Ivy Hypothesis. *Bilingualism: Language and Cognition*, 7(1), 49–69.

Bezcioglu-Goktolga, I., & Yagmur, K. (2018). Home language policy of second-generation Turkish families in the Netherlands. *Journal of Multilingual and Multicultural Development. 39*(1), 44–59.

Bialystok, E. (2018). Bilingual education for young children: Review of the effects and consequences. *International Journal of Bilingual Education and Bilingualism, 21*(6), 666–679.

Blackledge, A., & Creese, A. (2010). *Multilingualism: A critical perspective.* London, UK: Continuum.

Budiyana, Y. E. (2017). Students' parents' attitude toward Chinese heritage language maintenance. *Theory and Practice in Language Studies, 7*(3), 195–200.

Busch, B. (2012). The linguistic repertoire revisited. *Applied Linguistics, 33*(5), 503–523.

Caldas, S. (2012). Language policy in the family. In B. Spolsky (Ed.), *The Cambridge handbook of language policy* (pp. 351–373). Cambridge, UK: Cambridge University Press.

Canagarajah, A. S. (2011a). Translanguaging in the classroom: emerging issues for research and pedagogy. *Applied Linguistics Review, 2*, 1–28.

Canagarajah, A. S. (2011b). Codemeshing in academic writing: Identifying teachable strategies of translanguaging. *The Modern Language Journal, 95*, 401–417.

Canagarajah, A. S. (Ed.). (2013). *Literacy as translingual practice: Between communities and schools.* New York, NY: Routledge.

Carreira, M., & Kagan, O. (2017). Heritage language education: A proposal for the next 50 years. *Foreign Language Annals, 51*(1), 152–168.

Cenoz, J. (2017). Translanguaging in school contexts: international perspectives. *Journal of Language, Identity and Education, 16*(4), 193–198.

Cenoz, J., & Gorter, D. (2017). Minority languages and sustainable translanguaging: Threat or opportunity? *Journal of Multilingual and Multicultural Development, 38*(10), 901–912.

Cha, K., & Goldenberg, C. (2015). The complex relationship between home language proficiency and kindergarten children's Spanish and English oral proficiencies. *Journal of Educational Psychology, 107*(4).

Cho, G. (2000). The role of heritage language in social interactions and relationships: Reflections from a language minority group. *Bilingual Research Journal, 24*, 369–384.

Cook, V. (2001). Using the first language in the classroom. *Canadian Modern Language Review, 57*(3), 402–423.

Crawford, J. (2004). *Educating English learners: Language diversity in the classroom* (Vol. 5). Los Angeles, CA: Bilingual Education Services.

Creese, A., & Blackledge, A. (2010). Translanguaging in the bilingual classroom: A pedagogy for teaching and learning. *The Modern Language Journal, 94*, 103–115.

Creese, A., Blackledge, A., & Hu, R. (2018). Translanguaging and translation: The construction of social difference across city spaces. *International Journal of Bilingual Education and Bilingualism, 21*(7), 841–851.

Cummins, J. (1991). Interdependence of first- and second-language proficiency in bilingual children. In E. Bialystok (Ed.), *Language processing in bilingual children* (pp. 70–89). Cambridge, England: Cambridge University Press.

Cummins, J. (2005). A proposal for action: Strategies for recognizing heritage language competence as a learning resource within the mainstream classroom. *Modern Language Journal, 89,* 585–592.

Cummins, J., & Persad, R. (2014). Teaching through a multilingual lens: The Evolution of EAL Policy and Practice in Canada. *Education Matters, 2,* 3–40.

Daniel, S. M., & Pacheco, M. B. (2016). Translanguaging practices and perspectives of four multilingual teens. *Journal of Adolescent and Adult Literacy, 59*(6), 653–663.

De Houwer, A. (2007). Parental language input patterns and children's bilingual use. *Applied Psycholinguistics, 28,* 411–424.

Dorner, L. M., Orellana, M. F., & Li-Grining, C. P. (2007). "I helped my mom," and it helped me: Translating the skills of language brokers into improved standardized test scores. *American Journal of Education, 113*(3), 451–478.

Dorner, L. M., Orellana, M. F., and Jiménez, R. (2008). "It's one of those things that you do to help the family": Language brokering and the development of immigrant adolescents'. *Journal of Adolescent Research. 23*(5). 515–543.

Duarte, J. (2020). Translanguaging in the context of mainstream multilingual education. *International Journal of Multilingualism, 17*(2), 232–247.

Durán, L. (2017). Audience and young bilingual writers: Building on strengths. *Journal of Literacy Research, 49*(1), 92–114.

Durán, L., & Palmer, D. (2014). Pluralist discourses of bilingualism and translanguaging talk in classrooms. *Journal of Early Childhood Literacy, 14,* 367–388.

Duursma, E., Romero-Contreras, S., Szúber, A., Proctor, C. P., Snow, C., & August, D., (2007). The role of home literacy and language environment on bilinguals' English and Spanish vocabulary development. *Applied Psycholinguistics, 28,* 171–190.

Edelsky, C. (1986). *Writing in a bilingual program: Había una vez.* Norwood, NJ: Ablex.

Escamilla, K., & Hopewell, S. (2010). Transitions to biliteracy: Creating positive academic trajectories for emerging bilinguals in the United States. In J. Petrovic (Ed.), *International perspectives on bilingual education: Policy, practice, controversy.* Charlotte, NC: Information Age Publishing. (pp. 69–93).

Esquinca, A., Araujo, B., & de la Piedra, M. T. (2014). Meaning making and translanguaging in a two-way dual-language program on the U.S.-Mexico border, *Bilingual Research Journal, 37*(2), 164–181.

Flores, N., & Schissel, J. L. (2014). Dynamic bilingualism as the norm: Envisioning a heteroglossic approach to standards-based reform. *TESOL Quarterly, 48*(3), 454–479.

Fogle, L. W. (2013). Parental ethnotheories and family language policy in transnational adoptive families. *Language Policy, 12*(1), 83–102.

Fogle, L. W., & King, K. A. (2013). Child agency and language policy in transnational families. *Issues in Applied Linguistics, 19,* 1–25.

Francis, D. J., Lesaux, N. K., & August, D. (2006). Language of instruction. In D. August & T. Shanahan (Eds.), *Developing literacy in second-language learners: Report of the National Literacy Panel on language minority children and youth* (pp. 365–414). Mahwah, NJ: Lawrence Erlbaum.

Gandara, P., & Hopkin, M. (2010). *Forbidden language: English learners and restrictive language policies.* New York, NY: Teachers College Press.

García, E. E. (2005). *Teaching and learning in two languages: Bilingualism and schooling in the United States*. New York: Teachers College Press.

García, O. (2009). *Bilingual education in the 21st century*. Malden, MA: Wiley-Blackwell.

García, O. (2011). Educating New York's bilingual children: Constructing a future from the past. *International Journal of Bilingual Education and Bilingualism*, *14*, 133–153.

García, O. (2014). What is translanguaging? Expanded questions and answers for U.S. educators. In S. Hesson, K. Seltzer, & H. H. Woodley (Eds.), *Translanguaging in Curriculum and Instruction: A CUNY-NYSIEB Guide for Educators* (pp. 1–13). New York, NY: CUNY- NYSIEB.

García, O., & Leiva, L. (2014). Theorizing and enacting translanguaging for social justice. In A. Blackledge & A. Creese (Eds.), *Heteroglossia as practice and pedagogy* (Vol. 20, pp. 199–216). Heidelberg, Germany: Springer.

García, O., & Kano, N. (2014). Translanguaging as process and pedagogy: Developing the English writing of Japanese students in the US. In J. Conteh & G. Meier (Eds.), *The multilingual turn in languages education: Opportunities and challenges* (pp. 258–277). Bristol: Multilingual Matters.

García, O., & Wei, L. (2014). Translanguaging: Language, bilingualism and education. Basingstoke, UK: Palgrave Macmillan.

García, G. E., & Godina, H. (2017). A window into bilingual reading: The bilingual reading practices of fourth-grade, Mexican-American children who are emergent bilinguals. *Journal of Literacy Research*, *49*(2), 273–301.

García, O., & Lin, A. (2017). Translanguaging and bilingual education. In O. García, A. Lin, & S. May (Eds.) *Bilingual and Multilingual Education* (pp. 117–130). Springer.

García, G. E., McKoon, G., & August, D. (2006). Synthesis: Language and literacy assessment. In D. August & T. Shanahan (Eds.), *Developing literacy in second-language learners: A report of the National Literacy Panel on language minority children and youth* (pp. 583–596). Mahwah, NJ: Lawrence Erlbaum.

García, O., Johnson, S., & Seltzer, K. (2017). *The Translanguaging Classroom. Leveraging Student Bilingualism for Learning*. Philadelphia, PA: Caslon.

García-Mateus, S., & Palmer, D. (2017). Translanguaging pedagogies for positive identities in two-way dual language bilingual education. *Journal of Language, Identity, and Education*, *6*(4), 245–255.

Gee, J. P. (1996). *Social linguistics and literacies: Ideology in discourses* (2nd ed.). London: Taylor & Francis.

Gee, J. P. (2012). *Social linguistics and literacies: Ideology in discourses* (4th ed.). New York, NY: Routledge.

Genesee, F. (2008). Bilingual first language acquisition: Evidence from Montreal. *Diversite urbaine*, 9–26.

Genesee, F., Nicoladis, E., & Paradis, J. (1995). Language differentiation in early bilingual development. *Journal of Child Language*, *22*, 611–631.

Genesee, F., Geva, E., Dressler, C., & Kamil, M. L. (2006). Synthesis: Cross-linguistic relationships. In D. August & T. Shanahan (Eds.), *Developing literacy in second-language learning: Report of the National Literacy Panel on language minority children and youth* (pp. 153–174). Mahwah, NJ: Lawrence Erlbaum.

Gkaintartzi, A., Chatzidaki, A., & Tsokalidou, R. (2014). Albanian parents and the Greek educational context: who is willing to fight for the home language? *International Multilingual Research Journal, 8*(4), 291–308.

Glaser, B. G., & Strauss, A. L. (1967). *Discovery of grounded theory: Strategies for qualitative research*. Chicago: Aldine.

Gort, M. (2012). Evaluation and revision processes of young bilinguals in a dual language program. In E. B. Bauer & M. Gort (Eds.), *Early biliteracy development: Exploring young learners' use of their linguistic resources* (pp. 90–110). New York, NY: Routledge.

Gort, M., & Sembiante, S. (2015). Navigating hybridized language learning spaces through translanguaging pedagogy: Dual language preschool teachers' languaging practices in support of emergent bilingual children's performance of academic discourse. *International Multilingual Research Journal, 9*, 7–25.

Gravelle, M. (1996). *Supporting bilingual learners in schools*. Stoke-on-Trent, UK: Trentham Books.

Guardado, M., & Becker, A. (2015). "Glued to the family": The role of familism in heritage language development. *Language, Culture and Curriculum, 27*(2), 163–181.

Guerra (2012). From code-segregation to code-switching to code-meshing: Finding deliverance from deficit thinking through language awareness and performance. In P. Dunston & S. Fullerton (Eds.), *61st yearbook of the Literacy Research Association* (pp. 108–118). Oak Creek, WI: Literacy Research Association.

Hakuta, K., & Diaz, R. (1985). *Bilingualism and cognitive development: Three perspectives and methodological implications*. (CLEAR Technical Report 2). Los Angeles, CA: Center for Language Education and Research, University of California, Los Angeles.

Halliday, M. A. K. (1973). *Explorations in the functions of language*. London: Edward Arnold.

Heath, S. B. (1983). *Ways with words: Language, life, and work in communities and classrooms*. Cambridge: Cambridge University Press.

Heller, M. (2001). Undoing the macro/micro dichotomy: Ideology and categorization in a linguistic minority school. In N. Coupland, S. Sarangi, & C. N. Candlin (Eds.), *Sociolinguistics and social theory* (pp. 212–234). London, England: Routledge.

Hinton, L. (2008). Trading tongues: Loss of heritage languages in the United States. In A. Reyes & A. Lo (Eds.). *Beyond Yellow English: Toward a linguistic anthropology of Asian Pacific America: Toward a linguistic anthropology of Asian Pacific America* (pp. 331–346). Oxford: Oxford University Press.

Hopewell, S., & Escamilla, K. (2014). Biliteracy development in immersion contexts. *Journal of Immersion and Content-based Language Education. 2*(2), 181–195.

Hopewell, S., & Abril-Gonzalez, P. (2019). Por qué estamos codeswitching? Understanding language use in a second-grade classroom. *Bilingual Research Journal, 42*(1), 105–120.

Hua, Z., Wei, L., & Lyons, A. (2017). Polish shop(ping) as translanguaging space. *Social Semiotics, 27*(4), 411–433.

Jiang, Y. B., García, G. E., & Willis, A. I. (2014). Code-mixing as a bilingual instructional strategy. *Bilingual Research Journal*, 37(3), 311–326.

Jönsson, K., (2018). Translanguaging and multilingual literacies: Diary-based case studies of adolescents in an international school. *International Journal of the Sociology of Language*, 224, 85–117.

Keh, M. L., & Stoessel, S. (2017). How first is first? Revisiting language maintenance and shift and the meaning of L1/L2 in three case studies. *International Multilingual Research Journal*, 11, 101–114.

Kheirkhah, M., & Cekaite, A. (2015). Language maintenance in a multilingual family: Informal heritage language lessons in parent–child interactions. *Journal of Cross-Cultural and Interlanguage Communiciation*, 34(3), 319–346.

King, K. A., & Fogle, L. W. (2006). Bilingual parenting as good parenting: Parents' perspectives on family language policy for additive bilingualism, *International Journal of Bilingual Education and Bilingualism*, 9(6), 695–712.

Kondo-Brown, K. (2011). Maintaining heritage language perspectives of Korean parents, *Multicultural Education*, 19(1), 31–37.

Lanauze, M., & Snow, C. E. (1989). The relation between first and second language writing skills: Evidence from Puerto Rican elementary school children in bilingual programs. *Linguistics and Education*, 1(4), 323–339.

Lewis, C., Enciso, P., & Moje, E. B. (2007). Introduction: Reframing sociocultural research on literacy: Identity, agency, and power. In C. Lewis, P. Enciso, & E. B. Moje (Eds.), *Reframing sociocultural research on literacy: Identity, agency, and power*. New York, NY: Routledge.

Lewis, G., Jones, B., & Baker, C. (2012). Translanguaging: Developing its conceptualisation and contextualization. *Educational Research and Evaluation*, 18, 655–670.

Li, G. (2006). Biliteracy and trilingual practices in the home context: Case studies of Chinese-Canadian children. *Journal of Early Childhood Literacy*, 6(3), 355–381.

Liang, F. (2018). Parental perceptions toward and practices of heritage language maintenance: Focusing on the United States and Canada. *International Journal of Language Studies*, 12(2), 65–86.

Lindholm-Leary, K. J. (2001). *Dual language education*. Clevedon, UK: Multilingual Matters.

López, D. (1996). Language: Diversity and assimilation. In R. Waldinger & M. Bozorgmehr (Eds.), *Ethnic Los Angeles* (pp. 139–163). New York: Russell Sage Foundation.

Lü, C., & Koda, K. (2011). The impact of home language and literacy support on English-Chinese biliteracy acquisition among Chinese heritage language learners. *Heritage Language Journal*, 8, 119–231.

Lynch, A. (2014). The first decade of the Heritage Language Journal: A retrospective view of research on heritage languages. *Heritage Language Journal*, 11(3), 224–242.

MacSwan, J. (2017). A multilingual perspective on translanguaging. *American Education Research Journal*, 54(1), 167–201.

Martin–Beltran, M. (2010). The two-way language bridge: Co-constructing bilingual language learning opportunities. *The Modern Language Journal*, 94(2), 254–277.

Martínez, R. A., Hikida, M., & Durán, L. (2015). Unpacking ideologies of linguistic purism: How dual language teachers make sense of everyday translanguaging. *International Multilingual Research Journal, 9*(1), 26–42.

Martínez, R. A., Durán, L., & Hikida, M. (2017). Becoming "Spanish learners": Identity and interaction among multilingual children in a Spanish-English dual language classroom. *International Multilingual Research Journal, 11*(3), 167–183.

Martínez-Roldán, C. M. (2015). Translanguaging practices as mobilization of linguistic resources in a Spanish/English bilingual after-school program: An analysis of contradictions. *International Multilingual Research Journal, 9*(1), 43–58.

McCabe, M. (2016). Transnationalism and language maintenance: Czech and Slovak as heritage languages in the Southeastern United States. *International Journal of the Sociology of Language, 238*, 169–191.

Melo-Pfeifer, S. (2015). The role of the family in heritage language use and learning: Impact on heritage language policies, *International Journal of Bilingual Education and Bilingualism, 18*(1), 26–44.

Mertens, D. M. (2015). *Research and evaluation in education and psychology: Integrating diversity with quantitative, qualitative, and mixed methods* (4th ed.). Thousand Oaks, CA: Sage.

Min, H. (1997). *The code-switching behavior of three Mandarin-English speaking children.* Unpublished doctoral dissertation, University of Illinois, Urbana-Champaign.

Montrul, S. (2008). *Incomplete acquisition in bilingualism: Re-examining the age factor.* Amsterdam: John Benjamins.

Montrul, S. (2010). Current issues in heritage language acquisition. *Annual Review of Applied Linguistics, 30*, 3–23.

Montrul, S. A. (2018). Heritage language development: Connecting the dots, *International Journal of Bilingualism, 22*(5), 530–546.

Moro, L., Mortimer, E., & Tiberghien, A. (2019). The use of social semiotics multimodality and joint action theory to describe teaching practices: two cases studies with experienced teachers. *Classroom Discourse, 11*(3), 1–23.

Murphy, V. (2014). *Second language learning in the early school years: Trends and contexts.* Oxford: Oxford University Press.

Nagy, W. E., García, G. E., Durgunoglu, A., & Hancin-Bhatt, B. (1993). Spanish-English bilingual children's use and recognition of cognates in English reading. *Journal of Reading Behavior, 21*, 241–259.

Nam, K. M. (2017). How young children make sense of two different writing systems: Korean written in the Hangul alphabet, and English written in the Roman alphabet. *Journal of Early Childhood Literacy, 18*(4), 490–517.

Nesteruk, O. (2010). Heritage language maintenance and loss among the children of Eastern European immigrants in the USA, *Journal of Multilingual and Multicultural Development, 31*(3), 271–286.

Oh, J. S., & Fuligni, A. J. (2010). The role of heritage language development in the ethnic identity and family relationships of adolescents from immigrant backgrounds. *Social Development, 19*, 202–220.

Orellana, M. F., & García, O. (2014). Conversation currents: language brokering and translanguaging in school. *Language Arts, 91*(5), 386–392.

Orellana, M. F., Reynolds, J., Dorner, L., & Meza, M. (2003). In other words: Translating or "para-phrasing" as a family literacy practice in immigrant households. *Reading Research Quarterly, 38*(1), 12–34.

Oriyama, K. (2010). Heritage language maintenance and Japanese identity formation: What role can schooling and ethnic community contact play? *Heritage Language Journal, 7*(2), 76–111.

Otheguy, R., García, O., & Reid, W. (2015). Clarifying translanguaging and deconstructing named languages: A perspective from linguistics. *Applied Linguistics Review, 6,* 281–307.

Palmer, D. K., Martínez, R. A., Mateus, S. G., & Henderson, K. (2014). Reframing the debate on language separation: Toward a vision for translanguaging pedagogies in the dual language classroom. *The Modern Language Journal, 98,* 757–772.

Pan, B. A. (1995). Code negotiation in bilingual families: "My body starts speaking English." *Journal of Multilingual and Multicultural Development, 16*(4), 315–327.

Park, S. M., & Sarkar, M. (2007). Parents' attitudes toward heritage language maintenance for their children and their efforts to help their children maintain the heritage language: A case study of Korean-Canadian immigrants. *Language, Culture and Curriculum, 20*(3), 223–235.

Park-Johnson, S. (2017). Code mixing as a window into language dominance: Evidence from Korean heritage speakers. *Heritage Language Journal, 14*(1), 49–69.

Polinsky, M. (2011). Reanalysis in adult heritage language. *Studies in Second Language Acquisition, 33*(2), 305–328.

Polinsky, M., (2018). Bilingual children and adult heritage speakers: The range of comparison. *International Journal of Bilingualism, 22*(5) 547–563.

Polinsky, M., & Kagan, O. (2007). Heritage languages: In the "wild" and in the classroom. *Language and Linguistics Compass, 1*(5), 368–395.

Polinsky, M., & Scontras, G. (2019). A roadmap for heritage language research. *Bilingualism: Language and Cognition, 23*(1), 5–55.

Reyes, I. (2004). Functions of code switching in schoolchildren's conversations. *Bilingual Research Journal, 28*(1), 77–98.

Sanders-Smith, S. C., & Dávila, L. T. (2019). Progressive practice and translanguaging: Supporting multilingualism in a Hong Kong preschool. *Bilingual Research Journal, 42*(3), 275–290.

Sayer, P. (2013). Translanguaging, TexMex, and bilingual pedagogy: Emergent bilinguals learning through the vernacular. *TESOL Quarterly, 47*(1), 63–88.

Schmid, M. S. (2010). Languages at play: The relevance of L1 attrition to the study of bilingualism. *Bilingualism: Language and Cognition, 13,* 1–7.

Seals, C., & Peyton, J. K. (2017). Heritage language education: Valuing the languages, literacies and cultural competencies of immigrant youth. *Current Issues of Language Planning, 18*(1), 87–101.

Shibata, S. (2000). Opening a Japanese Saturday School in a small town in the United States: Community collaboration to teach Japanese as a heritage language. *Bilingual Research Journal, 24,* 465–474.

Shin, S. J. (2005). *Developing in two languages: Korean children in America.* Clevedon, UK: Multilingual Matters.

Shin, F. H., & Krashen, S. (1996). Teacher attitudes toward the principles of bilingual education and toward students' participation in bilingual programs: Same or different? *Bilingual Research Journal, 20,* 45–53.

Smith, P., & Murillo, L. (2015). Theorizing translanguaging and multilingual literacies through human capital theory. *International Multilingual Research Journal, 9,* 59–73.

Soltero-Gonzalez, L., & Butvilofsky, S. (2016). The early Spanish and English writing development of simultaneous bilingual preschoolers. *Journal of Early Childhood Literacy, 16*(4), 473–497.

Soltero-González, L., Escamilla, K., & Hopewell, S. (2012). Changing teachers' perceptions about the writing abilities of emerging bilingual students: towards a holistic bilingual perspective on writing assessment. *International Journal of Bilingual Education and Bilingualism, 15*(1), 71–94.

Song, K. (2016). "Okay, I will say in Korean and then in American": Translanguaging practices in bilingual homes. *Journal of Early Childhood Literacy, 16*(1), 84–106.

Spolsky, B. (2012). Family language policy—The critical domain. *Journal of Multilingual and Multicultural Development, 33*(1), 3–11.

Street, B. V. (1984). *Literacy in theory and practice.* Cambridge: CUP.

Street, B. V. (2001). The new literacy studies. In E. Cushman, G. R. Kintgen, B. M. Kroll, & M. Rose (Eds.), *Literacy: A critical sourcebook* (pp. 430–442). Boston: St. Martin's Press.

Street, B. V. (2003). The implications of the "New Literacies Studies" for literacy education. In S. Goodman, J. Maybin, & N. Mercer (Eds.), *Language, literacy, and education: A reader* (pp. 77–88). Stoke-on-Trent, UK: Trentham Books.

Swain, M. (2000). The output hypothesis and beyond: Mediating acquisition through collaborative dialogue. In J. Lantolf (Ed.), *Sociocultural theory and second language learning* (pp. 97–114). Oxford: Oxford University Press.

Szilagyi, J., & Szecsi, T. (2020). Why and how to maintain the Hungarian language: Hungarian-American families' views on heritage language practices. *Heritage Language Journal, 17*(1), 114–139.

Tracey, D. H., & Morrow, L. M. (2006). *Lenses on reading: An introduction to theories and models.* New York, NY: The Guilford Press.

Tse, L. (1998). Affecting affect: The impact of heritage language programs on student attitudes. In S. Krashen, L. Tse, & J. McQuillan (Eds.), *Heritage language development* (pp. 51–72). Culver City, CA: Language Education Associates.

Tse, L. (2001). *Why don't they learn English? Separating fact from fallacy in the U.S. language debate.* New York; London: Teachers College Press.

Valdés, G. (2001). Heritage Language Students: Profiles and Possibilities. In J. Peyton, J. Ranard, & S. McGinnis (Eds.), *Heritage languages in America: Preserving a national resource* (pp. 37–80). McHenry, IL: The Center for Applied Linguistics and Delta Systems.

Valdés, G. (2005). Bilingualism, heritage learners, and SLA research: Opportunities lost or seized? *Modern Language Journal, 89*(3), 410–426.

Velasco, P., & García, O. (2014). Translanguaging and the writing of bilingual learners. *Bilingual Research Journal: The Journal of the National Association for Bilingual Education, 37,* 6–23.

Veltman, C. (1983). *Language shift in the United States.* The Hague: Mouton.

Vihman, M. (1998). A developmental perspective on code-switching: Conversations between a pair of siblings. *International Journal of Bilingualism*, 2(1), 45–84.

Vygotsky, L. S. (1962). *Thought and language*. Cambridge MA: MIT Press.

Vygotsky, L. S. (1978). *Mind in society: The development of higher psychological processes*. Cambridge, MA: Harvard University Press.

Wei, L. (2011). Moment analysis and translanguaging space: Discursive construction of identities by multilingual Chinese youth in Britain. *Journal of Pragmatics*, *43*, 1222–1235.

Wei, L., & Wu, C. (2009). Polite Chinese children revisited: Creativity and the use of code-switching in the Chinese complementary school classroom. *International Journal of Bilingual Education and Bilingualism*, *12*(2), 193–211.

Wong-Fillmore, L. W. (1991). When learning a second language means losing the first. *Early Childhood Research Quarterly*, *6*(3), 323–347.

Worthy, J., Durán, L., Hikida, M., Pruitt, A., & Peterson, K. (2013). Spaces for dynamic bilingualism in read-aloud discussions: Developing and strengthening bilingual and academic skills. *Bilingual Research Journal*, *36*, 311–328.

Yazan, B., & Ali, I. (2018). Family Language Policies in a Libyan Immigrant Family in the U.S.: Language and Religious Identity. *Heritage Language Journal*. *15*(3), 369–388.

You, B. K. (2005). Children negotiating Korean American ethnic identity through their heritage language. *Bilingual Research Journal*, *29*, 712–721.

3 Pathway to translanguaging research
Creating translanguaging spaces

Introduction

This chapter introduces the methodological framework for the study so that readers of the book can understand how the translanguaging spaces were created in the research setting. The study employs the constructivist/interpretive paradigm (Mertens, 2015), which views that reality is socially constructed because the current study aims to understand the everyday translanguaging practices that the emergent bilingual students naturally displayed from their "perceptions and experiences" (Thanh & Than, 2015, p. 24). Since "the reality is socially constructed" (Mertens, 2015, p. 12), the constructivist/interpretive research paradigm with its focus on social construction, multiple participant meanings, and naturalistic phenomenon (Creswell, 2009) was appropriate for this research.

Based on the constructivist/interpretive paradigm, the study employs a qualitative discourse analysis methodology that combined micro- and macro-analyses. The micro-level analysis is needed to examine the speaker's language use, verbal interaction, or communication, whereas macro-level analysis is needed to analyze the surrounding sociocultural context that influences the speaker's language use and discourse (van Dijk, 1990). Bloome, Carter, Christian, Otto, and Shuart-Faris (2008) pointed out that the discourse analysis approach can help researchers examine the sociocultural orientation of language and literacy events in classrooms. Specifically, classroom discourse analysis focuses on communication systems by all the participants in the classroom setting (Cazden & Beck, 2003); thus, it helps researchers to closely examine what the students actually do with their languages (Saville-Troike, 2003; Gee, 2012) and how they use languages within specific events (Bloome et al., 2008). Because the purpose of this study was to investigate Korean emergent bilingual students' oral and written language use to understand the their "ways of behaving, interacting, and speaking" (Gee, 2012, p. viii), the discourse analysis approach serves as the appropriate methodological framework for this study.

The study further employs qualitative case study methodology (Stake, 1994, 2010) as part of the study to examine the role of the families in their children's language use by presenting mini-case studies of three 1st-graders whose parents present different attitudes and perspectives towards their children's bilingualism. The case study approach serves as the appropriate methodological tool to study complex phenomena within the different sociocultural contexts of each family (Creswell, 2009). For the longitudinal study, a constant comparative analysis method (Glaser & Strauss, 1967) was used to compare the focal 3rd-grade students' current language use and their earlier language use when they were in 1st grade.

Research context

This study primarily took place in a Korean heritage language (HL) school in a university town in the Midwest where 200,000 people reside. Approximately, 63% of the town population identified as non-Latinx white, 13% as Asian, and 15% as foreign-born. There were no Korean-English bilingual education programs in the local school districts. Korean parents who wanted to develop their children's HL learning in the town funded the Korean HL school. Thus, the school was private and designed for Korean students in the town to help their HL learning by providing formal instruction in Korean at each grade level. Most of the enrolled students were second-generation Korean-Americans who were born after their parents had immigrated to the U.S. Other students were first-generation Korean immigrant students, who were born in Korea and moved to the U.S. with their families. All the students at the school attended all-English classrooms during the school weeks and attended the Korean HL school on Saturdays. The school provided classes for Korean heritage students in preschool–grade 5. The classes at all grade levels met three hours per week on Saturdays, from 10:20 a.m. to 1:20 p.m. The school had recess for 15–20 minutes around 11:10 a.m. During recess, the students were offered snacks and had free-play time.

Participants

Students

At the time of data collection for this study, ten students were enrolled in 1st- and 3rd-grade classrooms at the school (five at each grade level). There were two sets of siblings in the 1st- and 3rd-grade classes. All the students were invited to participate, but the parents of a set of siblings did not agree to participate in the study. Thus, eight students (four in each grade) participated in this study. All eight students attended American schools taught in English on weekdays. Table 3.1 provides background information on the study participants. Pseudonyms are used for all the participants.

Three of the 1st-graders are females, and one is male. All of them were born in the U.S. and had been enrolled in the Korean HL school for

Table 3.1 Description of the students

		Age	Gender	Birthplace	Proficient Language	Time at Korean Language School
1st-graders	Joon	6.2	Male	U.S.	English	3 years
	Yuri	5.9	Female	U.S.	English	3 years
	Rena	6.3	Female	U.S.	English	1.5 years
	Nari	6.4	Female	U.S.	Korean	3.5 years
3rd-graders	Tomi*	8.4	Male	U.S.	English	5.5 years
	Julie*	8.6	Female	U.S.	English	5 years
	Suji	8.2	Female	U.S.	English	5 years
	Mina	8.8	Female	Korea	Korean	First semester

Note
An asterisk (*) indicates the focal 3rd-graders who participated in the pilot study as 1st-graders.

1.5–3.5 years. Three of them (Joon, Yuri, and Rena) identified themselves as English proficient but limited in Korean, and one (Nari) viewed herself as a balanced bilingual but more proficient in Korean than English.

Three of the 3rd-graders are females, and one is male. Three of them (Toni, Julie, and Suji) were born in the U.S. and had been enrolled in the Korean HL school for 5–5.5 years. The three students believed that they were more fluent in English than Korean. The three students regarded themselves as fluent English speakers, but they believed that their Korean was less competent than English. One of them (Mina) was born in Korea and recently had arrived in the U.S., and it was her first semester at the Korean HL school. She considered herself to be fluent in Korean but limited in English. Two English-proficient students (Toni and Julie) in the 3rd-grade class were selected as the focal students for the long-itudinal study as they had participated in the pilot study in Spring 2014; thus, I had collected their 1st-grade language use data. Toni and Julie's earlier language use (as 1st-graders) were analyzed compared to their current language use from the 3rd grade.

Parents

Seven parents (all mothers) out of a total of 14 parents (from eight students with a set of siblings in each grade) participated in this study. All but one of the mothers (Mina's; 3rd grade) were first-generation Korean immigrants. Mina's mother came to the U.S. with Mina for a short period time (for two years) as a visiting scholar. The other parents came to the U.S. when they were teenagers or between their late 20s to early 30s. There were four focal parents (two from the 1st grade and two from the 3rd grade) who agreed to participate in additional interviews and to keep journals about their children's language use at home. The two focal parents in the 1st-grade class were selected based on their children's self-reported language preference and proficiency: one child viewed himself as English proficient, and the other saw herself as Korean proficient. The two focal parents in the 3rd-grade class were the mothers of the pilot study participants.

Teachers

The teachers in the 1st- and 3rd-grade classes participated in the study. I was the 1st-grade teacher at the Korean HL school. I am from Korea, a native-Korean speaker, and bilingual in Korean and English. It was my fourth year of teaching 1st-graders at the school. At the time of the study, I was a doctoral candidate in bilingual and ESL education and held a master's degree in the same field, with a teaching certificate in the area of ESL education. The 3rd-grade teacher (Mrs. Joen) was a female, native

Korean speaker. She came to the U.S. two years before this study was conducted with her husband, who was pursuing his post-doctorate degree. Mrs. Joen had been a Korean language teacher in a public elementary school in Korea for five years. She self-reported her English proficiency as intermediate in terms of her listening comprehension skills and basic regarding her speaking proficiency. She had taught 2nd-graders during the previous year at the Korean HL School.

Researcher's positionality

This section helps the readers to understand my investment and role (teacher as a researcher) in this study since I held both positions as an insider (the classroom teacher) and an outsider (the researcher). Qualitative research requires the researcher's reflexivity to identify his or her experiences and understanding of the research site (Denicolo, 2016; Stake, 2010). I drew on my prior experiences as a teacher in the HL school to understand how the emergent bilingual students utilized their language and linguistic repertoires to participate in class activities and for their HL learning. I reflected on how I was making sense of the context of HL school by considering its role and purpose for both groups of the children (i.e., first-generation Korean immigrants and second-generation Korean Americans) and their language learning experiences as HL learners of emergent bilingual speakers.

Since I held positions as an insider (classroom teacher) and an outsider (researcher), I refer to myself as the 1st-grade teacher when I analyze my language use during instruction in the findings and as the researcher when I discuss the overall procedure of research. To avoid the potential biases (both as a teacher and researcher), which may impact the study, I tried not to disturb the natural ecology of the social world by expressing my own beliefs (Roman & Apple, 1990). In other words, even though one of my objectives was to collect the students' language use data in the classrooms, I identified my primary role as a classroom teacher to encourage the 1st-graders' classroom participation by facilitating their HL learning. Therefore, I tried to collect 1st-graders' language use data in a natural setting by foregrounding the students' learning over the data collection.

Data collection sources and procedures

The primary data collection occurred in a 1st-grade class and a 3rd-grade class at the Korean HL school during the spring semester of 2016. Secondary data (i.e., mothers' interviews) also were collected during the spring and summer in 2016 outside of the school (e.g., home setting). The longitudinal study includes data from the pilot study to compare the focal 3rd-graders' language use data when they were in the 1st-grade class.

First-grade classroom data

Instruction in the 1st-grade classroom was divided into three parts. For the first 50 minutes, the class focused on developing the students' Korean communicative skills by using a government-designated Korean text-book. The title of the book was *Kuk-uh* [the Korean language]. Then the students had 15–20 minutes of recess either outside or inside of the classroom depending on the weather condition. After recess, the class participated in book discussions after reading a Korean storybook and in-class writing for 45–50 minutes each. The students' language use in the classrooms was primarily collected during the book discussion and in-class writing time.

In terms of the language use in the 1st-grade classroom, the students were allowed to use English if they needed during the class discussions and when they communicated with one another. I, as the classroom teacher, understood that the students would spontaneously and unconsciously utilize their language repertoires both from Korean and English as bilingual speakers. Thus, I allowed the students to freely utilize their language resources when responding to my questions instead of asking them to stay in Korean only. In addition, I wanted them to participate in the class discussions as much as possible without a language barrier. I was concerned that the English-proficient students may not be engaged in class discussions if they were required to speak only in Korean. Although the main language of instruction was Korean, I, the classroom teacher, also used English and translanguaged in certain situations. For example, when the class did not understand my questions that were asked in Korean, I repeated them in English purposefully so that the class would stay engaged. Furthermore, as bilingual, I translanguaged unconsciously and instinctively when I interacted with my bilingual students.

Audio-recording of students' talk during the reading sessions

Since I predominantly talked during the first part of the class (when I used the government-designated Korean textbook), the audio-recordings occurred during the reading and writing class sessions only. The students' talk during the book reading and discussion sessions for 50 minutes were audio-recorded for 14 weeks, resulting in 700 minutes of audio recording. During the reading class sessions, I brought a book each week to read with the students and then held a book discussion with them. For the Korean storybook selection, I chose Korean picture books both in fiction (e.g., folktales, myths, legends) and non-fiction (e.g., informational, biography). I most often selected Korean folktales because the students did not have an opportunity to learn about stories from Korean folktales in their American schools. I also provided bilingual versions of the books if available to help the students comprehend the texts so that they did not feel that their limited competence in one of the languages prevented them from comprehending the stories.

Before reading aloud a book to the class, I did picture walks by showing the illustrations of the book and asked questions that could encourage the students' imagination about the stories in the chosen books. After I read aloud the book in Korean, the class read it again by taking turns, which promoted the students' reading fluency in Korean. Since Korean is phonetically clear unlike English, all the students were able to decode all the words from the book without difficulties. Yet, the English-proficient students were given additional time to read the books in English which is often provided on the other side of the bilingual version of books so that they can make sure their comprehension of stories from the books. Then the students were encouraged to participate in book discussions based on what they had read, and I usually initiated discussion questions to capture the students' attention.

Audio-recordings of student talk during the writing sessions

The students' talk during the writing sessions was audio-recorded over 14 weeks and later transcribed. During their compositions, the students often engaged in verbal communications with me (the teacher) and one another about their ideas or thoughts. The 1st-graders sometimes talked to themselves; thus, their self-talk was captured from the audio-recordings. During the writing sessions, I held writing conferences by meeting with each student individually when s/he completed his/her writing. I spent 5–10 minutes discussing their written texts and drawings that accompanied their writing. Each student's spoken language use during the writing conferences was audio-recorded and analyzed later. The total audio-recording of writing sessions, including their self-talk and writing-related talk during writing conferences, took 680 minutes.

Writing samples

After the students engaged in the book discussion each week, they were asked to provide their written responses to the book in Korean. The topics of writing each week varied depending on the story or genre of the books. Sometimes the students were asked to retell the stories by thinking about the characters, plots, or specific events. Other times, they were asked to choose their favorite scene or part of the story and address their reasons for their selection or to expand their thoughts about a particular scene or part. The students were also encouraged to provide drawings during their pre-writing, and other times they provided drawings based on what they had written about the books.

In addition, the 1st-graders were asked to complete two diary entries in Korean, along with drawings each week as their homework. For the diary entries, the students did free writing in Korean based on what they have done on a particular date. For both types of writing, the students were given sheets of paper that had lines for written texts and spaces for drawings; thus, all the 1st-graders' writing samples included drawings that described their writing. The 1st-graders were allowed to use both languages as needed when they engaged in their writing practices. A total of 131 writing samples (in-class writing and diary entries) with drawings were collected from the 1st-graders for 14 weeks.

Student interviews

The four 1st-grade students individually participated in two semi-structured open-ended interviews with me. The first interview with each student was conducted at the beginning of the study, and the second interview was conducted at the end of the study. For the first interview, I asked approximately ten interview questions about the students' language use at home (with parents, siblings, peers, etc.), language preferences in different contexts (e.g., at home, school, other public places) or different language domains (e.g., reading, writing, speaking), as well as how they identified their ethnic identity.

During the second interview, I asked questions based on a preliminary analysis of the individual student's translanguaging practices while speaking and writing. Since the second interviews were conducted in a retrospective way, I provided the students with examples of their oral and written translanguaging and asked them questions about their language use (e.g., Here, did you know the words that you wrote in the other language? Why did you switch languages here?). Each of the student interviews took about 15–20 minutes and were audio-recorded. When the interviews were conducted in Korean, they were transcribed in Korean and translated to English later. When the interviews were conducted in English or the student answered in English, they were transcribed in English and analyzed later.

Informal interviews with the 1st-graders also occurred naturally during the class sessions as follow-up conversations based on what I had observed in the classroom. For all the interviews, I initially asked the questions in Korean but translated the questions into English when the students did not understand. The students were allowed to respond with the language they preferred to use during the interviews.

Third-grade classroom data

The teacher (Mrs. Joen) in the 3rd-grade classroom taught her students using the government-designated Korean textbook during the first period of her lesson (approximately 50 minutes). Then the 3rd-graders in her class had recess for 15–20 minutes either outside or inside of the classroom depending on the weather condition. After recess, the 3rd-graders participated in reading and writing class sessions by reading Korean books and providing written responses in Korean about their chosen books for 45–50 minutes, respectively.

In terms of the language use in the 3rd-grade classroom, the students were encouraged to use Korean as much as possible. Yet, Mrs. Joen understood that the students needed to use English during the class discussions and when they communicated with each other. Unlike the 1st-grade classroom where I (as the teacher) selectively used English through translanguaging in certain situations, Mrs. Joen maintained speaking in Korean although the students asked the questions in English. Thus, it was often found that the 3rd-graders asked questions in English, and Mrs. Joen responded to their questions in Korean.

Audio-recordings of the third-grade class

Because I taught the students in my 1st-grade class at the same time that the 3rd-grade class was meeting, Mrs. Joen audio-recorded her class during the reading and writing sessions so that I could analyze the 3rd-graders' oral language use later. After teaching the Korean textbook, Mrs. Joen held reading and discussion sessions using a Korean storybook each week. Sometimes the 3rd-graders selected a book that they wanted to read from the school library under the teacher's guidance, read it individually, and orally presented the story of their chosen books to the class. Most often, the whole class read the same book that Mrs. Joen chose and participated in a book discussion about the story of the book. The students' oral responses during book discussions were audio-recorded for about 50 minutes each week for 14 weeks.

Then the 3rd-graders were asked to provide their written responses to the book that they had read during the reading session. Similar to the 1st-graders, the 3rd-graders engaged in verbal communications with the teacher and one another about their ideas or thoughts during their compositions. Mrs. Joen audio-recorded her students' talk when they engaged in writing tasks over 14 weeks. Yet, unlike the 1st-graders, the 3rd-graders rarely talked to themselves (loudly) while writing; thus, their self-directed talk was seldom captured from the audio-recordings.

Writing samples

After the students engaged in book discussions each week, they were asked to provide their written responses to the books in Korean. Mrs. Joen provided her students different writing prompt each week; thus, the students' writing genres and topics were varied (e.g., retelling the story, writing a letter to the main character, writing about a favorite scene with the reason). For the in-class writing, they were provided sheets of paper with lines for writing and spaces for drawing. Thus, the 3rd-graders were also encouraged to provide drawings that illustrate their writing.

Similar to the 1st-graders, the 3rd-graders also were asked to complete two diary entries per week at home as their homework. For the diary entries, the students did free writing in Korean based on what they have done on a particular date. The 3rd-graders prepared their own notebook for their diary entries, and all but Suji chose their notebooks that have lines only. Hence, diary entries from Suji always included drawings in her written texts, but other 3rd-graders' diaries were mainly comprised of written texts. A total of 133 writing samples were collected from the 3rd-graders over 14 weeks.

Teacher interview

The 3rd-grade teacher interview was conducted prior to data collection of the students' book discussions. During the interview, I asked Mrs. Joen about her instruction in her class and her teaching styles to understand her teaching philosophy as a HL teacher. I then asked her about her students' (the 3rd-grade participants in this study) language use, performance, and participation in class during the previous year when they were in her 2nd-grade class (except for Mina). She also had shared with me her class schedule for the 14 weeks of the study including class materials/resources that she planned to use. I conducted additional informal interviews with her (e.g., before/after class or during recess for 5–10 minutes each week) if needed to identify the context of her class activities to better understand the 3rd-grade students' language use data that I received from her class.

Student interviews

The interviews with the 3rd-graders took place twice either before or after school in the 1st-grade classroom. Each of the 3rd-graders parti-cipated in the first interview at the beginning of the semester and the second interview at the end of the semester. Similar to the interview with the 1st-graders, the first interviews with the 3rd-graders were about their language use, language preferences, as well as how they identified themselves in terms of their ethnic identity. During the second inter-views, each student received interview questions based on his/her lan-guage use from the audio-recordings and from his/her writing samples. During the interviews, the 3rd-graders were allowed to provide their responses either in English or Korean based on their language preference.

When I conducted the second interviews with the two focal students, I brought their 1st-grade language data (the analysis of their spoken language and writing samples) to show and ask them additional ques-tions regarding any changes in their language use over the years. The second interview with the focal 3rd-graders took about 20–30 minutes longer than the interviews with the other 3rd-graders. All of the 3rd-graders interviews were audio-recorded and transcribed later. I transcribed the audio-recordings in the languages that the students used. If they used Korean, I translated the transcripts into English before analyzing them.

First- and third-graders' talk during recess

I examined the 1st- and 3rd-grade students' Korean and English language use outside of the classroom by observing them during recess at the school. The 1st- and 3rd-graders usually played together on a playground under the guidance of their teachers during recess (for 10–15 minutes). I planned to take fieldnotes on their language use by focusing on specific students on certain days so that after 14 weeks of study, I would capture at least two to three days of each student's oral language use during recess. However, because of bad weather conditions (e.g., snow, rain, low temperature), the students only went outside 5 of the 14 Saturdays. When the classes decided to stay in the classrooms and have indoor recess, Mrs. Joen and I audio-recorded the students' talks so that I could capture the students' language use later by listening to the audio-recordings. There were 80 minutes of audio-recording during outside recess and 250 minutes of audio-recording during indoor recess (130 minutes in 1st grade and 120 minutes in 3rd grade).

Mothers' interviews

The mothers of the eight students participated in two semi-structured, open-ended interviews with me at the beginning and end of the semester. The initial interview focused on the family members' language use and literacy practices at home as well as the parents' attitudes towards and perspectives on their children's HL learning and bilingualism. I began the first interview with 20 questions that provided the mothers with an opportunity to share their life events and experiences in the U.S., such as their reasons to come to the U.S., their practices and activities at home, and their general philosophy toward their children's language learning and bilingualism. Throughout the interviews, I wanted to learn about how the parents' perspectives, beliefs, and language education philosophy had impacted their child(ren)'s language use, preference, and proficiency.

The second interviews were conducted after I completed analyzing the students' language use data since they were based on the analysis of the students' oral and written language use, the student interview results, and my own observations in the classroom (for the 1st-graders). The questions that I asked varied for each mother according to the analysis of each student's language use data. I had analyzed the results of the students' second interview before conducting the second parent interview so that I could share the students' interview responses to the mothers during the mother's interviews. Both the first and second interviews with the mothers were conducted for 60–180 minutes, depending on each mother's preferences and availability. All the interviews with the mothers were conducted in Korean and audio-recorded. I transcribed them in Korean first and then translated them to English before analyzing them.

Focal mothers' journals and interviews

Four focal mothers (two in each grade) agreed to keep journals about their child's use of Korean and English for this study. I asked the focal mothers to keep their journals on three different days per week (e.g., Sunday, Tuesday, and Thursday) during the data collection period. I provided the mothers with small notebooks and asked them to record their child's language use at home when s/he participated in activities with his/her family members. I gave the mothers several examples of events/activities that could capture the child's Korean and/or English language use (e.g., when they read Korean books to their child, when their child talked with their grandparents in Korea via Skype, when they watched Korean TV programs or movies with their child, or when their child invited their Korean friends to their house). I collected the mothers' journals at the end of the semester and had 24–30 journal entries from each mother. I analyzed the content of the journal entries before I conducted the second interviews with the focal mothers to discuss and learn more about what they had shared in their journals. That is, the four focal mothers' journal reports were used as an interview source. Accordingly, the focal mothers' interviews took longer than the interviews with the other mothers.

During the interviews with the 3rd-grade focal mothers, I brought their child's previous language use data (the analysis of their 1st-grade oral language use from the transcripts and writing samples that they composed when they were in 1st-grade class). I then shared with them their child's 3rd-grade language use data to show and discuss their child's language use over the years and their HL learning trajectory. By sharing the longitudinal data, I was able to further learn about the mothers' perspectives and philosophies on their children's Korean language and literacy learning while living in the U.S.

Comparison of the focal 3rd-graders' oral and written language use

For the focal 3rd-graders (Toni and Julie), I previously had collected and analyzed their oral language use data when they were in 1st grade. I re-visited their 1st-grade oral language use to compare to their 3rd-grade language use to learn about the patterns of their oral language use over time. For their 1st-grade written language use, I had collected their

1st-grade writing samples for my pilot study but did not analyze them at that time because they were not part of the earlier study. For the current study, I analyzed their 1st-grade writing samples to compare their 3rd-grade writing and further document the patterns of their written language use over the years. When I was their 1st-grade teacher, I let the class use English if they needed to do so during their compositions. As anticipated, Toni and Julie had employed both Korean and English in their writing samples; thus, I had collected Toni's and Julie's 1st-grade writing samples that were written both in Korean and English.

Data analysis

The transcripts of audio-recordings and writing artifacts were the main resources for this qualitative study to examine the students' oral and written language use and their translanguaging practices. The transcripts of the parents' interviews and the focal mothers' journals were analyzed to corroborate the students' language use findings and to further learn about the parents' practices and attitudes toward their children's language learning and bilingualism. For the longitudinal study, the focal 3rd-grade students' language use data was compared to their 1st-grade language use to explore any observed different language use patterns over time.

To address Research Questions 1 and 3—the 1st- and 3rd-graders' oral and written language use and their translanguaging practices—the transcripts of their class interactions, which included oral responses during book discussions, writing-related talk during writing compositions, and the nature of talk during recess, were analyzed for their spoken language use. For the students' written language use, their writing samples, including drawings and text labels from their in-class writing and diary entries, were analyzed. Each student's language use (both oral and written) was examined based on whether s/he used Korean, English, or translanguaging. Next, the number of their utterances and written sentences that were in Korean, English, and mixed in the two languages was computed for the students in each grade. Then, their use of translanguaging was closely examined to find its function for each occurrence. Throughout the students' translanguaging, the functions of their translanguaging were organized into the following four categories: sociolinguistic competence, metalinguistic awareness, metacognitive insight, and sociocultural understanding.

The students' use of translanguaging was coded as for their sociolinguistic competence (Canale & Swain, 1980) when they used languages with the appropriate social meanings for communication situations. According to Canale and Swain (1980), sociolinguistic competence refers to the ability to use language(s) appropriately in different communicative situations and in various social contexts. It indicates the speaker's knowledge of the target language, which involves linguistic awareness when it comes to literacy activities (van Compernolle & Williams, 2012). Mizne (1997) argues that sociolinguistic competence required speakers to have a higher level of knowledge than linguistic competence. That is, linguistic competence describes learners' abilities in the grammatical aspects of language, including grammar, pronunciation, and vocabulary in the target language. Yet, sociolinguistic knowledge further requires speakers to understand the social situation in which they are speaking; thus, they have to achieve when/how to manipulate their speeches to make them appropriate to the situation. Accordingly, even if they speak with perfect grammar, their speech might not be appropriate or could convey different/unintended meanings in the social situation in which they are speaking (Genesee & Nicoladis, 2006). Thus, I defined sociolinguistic purposes as those instances in which bilingual students employed oral translanguaging appropriately according to the communicative situation and social context (Canale & Swain, 1980).

The students' use of translanguaging was coded as for their meta-linguistic awareness when they demonstrated their understanding of their language use and their ability to apply their linguistic knowledge (Bialystok, 1991). Children's metalinguistic awareness is defined as their ability to know about their language(s), which includes phonemic aware-ness (the ability to manipulate individual phonemes), syntactic knowledge (the ability to identify the structure of language), and pragmatic skills (the ability to use language appropriately in social contexts) (Barac, Bialystok, Castro, & Sanchez, 2014; Lightsey & Frye, 2004; Snow, Burns, & Griffin, 1998). According to Bialystok (1991), metalinguistic awareness indicates learners' ability to reflect upon their language use and to manipulate their own language-processing skills. Bialystok further described metalinguistic awareness not only as of the speaker's understanding of their language use but also as a writer's ability to apply their linguistic knowledge. I drew from the researchers' definitions of metalinguistic awareness to arrive at a cate-gory that focused on bilingual students' understanding of their language use and application of their linguistic knowledge to reflect on "the properties of language" (Galambos & Hakuta, 1988, p. 91).

The students' use of translanguaging was also coded as for their me-tacognitive insight (Meichenbaum, 1985) when they engaged in inner speech. According to Meichenbaum, metacognitive skills indicate the ability to reflect on, evaluate, and manipulate one's cognitive process or thinking. Fogarty (1994) argued that the process of metacognition involves 1) planning before approaching the learning task, 2) monitoring understanding by taking necessary steps to solve problems, 3) evaluating results, and 4) modifying the outcomes as needed. Metacognitive awareness is different from metalinguistic awareness because it involves self-thinking processes in which learners can self-assess and self-correct in response to their own evaluation to complete the task. That is, students who acquire metacognitive skills can think about their own thinking processes to resolve the problem or perform the task successfully through the self-assessing process (Meichenbaum, 1985). I defined metacognitive awareness as self-thinking processes that involve speakers' inner speech in which they self-assessed or self-corrected in response to their own evaluation to complete a task.

Sociocultural awareness indicates the learner's understanding of the societies and cultures of the target language as well as the appropriate contexts in which the language is used (Gumperz, 1979). Students' sociocultural understanding might appear to be similar to the previous definition of sociolinguistic awareness. Yet, sociocultural knowledge involves students' understanding of cultural aspects (e.g., from their own cultural experiences) in addition to communicative skills and linguistic knowledge (Halliday, 1973). Hence, sociocultural knowledge is regarded as speakers' understanding of culturally specific norms and values when engaging in speech events and performance beyond their verbal skills. Given the interrelated nature of culture and language (Halliday, 1973), I coded sociocultural knowledge when the bilingual students demonstrated their understanding of culturally specific events that include cultural values, beliefs, and norms (Gumperz, 1979).

To address Research Question 2—the parents of 1st-graders' attitudes toward bilingualism and their home practices to support their children's HL learning—the mothers' interview results were analyzed to learn about how the parents' attitudes and perspectives had influenced their children's language use. The interview transcripts with the mothers were also analyzed to learn about the sociocultural influence on their children's language use and development. The mothers' interview results revealed other sociocultural contexts (e.g., family's immigration status and future residency, the role of siblings, amount of interaction with other Korean relatives) that also played a pivotal role in their children's languages use and learning. The two focal parents' journals were also analyzed to understand additional information about the family's general practices related to their children's HL learning at home.

To seek the answer for Research Question 4—the comparison of the two focal 3rd-graders' oral and written language use to their earlier use as 1st-graders—the focal 3rd-grade students' language data when they were in my 1st-grade class (which I had previously collected for the pilot study) was analyzed again and compared to their current language use (as 3rd-graders) to document the pattern of their HL use over time. In other words, for this longitudinal study, I compared their language use in the past to their current language use so that I could learn about my former students' language use and development over the years.

For Research Question 5—the family and sociocultural influences on the focal 3rd-graders' longitudinal language use—the interview transcripts with the mothers of the focal 3rd-graders and their journal reports were analyzed to identify any regular practices that the families performed at home. The interview results provided additional information about the focal families' home language use and relevant language and literacy practices that possibly influence on their children's longitudinal language use and the different patterns in their language use between 1st and 3rd grade. A constant comparative analysis method (Strauss & Corbin, 1998) was used throughout the longitudinal finding chapter. Glaser and Strauss (1967) claimed that a constant comparative analysis method can be used to identify features of the experience or phenomenon of interest because "[it] compares each incident in the data with other incidents appearing to belong to the same category, exploring their similarities and differences" (Spiggle, 1994, p. 494). The patterns of consistencies or differences in the focal students' language use were identified by using an inductive constant comparative analysis method.

Overall, a triangulation method (Bogdan & Biklen, 2003) was used in this study by investigating all the data (transcripts of the students' classroom interactions, students' writing samples, fieldnotes during recess at the school, mother and student interview results, and focal mothers' journals) to "minimize misperception and the invalidity of my conclusions" (Stake, 2010, p. 120). Agar (1996) argued that "an isolated observation cannot be understood unless you understand its relationships to other aspects of the situation in which it occurred" (p. 125). In line with the researchers' arguments, a holistic perspective was implemented when analyzing all the data as well as discussing and reporting the results in this book.

References

Agar, M. (1996). *The professional stranger: An informal introduction to ethnography*. San Diego, CA: Academic Press.

Allard, E. (2017). Re-examining teacher translanguaging: An ecological perspective. *Bilingual Research Journal*, *40*(2), 116–130.

Alvarez, S. (2014). Translanguaging *Tareas*: Emergent bilingual youth as language brokers for homework in immigrant families. *Language Arts*, *91*(5), 326–339.

Barac, R., Bialystok, E., Castro, D., & Sanchez, M. (2014). The cognitive development of young dual language learners: A critical review. *Early Childhood Research Quarterly*, *29*(4), 699–714.

Bialystok, E. (1991). Metalinguistic dimensions of bilingual language proficiency. In E. Bialystok (Ed.), *Language processing in bilingual children* (pp. 113–140). London, England: Cambridge University Press.

Bialystok, E., Craik, F. I., Klein. R., & Viswanathan, M. (2004). Bilingualism, aging, and cognitive control: Evidence from the Simon task. *Journal of Psychology Aging*, *19*(2), 290–303.

Bloome, D., Carter, S. P., Christian, B. M., Otto, S., & Shuart-Faris, N. (2008). *Discourse analysis and the study of classroom language and literacy events: A microethnographic perspective*. New York, NY: Routledge.

Bogdan, R., & Biklen, S. (2003). *Qualitative research for education: An introduction to theories and methods*. New York: Allyn and Bacon.

Bokamba, E. G. (1989). Are there syntactic constraints on code-mixing? *World Englishes*, 8, 277–292.

Canale, M., & Swain, M. (1980). Theoretical bases of communicative approaches to second language teaching and testing. *Applied Linguistics*, 1, 1–47.

Cazden, C., & Beck, S. (2003). Classroom discourse. In A. C. Graesser, M. A. Gernsbacher, & S. R. Goldman (Eds.), *Handbook of discourse processes* (pp. 165–197). Mahwah, NJ: Lawrence Erlbaum Associates Publishers.

Creswell, J. (2009). *Research design: Qualitative, quantitative, and mixed methods approaches* (3rd ed.). Thousand Oaks, CA: Sage.

Denicolo, P. C. (2016). "School within a school": Examining implementation barriers in a Spanish/English transitional bilingual education program. *Bilingual Research Journal*, 39(2), 91–106.

Fogarty, R. (1994). *How to teach for metacognition*. Palatine, IL: IRI/Skylight Publishing.

Galambos, S. J., & Hakuta, K. (1988). Subject-specific and task-specific characteristics of metalinguistic awareness in bilingual children. *Applied Psycholinguistics*, 9(2), 141–162.

Gee, J. P. (2012). *Social linguistics and literacies: Ideology in discourses* (4th ed.). New York, NY: Routledge.

Genesee, F., & Nicoladis, E. (2006). Bilingual acquisition. In E. Hoff & M. Shatz (Eds.), *Handbook of language development*, Oxford, England: Blackwell.

Glaser, B. G., & Strauss, A. L. (1967). *Discovery of grounded theory: Strategies for qualitative research*. Chicago: Aldine.

Grumperz, J. J. (1979). The Retrieval of sociocultural knowledge in conversation. *Poetics Today*, 1(2), 273–286.

Halliday, M. A. K. (1973). *Explorations in the functions of language*. London: Edward Arnold.

Lightsey, G. E., & Frye, B. J. (2004). Teaching metalinguistic skills to enhance early reading instruction. *Reading Horizons*, 45(1), 27–37.

Meichenbaum, D. (1985). Teaching thinking: A cognitive-behavioral perspective. In S. F. Chipman, J. W. Segal, & R. Glaser (Eds.), *Thinking and learning skills, Vol. 2: Research and open questions*. Hillsdale, NJ: Lawrence Erlbaum Associates.

Mertens, D. M. (2015). *Research and evaluation in education and psychology: Integrating diversity with quantitative, qualitative, and mixed methods* (4th ed.). Thousand Oaks, CA: Sage.

Mizne, C. A. (1997). Teaching sociolinguistic competence in the ESL classroom. Senior Thesis Projects, 1993–2002. Available at: http://trace.tennessee.edu/utk_interstp2/20.

Roman, L. G., & Apple, M. (1990). Is naturalism a move away from positivism? In E. W. Eisner & A. Peshkin (Eds.). *Qualitative inquiry in education* (pp. 38–73). New York: Teachers College Press.

Saville-Troike, M. (2003). *The ethnography of communication: An introduction* (3rd ed.). Malden, MA: Blackwell.

Snow, C. E., Burns, S. M., & Griffin, P. (Eds.). (1998). The process of learning to read. *Preventing reading difficulties in young children* (pp. 41–84). Washington, D.C.: National Academy Press.

Spiggle, S. (1994). Analysis and interpretation of qualitative data in consumer research. *Journal of Consumer Research*, *21*(3), 491–503.

Stake, R. E. (1994). Case studies. In N. K. Denzin & Y. S. Lincoln (Eds.), *Handbook of qualitative research* (pp. 236–247). Thousand Oaks, CA: Sage.

Stake, R. E. (2010). *Qualitative research: Studying how things work.* New York, NY: Guilford Press.

Stanovich, K. E., & West, R. F. (1989). Exposure to print and orthographic processing. *Reading Research Quarterly*, *24*(4), 402–433.

Strauss, A., & Corbin, J. (1998). *Basics of qualitative research: Techniques and procedures for developing grounded theory* (2nd ed.). Thousand Oaks, CA: Sage.

Street, B. V. (1984). *Literacy in theory and practice*, Cambridge: CUP.

Street, B. V. (2001). The new literacy studies. In E. Cushman, G. R. Kintgen, B. M. Kroll, & M. Rose (Eds.), *Literacy: A critical sourcebook* (pp. 430–442). Boston: St. Martin's Press.

Street, B. V. (2003). The implications of the "New Literacies Studies" for literacy education. In S. Goodman, J. Maybin, & N. Mercer (Eds.), *Language, literacy, and education: A reader* (pp. 77–88). Stoke-on-Trent, UK: Trentham Books.

Thanh, N., & Than, T. (2015). The interconnection between interpretivist paradigm and qualitative methods in education. *American Journal of Educational Science*, *1*(2), 24–27.

van Compernolle, R. A., & Williams, L. (2012). Reconceptualizing sociolinguistic competence as mediated action: Identity, meaning-making, agency. *Modern Language Journal*, *96*(2), 234–250.

van Dijk, T. A. (1990). Social cognition and discourse. In H. Giles and R. P. Robinson (Eds.), *Handbook of social psychology and language*, (pp. 163–183). Chichester: Wiley.

Veltman, C. (1983). *Language shift in the United States.* The Hague: Mouton.

4 Oral and written language use and translanguaging functions of 1st-grade Korean bilingual students across school and home contexts

1st-graders' views of their language use, preferences, and proficiencies

Before investigating the 1st-graders' classroom language use, their home language use, language preferences, and self-reported language proficiencies were examined from the interviews with each 1st-grader. All the students answered that they primarily used Korean with their parents at home, but if they had older siblings, they used English with them. Joon, Yuri, and Rena all had older sibling(s) and reported that they used English with their siblings. On the other hand, Nari reported that she used only Korean with her younger brother.

In terms of their language preference, three of the students (Joon, Yuri, and Rena) reported that they preferred to speak and write in English because it was easier than Korean. For instance, Joon stated, "I like English (more than Korean) because English is easier (than Korean) when I speak." In contrast, Nari answered that she preferred to speak and write in Korean. Unlike Nari whose answers about her home language use and preference coincided, the other three students said that they actually preferred to use English although the language they spoke with their parents was primarily Korean.

In terms of their language proficiency, the first three students (Joon, Yuri, and Rena) reported that their English skills were many times better than their Korean skills (10, 2, and 3 times, respectively). For instance, Joon, who self-evaluated his English language proficiency 10 times higher than his Korean proficiency, stated, "I am way better in English (than Korean). But my Korean is bad." On the other hand, Nari saw herself as a more fluent speaker in Korean than English. Nari stated during the interview that she liked Korean a little more than English. Yet, she also stated that she was strong in English, including her reading and writing skills, explaining, "I think that I am good at English, too. I like English reading and writing. I am good at English reading and writing."

The four 1st-graders' answers showed differences (Joon, Yuri, Rena vs. Nari) in their language proficiency not only from the content of their responses but also from their choices of languages in answering. The first three students often spoke English or inserted English words when they responded to the questions that were asked in Korean, whereas Nari maintained speaking in Korean when she provided all her answers. That is, their language use corroborated their answers when they identified themselves as proficient English speakers (Joon, Yuri, and Rena) and proficient Korean speaker (Nari). Accordingly, I refer to the first three students (Joon, Yuri, and Rena) as English proficient and Nari as a Korean-proficient student throughout this chapter. The following section displays the students' oral language use in their HL classroom and illustrates how their actual language use substantiates their views about their respective language proficiencies.

1st-graders' oral language use in the classroom

This section presents findings on how the 1st-graders used their languages to orally communicate in an HL classroom. Although the students were encouraged to speak in Korean, they were allowed to use both languages (Korean and English). Table 4.1 shows the frequency of 1st-graders' oral language use in English and Korean when they engaged in classroom interactions. It also illustrates each student's translanguaging practice with its incidence.

As shown in Table 4.1, the three English proficient students (Joon, Yuri, and Rena) used more English (34%, 29%, 31%, respectively) than Korean (15%, 21%, 21%, respectively) when they talked in class. The three students' spoken language showed the use of translanguaging in their utterances, with their translanguaging occurring both at the word- and sentence-levels. The English-proficient students often initiated speaking in Korean but incorporated English words into their Korean statements (e.g., "우리 recess 언제해요?" [When do we have recess?]). They sometimes switched entirely from one language to the other. However, their use of word-level translanguaging (inserting English words in Korean speech) was observed more often (46%, 45%, 45% for Joon, Yuri, and Rena, respectively) than their sentence-level translanguaging. Interestingly, their use of translangauging in their oral speech was greater than their discourse in either language. When they employed word-level translanguaging in each language, they translanguaged for 51%, 50%, and 48% (for Joon, Yuri, and Rena, respectively). Close analysis revealed that most of their word-level translanguaging occurred in their Korean speech as they often incorporated English words while speaking in Korean; whereas, they rarely inserted Korean words in their English speech. Thus, their Korean word-level translanguaging in their English statements was seldom observed (5%, 5%, 3%, respectively).

On the other hand, Nari predominantly used Korean. As shown in Table 4.1, 93% of her utterances were in Korean, and she rarely initiated

Table 4.1 First-graders' oral language use in the classroom

	Korean[a]	English[b]	Word-Level Translanguaging[c] (English Words in Korean Speech)	Word-Level Translanguaging[c] (Korean Words in English Speech)	Total	Frequency of Translanguaging at Sentence Level[d] (Korean to English)	Frequency of Translanguaging at Sentence Level[d] (English to Korean)
Joon	98 (15%)	212 (34%)	292 (46%)	32 (5%)	634 (100%)	45 times	26 times
Yuri	132 (21%)	180 (29%)	280 (45%)	29 (5%)	621 (100%)	31 times	19 times
Rena	87 (21%)	131 (31%)	191 (45%)	13 (3%)	422 (100%)	37 times	17 times
Nari	632 (93%)	14 (2%)	32 (4%)	4 (1%)	682 (100%)	8 times	6 times

[a] Spoke exclusively in Korean.
[b] Spoke exclusively in English.
[c] Intrasentential switching within a single utterance.
[d] Intersentential switching between the utterances.

Notes: The frequency of students' sentence-level translanguaging was provided, but the numbers were not counted in the total because the sentences were already included in the first two columns.

her speech in English (2%). Only 4% of her translanguging was presented at the word level when she inserted English words in her Korean speech. Overall, Nari's use of translanguaging was not just quantitatively but also qualitatively different from those of the English proficient students. In the section below, close analysis of the three English-proficient students' (Joon, Yuri, and Rena) translanguaging in their spoken language is presented followed by a close analysis of the Korean-proficient student's (Nari) translanguaging.

Functions of oral translanguaging among the English-proficient students

Close analysis of the three English-proficient students' oral language use revealed that they engaged in translanguaging practices for 1) sociolinguistic knowledge, 2) metalinguistic awareness, 3) metacognitive insight, and 4) sociocultural understanding. As stated, the English-proficient students' oral translanguaging primarily occurred when they incorporated English words or phrases while speaking in Korean; whereas, when they spoke in English, they rarely inserted Korean lexical items in their English speech.

English-proficient bilingual students' sociolinguistic knowledge

The bilingual students' sociolinguistic knowledge was defined as the ability to use their entire languages with the linguistic knowledge and appropriate social meanings for the communicative situation (Canale & Swain, 1980; van Compernolle & Williams, 2012). There were five subcategories when the students translanguaged in this area: 1) bilingual's flexible use of dual lexicon to reflect their language preference, 2) quicker lexical access to a particular language, 3) the borrowing of lexical items for unknown equivalent words, 4) the expression of bilingual identities, and 5) the influence of interlocutors. The majority of the English-proficient students' translanguaging functioned as sociolinguistic knowledge (49%, 48%, 57% for Joon, Yuri, and Rena, respectively) out of the four different functions (see Appendix A). The three students' use of translanguaging for sociolinguistic functions was observed both at the word- and sentence-levels in their speech.

Figure 4.1 shows an example of how Yuri used dual lexicons in her speech to demonstrate her language preference when she shared what she did in her American school. Although Yuri incorporated English words in her Korean speech, she stated during the interview that she knew all the corresponding words in Korean. In the interview, she indicated that she employed the English words because she preferred to speak some words in English, not because she did not know the equivalent words in Korean, stating: "Sometimes I prefer speaking in English for words that I

Yuri:　　나 school 가는 거 좋은데 왜냐하면 나 friends 많이 있고, playground 에서

노는 거 좋아서.

[I like going to school because I have many friends there, and I enjoy having fun

in the playground.]

Figure 4.1 Flexible use of bilingual lexicon to demonstrate language preference.

often use in English." Her response implies that she had access to the
vocabulary in both languages (dual-language lexicon) and utilized the
language in which she usually spoke for certain words. (English translations are provided within the brackets. Translanguaged words are
underlined in the English translation.)

Figure 4.2 displays Joon's use of translanguaging when he had quicker
lexical access to his dominant language. As shown, Joon employed word-
level translanguaging when he talked about the plot of a book since he
previously watched its movie version. During the interview, he explained
that he spoke the words in English rather than in Korean because "the
English words came to my mind first," indicating quicker lexical access
to English.

Joon:　　나 이 story 아는데 왜냐하면 나 movie 봤어. 이거 엄청 funny 해.

[I know this story because I watched the movie. This is very funny.]

Figure 4.2 Quicker lexical access in a more proficient language.

Figure 4.3 exhibits Rena's translanguaging when she borrowed lexical
items from English for unknown equivalent words in Korean. The words
that Rena translanguaged include English loanwords (e.g., lemonade,
popcorn), English words that do not have Korean equivalents (e.g., book
buddy), and Sino-Korean words (e.g., field trip), which originated from
Chinese characters and derived mainly from literary Chinese. Rena
borrowed her vocabulary knowledge from English for the English
loanwords in her Korean utterances, which seems reasonable. Utilizing
her English vocabulary knowledge for the English loanwords in her
Korean utterances seems reasonable. Yet, Rena stated that she did not
know the words for "book buddy" and "field trip" in Korean during the
interview. Beyond the translanguaging examples in the previous Figures,
Rena employed English when she did not know the corresponding words
or there is no equivalent word in Korean so that she could complete her
utterances. (Italics indicate the words Rena did not know in Korean).

Rena: 나 어제 park 가고, lemonade 랑 popcorn 먹었어요. 그리고 book buddy 랑 field trip 가고.

[Yesterday I went to the park and had lemonade and popcorn. I went on a field trip with my book buddy.]

Figure 4.3 Borrowing words from English for unknown and non-existing Korean words.

Figure 4.4 provides another example of how Rena expressed her bilingual identity through translanguaging. Rena visited Korea during the data collection period of the study, and her mother enrolled her in an elementary school in Korea for a month. In turn 1, Rena described in Korean how difficult it had been for her to attend a school in Korea. The teacher responded in Korean to praise Rena's English (line 2) to which Rena translanguaged and replied in English (line 3). Her translanguaging into English indicates that she had reacted in the language for which she was given a compliment, suggesting that she was conveying her identity as a bilingual.

1. Rena: 친구들이 laugh at me 했어, 나 한국말 잘못해서.

   [My classmates laugh[ed] at me because I didn't speak Korean well.]

2. T: 그런데 리나는 영어 잘 하잖아. 그럼 영어 알려주면 되지.

   [But you are good at English. Then, you could teach them English.]

3. Rena: Yes, I am good at English. I teach my friend in my class.

Figure 4.4 Expression of bilingual identity through translanguaging.

The English-proficient students also responded to the interlocutors' use of translanguaging, demonstrating another sociolinguistic function. The example in Figure 4.5 displays how Yuri translanguaged by considering her interlocutors' different language use during recess. Yuri was playing a card game using English with her peer (Hana; English-proficient child) who did not participate in this study. Before the teacher joined their conversation, Yuri spoke to Hana using English only. When the teacher interrupted their game to ask how to play it in Korean (turn 1), Yuri switched her language into Korean to respond and explain the game rule to the teacher (turn 2). Then, she switched back to English as she was

1. T: 왜? 세븐 가졌어? 설명해 줄 수 있어?

            [Why did you give her a seven card? Can you explain it to me?]

2. Yuri: (to me) 선생님, 이렇게 열 개 카드 주는 거예요. King 은 아무거나 할 수

            있어요. 그래서 여기 놓아 돼요...

            [Teacher, I will give her 10 cards. King can be anything. So, I will put it here...]

3. Yuri: (to Hana) You got A. So, you can only witch. This is already opened.

Figure 4.5 Response to interlocutors to sustain a bilingual conversation.

talking to Hana to continue their card (turn 3). It has shown that Yuri chose English when speaking to her English-speaking peer but used Korean when speaking to the teacher by flexibly moving across her languages. That is, Yuri flexibly conducted sentence-level translanguaging to sustain a bilingual conversation as she appropriately responded to each of the interlocutors in the languages they employed.

English-proficient bilingual students' metalinguistic awareness

Metalinguistic awareness refers to speakers' understanding of their language use and their ability to apply their linguistic knowledge (Bialystok, 1991). The English-proficient students' use of translanguaging as a metalinguistic awareness function occurred when 1) applying prior knowledge to create a new word, 2) elaborating on their understanding of concepts, 3) demonstrating their comparative linguistic knowledge of Korean and English, and 4) regulating their own language use to make jokes. The English-proficient students' translanguaging sometimes functioned as metalinguistic awareness (32%, 36%, 27% for Joon, Yuri, and Rena, respectively), and their uses of translanguaging for metalinguistic awareness were mainly observed at the word level (see Appendix A).

Figure 4.6 shows Joon activated his prior knowledge to create a new word by differentiating two English words: rabbit and bunny. When Rena answered the teacher's question, she provided the English word "bunny" for the word "rabbit" in Korean, which seems plausible since there is only one word that describes both rabbit and bunny in Korean. Yet, Joon reacted to Rena's response by stating that bunny and rabbit are not the same because of their different appearances in terms of size (turn 3). Joon's metalinguistic insight seemed to emerge when he heard the two words. To substantiate his idea, Joon provided another example in terms of similar looking animals having different names (turn 4). Then, in responding to the teacher's question (turn 5), Joon came up with an idea and eventually created a new word for bunny by adding the adjective "baby" to the word "rabbit" in Korean (turn 6). The process of his thinking, which involved the translanguaging practice, suggested that Joon was applying his prior knowledge to create a new word in Korean using his metalinguistic awareness.

1. T: 여기 이야기에서 누가 꾀를 낸 거야?

   [Who made a trick in this story?]

2. Rena: 토끼. Bunny.

   [Rabbit. <u>Bunny</u>.]

3. Joon: Bunny 아니야. 토끼는 rabbit 이야. Rabbit 은 크고 Bunny 는 작고 cute 해.

   [It is not <u>bunny</u>. Rabbit is <u>rabbit</u>. <u>Rabbit</u> is bigger, but <u>bunny</u> is smaller and <u>cute</u>.]

   …

4. Joon: It is similar to crocodile and alligator. They look the same, but I know that they are different. I know that their teeth are different. Crocodile has a longer body and mouth. Alligator is shorter and fatter…

5. T: 그럼 bunny 는 한글로 뭐라고 하면 돼?

   [Then, how can we call <u>bunny</u> in Korean?]

6. Joon: Bunny 는 small and cute 토끼. 그럼 애기 토끼.

   [<u>Bunny</u> is a <u>small and cute</u> rabbit. Then it is a baby rabbit.]

Figure 4.6 Application of prior knowledge to create a new word.

Figure 4.7 shows how Yuri elaborated on her understanding of concepts through translanguaging. Yuri had incorporated English words "grain," "dairy," and "protein" in her earlier Korean statements. The example below illustrates the conversation between the teacher and Yuri when the teacher checked on whether Yuri knew how to say the translanguaged words in Korean (turns 1, 3, and 5). As displayed, Yuri did not provide the equivalent words in Korean because she did not know the words in Korean. However, she successfully provided examples of the food categories (turns 2, 4, and 6), which demonstrated her understanding of the concepts for the words. In other words, although she did not know the equivalences in the named language (Korean), she was able to exhibit her understanding of concepts through translanguaging utilizing her metalinguistic awareness.

1. T: Grain 한국말로 뭐라고 해?

   [How do you say <u>grain</u> in Korean?]

2. Yuri: 몰라요. 근데 it's like rice and bread. 쌀 이랑 빵.

   [I don't know. But, <u>it's like rice and bread</u>. Rice and bread.]

3. T: 그럼 Dairy 는 알고 있어?

   [Then do you know <u>dairy</u> in Korean?]

4. Yuri: Dairy 는 우유랑 아이스크림 그리고 요거트.

   [<u>Dairy</u> is Milk, ice cream, and yogurt.]

5. T: Protein 은 한국말로 뭐라고 할 수 있지?

   [How can you say <u>protein</u> in Korean?]

6. Yuri: Meat 같은 거. 어.. 고기.

   [Like <u>meat</u>. Um…Meat.]

Figure 4.7 Elaborating on the concepts for unknown Korean words.

Figure 4.8 illustrates how Rena utilized her metalinguistic awareness to differentiate English and Korean by applying what she knew about speaking in both languages. As displayed, Rena translanguaged to point out the specific language feature from English—intonations—to compare the two languages that she knew. Rena's statement, which included her use of translanguaging for the particular language feature, suggest that she understood the differences between the two languages and further applied her linguistic knowledge to compare the two languages.

Rena: 영어는 나 말할 때 up and down pitch 있는데, 한국말은 없어요.

   [English has <u>up and down pitch</u> when I speak, but Korean does not have it.]

Figure 4.8 Comparing different linguistic features between two languages.

Figure 4.9 illustrates an example by Joon when he was making a joke using translanguaging. Joon began to retell the story of the Korean folktale *Brother and Sister Who Became Sun and Moon* in Korean (line 1), but he switched his language into English when he provided the

1. Joon: ⋯ 아이들이 도망가고 나무로 올라갔는데 호랑이가 못 올라 갔어 왜냐하면

   [The children ran away and climbed the tree, but the tiger could not climb the

   tree because...]

2. Joon: He is so fat, way too fat. He is 10,000 pounds (laugh). I am kidding.

Figure 4.9 Making a joke to exaggerate the story.

reason why the tiger (the character from the book) could not climb the tree (line 2). Joon's statement in English was not accurate based on the story in the book. His following statement, "I am kidding," and his nonverbal communication—laughing—indicate that he was trying to make fun rather than transmitting correct information. Joon seemed to purposefully choose English as he was playing with language to make a joke by exaggerating the story, which suggests that his translanguaging functioned for adding a sense of humor.

English-proficient bilingual students' metacognitive insight

Bilingual children use their metacognitive insight when they reflected on, evaluated, and/or manipulated their thinking about their language use (Fogarty, 1994; Meichenbaum, 1985). The English-proficient students' uses of translanguaging for metacognitive insight were occasionally observed (10%, 7%, 10% for Joon, Yuri, and Rena, respectively), and their use of translanguaging as a metacognitive awareness function occurred when they engaged in inner speech. In addition, their translanguaging practices for this function were discovered at the sentence-level only as the students entirely switched their languages (mainly from Korean to English) through self-directed talk (see Appendix A).

Figure 4.10 illustrates how Yuri articulated her self-talk through translanguaging. During class discussion, the teacher asked the class what they were learning during the science class in their American school (turn 1). Yuri responded in Korean that she had learned about the human body (turn 2). In responding to the teacher's follow-up question about what she had learned about the human body (turn 3), Yuri translanguaged into English and asked herself a question by engaging in self-talk (turn 4). Yuri's inner speech indicates the process of internalization as she moved from interpersonal dialogues with the teacher to intrapersonal speech to herself. This form of internalized and self-directed dialogue, which involved translanguaging, demonstrated her metacognitive insight.

1. T: 학교에서 science 시간에는 뭐 배워?

    [What did you learn during the <u>science</u> class in your American school?]

2. Yuri: 저는 몸.

    [I learned about the body.]

3. T: 몸? 사람 몸에 대해? 뭐 배웠는지 기억나?

    [Body? About human body? Do you remember what you have learned about?]

4. Yuri: (to herself) Um… What did I learn about? Let me see…

Figure 4.10 Engaging in self-talk through translanguaging.

English-proficient bilingual students' sociocultural understanding

Sociocultural knowledge is regarded as speakers' understanding of culturally specific values, beliefs, and norms (Halliday, 1973). The translanguaging practices for sociocultural understanding emerged when they inserted culturally familiar or relevant words. The students' translanguaging was mainly observed in their English discourse as they referred to the Korean teacher or school activities, Korean family members, and Korean linguistic or cultural practices. Although their uses of translanguaging for this function were rarely observed (9%, 9%, 6% for Joon, Yuri, and Rena, respectively; see Appendix A), their translanguaging for the sociocultural function seemed to play an essential role as their use of Korean added cultural meanings to their English speech.

Figure 4.11 illustrates the students' use of translanguaging in their English speech when referring to culturally appropriate names for family members. In lines A–C, each student incorporated Korean when s/he referred to his/her family members in their English statements. The Korean words that s/he used were "mom, dad, sister, grandmother, and aunt." Analysis of the interview data showed that the students mostly referred to their close family members in Korean. For instance, Joon stated that "I always say mom, dad, and sister because I have called them that way since when I was very young." Joon seemed to understand that referring to his family members by using Korean was his natural habit or normal practice. Even though the three students preferred to speak in English, they were more likely to choose to use the words from Korean when they referred to their family members. (Bold fonts in English translations indicate the words that the students translanguaged in Korean).

A. Joon: I am going to go to Chicago next week with my family, 우리 엄마, 아빠, 누나.

[I am going to Chicago next week with my family, **my mom, dad, and sister**].

B. Yuri: I wish 나 할머니 would live long.

[I wish **my grandmother** would live long.]

C. Rena: I will see 고모 today. She likes me a lot...

[I will see my **aunt** today. She likes me a lot...].

Figure 4.11 Inserting Korean for culturally appropriate referents.

Figure 4.12 displays how each student translanguaged into Korean when stating the words that were related to Korean language learning and Korean cultural practices/activities. In line A, Rena inserted the Korean word for "Korean dictation test" while speaking in English. Since there was a Korean dictation test at the beginning of the class every week at the school, Rena appeared to be more familiar with using the word in Korean. Line B shows how Yuri included the word for "honorifics" in Korean when speaking in English. The word "honorifics" is not commonly used in English, but it is required to use in the Korean language, which can indicate the speaker's sociocultural knowledge. In line C, Joon uttered his responses in English but translanguaged into Korean for the Korean activity that he practiced, Taekwondo, and for the names of Taekwondo moves. Because his Taekwondo instruction was delivered in Korean, Joon naturally translanguaged when he referred to the terms that are related to

A. Rena: I didn't study 받아쓰기 for today because I was busy.

[I didn't practice **Korean dictation test** for today because I was busy.]

B. Yuri: When I was in kindergarten, I learned 존댓말. So I know it.

[When I was in kindergarten, I learned **Korean honorifics**. So I know it.]

C. Joon: I can run fast way too fast. I do 태권도, too. Actually, I know how to do 발차기 and 격파.

[I can run fast way too fast. I do **Taekwondo**, too. Actually, I know how to do **kicks** and **breaking**.]

Figure 4.12 Incorporating Korean words for culturally based referents.

the Korean activity of Taekwondo. The examples illustrate that the students were using their sociocultural knowledge through translanguaging, which demonstrates that they were socioculturally competent.

Functions of oral translanguaging by the Korean-proficient student

There were relatively few times when Nari, the Korean-proficient student, used translanguaging in her oral speech. Although she engaged in less translanguaging than the other three 1st-graders, her translanguaging practices characterized each of the four major functions: sociolinguistic, metalinguistic, metacognitive, and sociocultural.

Korean-proficient bilingual student's sociolinguistic knowledge

Nari translanguaged for sociolinguistic purposes, accounting for 50% of her translanguaging (see Appendix A). Among the five sociolinguistic practices that were discovered from the English-proficient students' translanguaging, Nari only demonstrated two of the five sociolinguistic practices. Close analysis revealed that Nari used translanguaging when 1) she responded to interlocutors for code alignment and 2) there were no corresponding words in Korean.

Figure 4.13 displays evidence of Nari's use of translanguaging by inserting the English word "strong" into her Korean speech (turn 3) when responding to the teacher's question (turn 2). Yet, close analysis displays that Nari repeated the English word after hearing her peer (Yuri) say the word "strong" in English in the earlier statement (turn 1). Nari demonstrated that she knew how to say the word "strong" in Korean, so this example indicates that Nari conformed to a principle of *code alignment* (Sayer, 2013) to her peer's use of the English word. Her peer's word-level translanguaging appeared to sanction her own in this communicative event.

1. Yuri: 호랑이가 이겨요 왜냐하면 호랑이는 strong 해서

    [Tiger wins because the tiger is <u>strong</u>.]

2. T: 근데 여기서는 할머니가 왜 이겼지?

    [But why did the grandmother win in this story?]

3. Nari: 호랑이가 strong 한데 할머니가 똑똑해서 이겼어요.

    [Although the tiger was <u>strong</u>, the grandmother won because she was smart.]

Figure 4.13 Code alignment with peer's bilingual language use.

Analysis of Nari's oral language data revealed that she tended to repeat English words in her Korean speech after she had heard others using the English words, but it was discovered that she spoke the same words that she had translanguaged in Korean in other times. For example, Nari verbally used the same words ("artist" and "strong") in Korean in different communicative events; she spoke, "나는 커서 화가가 되고 싶어요" [I want to be an artist in the future] and "호랑이는 더 힘세요. 원래는 이겨요" [The tiger is stronger than the grandmother, thus it is taken for granted that the tiger wins]. The underlined words "화가" and "힘세요" in her Korean speech are the Korean words for "artist" and "strong." Although Nari did not seem to ever use English without someone else using it first, it appeared to be easy for Nari, as a bilingual, to instinctively repeat the English words when she heard the words in English because she knew the words in both languages.

Figure 4.14 presents Nari's individual utterance when she incorporated English words while speaking in Korean. In line A, Nari read aloud a book to the class. When the first passage introduces the main character's name "Mary," Nari mentioned the other English proper noun ("Saint Mary") and selectively uttered them in English. Similarly, in line B, Nari used English for the name of the academy that she went to. Using English seemed to be inevitable in these utterances since the words are proper nouns that indicate specific people and places. In line C, Nari used the English word "playdate" in her utterance, but there is no corresponding word for "playdate" in Korean. The examples in Figure 4.14 displays Nari using English for proper nouns and non-existing Korean equivalents, which indicates that Nari, as a bilingual, was utilizing her English vocabulary knowledge when necessary while speaking in Korean.

A. Mary 랑 Saint Mary 의 Mary 랑 똑같애요.

[Mary is the same as Mary in Saint Mary.]

B. 어제 친구들이랑 I-Power 갔어요.

[I went to I-Power to learn gymnastics.]

C. 친구랑 playdate 하는데 친구가 늦어서 오래 기다렸어요.

[I waited for a long time since my friend was late for our playdate.]

Figure 4.14 Translanguaging into English for proper nouns that do not exist in Korean.

Korean-proficient bilingual student's metalinguistic awareness

Nari's translanguaging that functioned for metalinguistic awareness characterized 28% of her translanguaging practices (see Appendix A). Her translanguaging for this function mostly occurred when she was interacting with other classmates during recess. Figure 4.15 shows evidence of Nari's translanguaging during recess that demonstrates her metalinguistic awareness. In line 1, Nari initiated a question in Korean to ask the class if there was anyone who wanted to smell her scented crayons. Yet, as her classmates responded to her in English, Nari translanguaged into English to interact with her English-proficient peers (turn 4). Since Nari knew that her classmates were more fluent in English than Korean, she purposefully translanguaged into English for code alignment. Indeed, Nari explained during the interview that she not only acknowledged that she needed English to communicate with her peers but also understood that she was encouraged to use Korean during the class, stating "I know that other kids use English only. I want to talk to them using English. But in class, I know that I have to use Korean." Since Nari understood when to utilize which languages depending on the different contexts and interlocutors, her use of translanguaging appeared to function as her metalinguistic awareness.

1. Nari: Who want to smell it?

2. Yuri: I want to. Smells like a banana!

3. Rena: Smells like coffee this one. Oh my gosh. Awesome!

4. Nari: That's my favorite! Do you want to smell the orange one here?

Figure 4.15 Communicating with English proficient peers by using English.

Korean-proficient bilingual student's metacognitive insight

The third most frequent translanguaging purpose was for metacognitive insight, which represented Nari's translanguaging 14% of the time (see Appendix A). Nari, who rarely translanguaged, did so when she talked to herself. In Figure 4.16, she employed Korean to express her physical discomfort to the Korean teacher (turn 1). Yet, right after that, she translanguaged into English to express and elaborate on how she felt and what she needed (turn 2). Nari's use of English to voice a complaint appeared to avoid any disrespect to the teacher because it was not presented in Korean. During the interview, Nari stated, "In class, I know that I have to use Korean, especially for the teacher."

1. Nari: 선생님, 저 너무 더워요.

   [Teacher, I am very hot.]

2. Nari: (to herself) I am hot. I need a fan.

Figure 4.16 Respectful bilingual private speech.

Korean-proficient bilingual student's sociocultural understanding

Like the other 1st-graders, Nari occasionally translanguaged for socio-cultural purposes (8%) when she employed culturally relevant Korean words in her English speech (see Appendix A). Nari translanguaged in her English discourse when she referred to the Korean teacher and her Korean family members. Figure 4.17 illustrates Nari's use of word-level translanguaging into Korean when referring to the teacher. Unlike students in the U.S. who call their teachers by their last names, Korean children are supposed to use the term "teacher" in Korean to refer to their teachers. This example exhibits that Nari was using her socio-cultural knowledge by translanguaging the culturally specific term into Korean. (Bold fonts in English translations indicate the word that Nari translanguaged in Korean).

Nari: "Or, 선생님 can be a judge."

             [Or, the teacher can be a judge.]

Figure 4.17 Use of culturally appropriate referent in Korean.

First-graders' language use when writing

The 1st-graders' written language uses were also analyzed from their writing samples, which displayed their use of Korean, English, and trans-languaging. Compared to their oral translanguaging practices, all four students used much less translanguaging when writing than they did when orally communicating. Table 4.2 shows each student's written language use from their in-class writings and their diary entries as homework. It illustrates the frequency of 1st-graders' written language use in English and Korean and their translanguaging practice with its incidence.

The three English-proficient students were more likely to stay in Korean when they wrote, compared to when they talked. Joon used Korean 76% of the time when writing, whereas he used Korean only 15% of the time when he spoke. Similarly, Yuri's writing samples show that she composed

Table 4.2 First-graders' written language use from writing samples

	Total Number of Writing Samples	Korean-Only Sentence	English-Only Sentence	Word-Level Translanguaging (English Words in Korean Sentences)	Word-Level Translanguaging (Korean Words in English Sentences)	Total	Translanguaging at Sentence Level[a] (Korean to English)	Translanguaging at Sentence Level[b] (English to Korean)
Joon	33	145 (76%)	5 (2%)	39 (21%)	3 (1%)	192	0	0
Yuri	31	160 (74%)	11 (5%)	44 (20%)	2 (1%)	217	7	0
Rena	29	80 (58%)	15 (11%)	40 (29%)	3 (2%)	138	12	4
Nari	39	206 (99.5%)	0	1 (0.5%)	0	207	0	0

a   The frequency of the 1st-graders' sentence-level translanguaging from Korean to English.
b   The frequency of the 1st-graders' sentence-level translanguaging from English to Korean.
Notes: The numbers of the students' written sentences were counted in the table.

74% using Korean, but she used only 21% of Korean when she spoke. Rena's writing samples display that she used Korean relatively less (58%) than the two other students (Joon and Yuri), but compared to her oral language use (21%), Rena also employed more Korean than English when writing. The three English-proficient students rarely provided Korean word-level translanguaging in their English sentences (1%, 1%, 2%, respectively). Yet, they occasionally inserted English words into their Korean sentences (21%, 20%, 29%, respectively).

Meanwhile, Nari (the Korean-proficient student) produced almost all of her writing in Korean. As displayed in Table 4.2, Nari provided only one English word throughout her 39 writing pieces with 206 sentences. Nari's writing samples also show that her use of English in her writing was less often (0.5%), compared to her use of English in her oral language communication (7%). Although Nari's writing displays only one incidence of direct translanguaging, she employed English phonology to write English words with Korean characters, which is known as transliteration, a type of written translanguaging practices.

Functions of written translanguaging among the English-proficient students

The English-proficient students' use of translanguaging was less observed in their writing than their oral language data; however, their word-level translanguaging was still found in the students' writing samples (21%, 20%, 29% for Joon, Yuri, and Rena, respectively). How the English-proficient students used translanguaging when they wrote was examined according to the four categories found in their oral speech: 1) sociolinguistic knowledge, 2) metalinguistic awareness, 3) metacognitive insight, and 4) sociocultural understanding.

English-proficient bilingual writers' sociolinguistic knowledge

The majority of the English-proficient students' translanguaging in writing functioned as sociolinguistic knowledge (50%, 64%, 70% for Joon, Yuri, and Rena, respectively) (see Appendix B). There were three subcategories when the students translanguaged in this area while writing: 1) quicker lexical access to a particular language, 2) bilingual's flexible use of dual lexicon, and 3) ensuring reader's understanding using English.

In Figure 4.18, Joon demonstrated translanguaging for quicker lexical access (i.e., using the word in the language that first came to mind) when he drafted a written response to the Korean folktale, *The Tiger and the Persimmon*. He wrote the English noun "baby" twice in the Korean text as a placeholder, later striking it out and writing the Korean word for baby when he remembered it. When he used lines to indicate the deletion of the English word "baby," his translanguaging was semiotic and multimodal

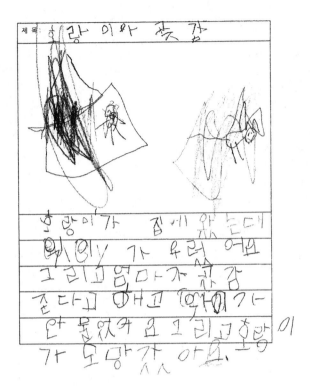

Title: The tiger and persimmon

When the tiger came to the house, the <u>baby</u> was crying. And the mom said (to the baby) that you would be given persimmon, and the <u>baby</u> stopped crying. Then the tiger ran away.

Figure 4.18 Quicker lexical access in a more proficient language.

(Busch, 2012; Durán, 2017; Kress, 2015). During the interview, Joon explained that he wrote the word "baby" in English because he could not think of the word in Korean, but remembered it after completing the draft (translated into English): "I just didn't remember the Korean word at that time, but I remembered it after finishing this [the draft]." His statement indicates that the Korean word for "baby" was not accessed by him at that moment during his first draft. Rather, he had quicker lexical access to the English word. Thus, employing his bilingual resources through translanguaging let him complete his draft so that he could render it into Korean later when he revisited his text, which demonstrated his sociolinguistic competence. (English translations of the students' Korean writing samples are provided above the figures. The words or sentences that students wrote in English are underlined in the English translation.)

Figure 4.19 displays how Rena drew from her dual lexicon to initiate and complete her written texts. Rena wrote the title ("My favit anmul") and the first sentence in English ("I like a Rabbit"). Then she switched the language into Korean for the next four sentences, employing translanguaging to describe a rabbit ("is wite [white].... Big Ears."). During the interview, Rena explained that she thought her Korean writing was weaker than her English writing, stating "I need help from English when I write in Korean, but I don't need [help from Korean] when I write in English." Indeed, Rena was the student who sometimes asked whether she could write in English during in-class writing. In fact, when the class was allowed to choose the language in which to write, Rena always chose to write in English. Rena often drew from her dual lexicon to initiate and complete her written texts because, as Rena explained, she relied on English when needed while writing in Korean. Rena's use of her dual-language lexicon to complete her writing illustrated a sociolinguistic purpose because she translanguaged to develop her writing or the topic of her writing.

Title: <u>My Favorite Animal</u>

<u>I like a rabbit.</u> A rabbit eats grass. And its color <u>is white</u>.
And it has <u>big ears</u>. And it is cute.

Figure 4.19 Utilizing dual lexicon to initiate and complete her written texts.

Figure 4.20 shows how Yuri composed her diary entry in Korean and then in English to ensure the reader's understanding. As shown, Yuri

Figure 4.20 Translanguaging to ensure the reader's understanding.

employed translanguaging by translating what she had written in Korean to English so that a bilingual reader could understand what she had written in Korean. During the interview, Yuri explained the reason why she wrote in English what she already had written in Korean because she was unsure of her Korean and wanted to make sure that the reader understood what she had written (translated into English): "I was not sure about my Korean writing so I rewrote them in English … because I am good at English. And if I make many mistakes in Korean but rewrite them in English, one can know what I write about." As shown, she wrote in English above and at the end her Korean writing using space to signal her multimodal translanguaging (Durán, 2017). Because she was paying attention to her audience and her translanguaging to communicate with her audience, the employment of her translanguaging served as a sociolinguistic purpose.

English-proficient bilingual writers' metalinguistic awareness

Out of the four functions, metalinguistic awareness was characterized as the second most frequent function throughout the three English-proficient students' translanguaging practices (41%, 30%, 25% for Joon, Yuri, and Rena, respectively; see Appendix B). There were four subcategories when the students translanguaged in this area while writing: 1) Distinguishing places for texts (in Korean) and drawings (in

English), 2) organizing ideas using English before composing in Korean, 3) expanding thoughts using English, and 4) explaining a concept using English.

Throughout their writing samples, the English-proficient students employed two languages in or across the titles, drawing spaces, and written texts. The writing samples by the students display that they mainly used Korean when they composed the texts in the body but often used English for titles and drawing spaces. Specifically, analyzing the three English-proficient students' use of Korean and English in their texts versus drawing spaces reveals that they used more translanguaging when they wrote in the drawing spaces (58%, 55%, 48% for Joon, Yuri, and Rena, respectively) than in the main texts (27%, 32%, and 38%, respectively).

The English-proficient students' answers during the interviews explained the reason why they tended to write the text in Korean but often used English in the drawing spaces. For example, Joon explained that writing at the Korean HL school should be in Korean, but the text labels around their drawing were not "real writing," stating: "I know that I have to write this (in-class writing task) in Korean because I was asked to write them in Korean. But, because they (text labels or caption writing) are not real writing, I wrote them in English." Rena also wrote her texts mostly in Korean but often employed English for the text labels when describing her drawings. Her text labels often included English proper nouns (e.g., names of places or people), which Rena considered as "special words." She explained that "I use Korean often when I write in the Korean language school, but these are special words next to my drawing; thus, I wrote them in English."

Similarly, Yuri seemed to understand that she should write the homework at the Korean language school in Korean, stating: "Because I have to write this (diary entries) in Korean because it is Korean homework. This will be read by the Korean teacher, so I have to write it in Korean only." Yuri presented a lot of speech bubbles around her drawings (e.g., Yay! No way! This is fun!) in her writing samples (i.e., 25 times in 33 writing samples), and mainly used English in the bubbles. Yuri explained, "I used English because this (the content in her speech bubble) is what my friend said, and this is what my sister said ...." The three students' statements and the translanguaging pattern from their writings exemplified their metalinguistic understanding since they were able to identify their own language use and regulate their language choices for different spaces in their compositions.

Joon's writing sample in Figure 4.21 shows how he used translanguaging when he responded to the Korean folktale, *The Lazy Man Who Became a Cow*. Joon first provided the title in English. Then, in the first line of the text, he printed "lazy," "bad," and "lay down" in English before using the equivalent Korean words to write his response to the folktale. This suggests that he was trying to come up with the lazy man's

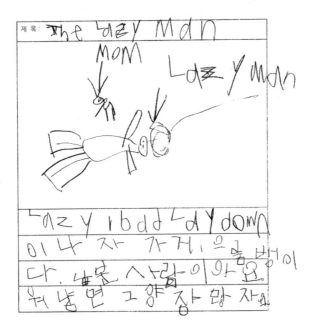

Title: <u>*The Lazy Man*</u>

<u>*Lazy, bad, lay down.*</u>*The man is a lazy person.*
He is a bad person because he just sleeps all the time.

Text labels: <u>*Mom*</u>, <u>*Lazy Man*</u>

Figure 4.21 Translanguaging to plan and draft his writing.

characteristics in English before he actually composed. During the interview, Joon explained the process that he had employed: "It [the words in the first line] is not my actual writing. I was thinking in English first. Look, here. I write them in Korean [the text]." After his composition in Korean, Joon translanguaged into English again to provide texts in his drawing. Joon seemed to understand that English could be used when organizing his thoughts, but that the text should be written in Korean. In other words, Joon was aware of how he self-regulated or controlled his language choices, which demonstrates his metalinguistic awareness.

Figure 4.22 shows Rena's written response to a Korean folktale *The Brother and Sister Who Became Sun and Moon.* Although Rena wrote the first three sentences in Korean, she translanguaged to complete her writing by stating three additional ideas in an English run-on sentence. During the writing conference, Rena implied that she initially wrote her response in Korean but got tired and employed English at the end: "I know that I had to write in Korean. I tried to write it in Korean until here and used English only for one sentence at the end." Her response

제목: 해와 달이된 오누이

엄마 떡가지로 그른대 호랑이
나타서요. 호랑이 엄마 주거서요.
인재 호랑이가 엄마 옷을 이버서요.
Children thot the tiger was her mom
and then she saw the tail it was not
mom.

Title: The Brother and Sister Who Became Sun and Moon

The mom brought rice cakes (for her children) but met the tiger.
The tiger killed the mom. The tiger wore the mom's clothes.
Children thought that the tiger was their mom and then they saw
the (tiger's) tail [but] it was not (their) mom.

Figure 4.22 Using metalinguistic insight to expand thoughts.

indicates that she acknowledged that she was encouraged to write in Korean. Rena's translanguaging during writing in this particular example demonstrates her metalinguistic awareness because she knew that she had switched languages to expand her thoughts to complete the text.

In her diary sample in Figure 4.23, Yuri wrote what happened when her sister made fun of her father. Her writing shows that she employed her bilingual resources to write the English word "prank" in the Korean text. After she completed her diary entry in Korean, she implemented two other translanguaging practices; she wrote in English to elaborate on what the prank involved and multimodal written translanguaging (Durán, 2017) when she placed the English writing outside the official writing space. During the interview, Yuri explained, "I wrote my diary in

Figure 4.23 Translanguaging to differentiate official from unofficial writing.

Korean, but this [the English sentences] is not part of my diary. I just explained this (pointing to the English word prank)." Yuri appeared to understand that by writing in English in the unofficial space below the entry, she could explain the prank in more detail for a bilingual audience without causing any embarrassment. Yuri's choice of languages for official and unofficial communication was an example of how she employed translanguaging for a metalinguistic purpose.

English-proficient bilingual writers' metacognitive insight

The students used translanguaging when they engaged in an inner speech during or after writing. Yet, only two translanguaging examples for metacognitive function were found in each of Yuri's and Joon's writing samples when they engaged in meta-talk (verbal reflection) to evaluate and to problem-solve their writing, accounting for 2% each (see Appendix B).

In Figure 4.24, Joon engaged in translanguaging when he wrote the text, misspelling the English words "dragonfly" and "wing" in the sentences, but completing the text in Korean. In addition, he engaged in oral translanguaging when he evaluated his written work through self-talk or what Swain (2010) called metatalk, verbal reflection about his writing. When Joon read aloud in Korean the essay that he had written on dragonflies, he noticed that he had forgotten to write the object in the second to the last sentence (the forgotten object is indicated by three hyphens; Joon's comments were in Korean but translated into English): "They eat ---. They can fly." Then, he exclaimed in English: "Oh, I forgot. Small insects. They eat small insects." After verbalizing in English what dragonflies eat, he wrote the Korean words (with a thicker pen) for small insects in the margin below the text. The type of translanguaging implemented in this example—English verbalization to Korean writing—appeared to involve mental translation. Joon's metatalk

Title: Animal

Dragonfly[ies] are small. They are cute. Their wing[s] help them to fly fast. Their eyes are scary. They eat (small insects). They can fly.

Figure 4.24 Engaging in metatalk to solve the problem.

demonstrated metacognitive insight about what was missing from his writing, allowing him to complete his writing correctly.

Similar to Joon's example, Yuri's writing-related talk also showed that she used a translanguaging strategy when she engaged in private speech. When Yuri was writing about her three wishes during in-class writing, it was observed that Yuri was talking to herself about the fact that she did not know how to write the Korean word for "twin." She stated, "I don't know how to write the word 'twin' in Korean. I know how to say it in Korean but don't know how to write [it].... I will write it in English then! (said the word in English) Twin!" That is, although Yuri verbally articulated the word "twin" in Korean, she was not sure about the correct spelling of it in Korean. In Figure 4.25, there is some evidence that Yuri erased how she initially wrote "twin" in Korean before she reproduced it in English. As presented in Joon's writing-

Title: <u>My wishes</u>

I want to be <u>twin</u>[s] with my friend. I wish my sister had not had <u>cat allergie</u>[s]. I want to have a big house. It would be fun.

Text labels: 나 [Me], 소리 [Sori (Name of Friend)], 언니 [Sister], <u>No Allergie!</u>, <u>Cat</u>

Figure 4.25 Translanguaging to problem solve her writing.

related talk in the previous example, Yuri appeared to engage in self-directed dialogue or metatalk (Swain, 2010), which involved translanguaging, to resolve her writing problem. She also employed multimodal translanguaging (Durán, 2017) in the drawing space above the text when she combined written translanguaging with drawings and speech bubbles to convey meaning. This translanguaging example suggests that Yuri utilized her linguistic repertoires from English using her metacognitive insight to complete her sentence, rather than giving up or not using the uncertain Korean word.

English-proficient bilingual writers' sociocultural understanding

Similar to the students' oral language use discussed earlier, the English-proficient students used translanguaging in their writing to present their

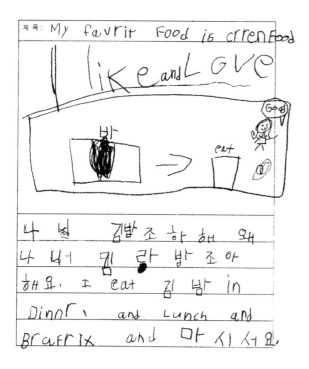

Title: <u>My favorite food is Korean food</u>

I like kimbab [Korean food item] because I like seaweed and rice.
I eat kimbab in <u>dinner, lunch and breakfast and</u> (it is) delicious.

Text labels: <u>I like and Love</u>, 밥 *[rice], <u>eat, Good</u>*

Figure 4.26 Employing Korean for culturally specific words.

sociocultural knowledge. This function of translanguaging was discovered when the students employed culturally familiar or culturally relevant words in their writing. Similarly, the same sociocultural translanguaging function was found in the English-proficient students' writing when they particularly chose to write some words in Korean within their English sentences or around their English text labels for cultural purposes. Only a few translanguaging examples for the sociocultural function were found in the English-proficient students' writing (7%, 4%, 5% for Joon, Yuri, and Rena, respectively; see Appendix B).

Figure 4.26 shows Rena's in-class writing when she wrote about her favorite Korean food, engaging in translanguaging for the sociocultural purpose. Rena employed multimodal translanguaging (Durán, 2017) in the drawing space when she combined written translanguaging with drawings and a speech bubble. As shown, Rena translanguaged when she provided the title in English. In the text, she wrote the first sentence in

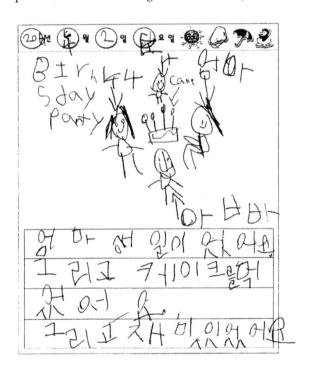

It was my mom's birthday. And we ate a birthday cake.
And it was fun.

Text labels: Birthday Party, 누나 [Sister], 나 [Me], Cake,
엄마 [Mom], 아빠 [Dad]

Figure 4.27 Selecting Korean to refer to family members.

Korean to describe her favorite Korean food. Next, she translanguaged into English to start the second sentence but incorporated the Korean word "김밥 [kimbab]," a Korean dish, to explain when she eats it. Her use of translanguaging into Korean for a cultural reference "kimbab" demonstrates her sociocultural knowledge because the word "kimbab" is the name of the particular Korean food item.

Similarly, Figure 4.27 shows how Joon's translanguaging demonstrates his sociocultural knowledge from Korean. Joon wrote his diary entry all in Korean, but he primarily chose English when providing text labels around his drawing ("birthday party" and "cake"). Yet, he translanguaged into Korean when he referred to his family members in his drawings: 엄마 (mom), 아빠 (dad), 누나 (sister). This was found to be a common translanguaging pattern in their oral responses because they were more likely to refer to their family members in Korean in their English discourses. A similar example was discovered in this particular writing sample implies that Joon employed the language that best reflected his thinking about his family members while writing. This finding implies that his translanguaging into Korean for his family members occurred because of his sociocultural understanding in Korean.

Functions of written translanguaging by the Korean-proficient student

As shown in Table 4.2, Nari composed 38 pieces of writing using only Korean, plus one writing sample that presents her use of translanguaging (for a total of 39 writing samples with 207 sentences; 99.5% in Korean). The only time that Nari translanguaged to write in both languages was when she introduced her English and Korean names. Overall, Nari's translanguaging functioned both as sociolinguistic knowledge (50%) and metalinguistic awareness (50%) (see Appendix B).

In Figure 4.28, Nari employed translanguaging practices when she wrote both in the text and in the drawing. She used transliteration, in which bilingual individuals utilize the phonology from one language to write characters in the other language (García, Johnson, & Seltzer, 2017) to write her English name with Korean letters in the text (케더린; see the word right before her English name in the text). She also utilized multimodal written translanguaging (Durán, 2017) to put her English name in parentheses in the text. This finding demonstrates that Nari was able to use her phonological awareness from English and linguistic features in Korean to transcribe the word in Korean, which indicates that she used her sociolinguistic knowledge through translanguaging. The placement of her translanguaging in the drawing with the two smiling faces seemed to indicate that she liked both her English and Korean names. Her use of parentheses to offset

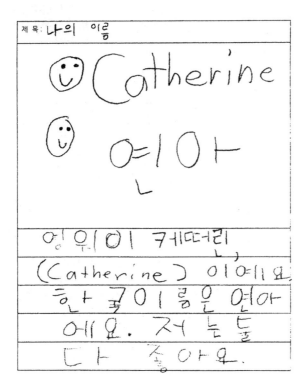

Title: My names

My English name is <u>Catherine</u> (Catherine).
My Korean name is Nari. I like them both.

Figure 4.28 Utilizing written transliteration to introduce her English name.

her English name in her Korean writing seemed to signal that this writing was not part of her "official" Korean writing, demonstrating metalinguistic awareness.

Nari's explanation for the reason why she transliterated by using English phonology to write her English name in Korean characters demonstrated her sociolinguistic competence because she was paying attention to her audience. During a writing conference, Nari explained that she wrote her English name by using Korean characters in the text so that monolingual Korean speakers would know how to pronounce it (translated to English): "If I write it only in English, people who do not know English would not know how to pronounce my English name." Overall, Nari drew from her dual lexicon to write her name in both languages in the drawing space, transliterated to write her English name with Korean characters in the text and employed multimodal written translanguaging both in the drawing (including the symbol of smiling faces) and text (using parentheses for the English name).

Although Nari provided English only once throughout her writing samples, there is evidence that Nari engaged in translanguaging that involved transliteration, in which she employed English phonology to write English words with Korean characters. Nari's written work showed that she transliterated for English proper nouns (e.g., her friends' English names and her English name), English words that she did not know in Korean (e.g., gymnastics), and English words that did not exist in Korean (e.g., playdate). Consistent with her interpretation of the Korean norms at the Korean HL school, Nari seemed to assume that she should be writing for an audience of monolingual Korean readers; thus, she wrote English words with Korean characters. Her use of transliteration demonstrates both her sociolinguistic knowledge and metalinguistic awareness because she acknowledged her Korean audiences and applied her knowledge by controlling/manipulating her languages.

Case studies of three 1st-grade students

In this section, I share mini-case studies of three of the four 1st-graders (Joon, Rena, and Nari) to discuss sociocultural influences on the Korean bilingual 1st-graders' language use. The findings are drawn from two semi-structured interviews with each of the three children's mothers and two of the focal mothers' journals about their children's (Joon and Nari) daily language use, which illustrates the parents' perspectives and attitudes towards their children's bilingualism as well as their practices at home for their children's language use and learning.

Joon, the second-generation, male English-proficient speaker

Joon's father and mother had moved to the U.S. seven years ago when the father started his graduate study. Both Joon and his older sister Suji (one of the 3rd-graders in this study) were born in the U.S. and began their initial schooling in the U.S. During school breaks, the family has visited Korea on an annual basis and stayed there for about a month each year. Joon's mother said that Joon improved his Korean communicative skills while in Korea because he had opportunities to meet and talk with his relatives and other Koreans. Because the parents do not hold permanent residency in the U.S., the family's future residency was unsure and would depend on the father's future occupation. The father preferred to find a job in the U.S. since both father and mother agreed that the education system in the U.S. would be better for their children.

"Both Korean and English are important."

The mother believed that where the family would live in the future plays a pivotal role in the parents' attitudes toward their children's language learning. Yet, since Joon's parents are unsure about their future residency, they think it is important for their children to learn and master both Korean and English. The mother stated:

> Learning Korean is very important for my children. Since we (her husband and her) do not know exactly whether we will stay in the U.S. or go back to Korea, learning and mastering both languages are critical for our children. It is true that if we will stay here [U.S.], English might be more important for our children, but if we will go back to Korea, Korean would be more important for them to learn.

Although the mother stated that the family's future residency would be an important factor to decide which language they focus more on their children, Joon's mother valued Korean language learning because heritage language is a part of her children's identity as Koreans beyond the ability to communicate with Korean family members. She explained:

> Korean is crucial not just for communication, talking with grandparents, for instance, but also for their heritage identity as Koreans. I believe that although my children would identify themselves as Americans, mastering Korean should be necessary. I hope that they should be able to use Korean freely and fluently while living in the U.S.

Different views on Joon's Korean and English proficiencies

Joon was the student who viewed his English proficiency as much stronger than his Korean proficiency. Joon's mother had a different opinion about her child's Korean and English proficiency. During the interview, she mentioned that she was surprised to hear that Joon thinks his English skills are much higher than his Korean skills:

> I think that Joon was optimistic and overly confident about his English proficiency but less generous and confident about his Korean proficiency …. I think his Korean is better than how he evaluated it, but his English is less developed than what he reported. Even though Joon believes he is better in English than in Korean, this might apply to his listening and speaking skills. In terms of literacy skills, since he has not fully acquired English grammar and spelling, it is hard to say that his English literacy is better than his Korean literacy.

The mother then reported that Joon used to feel more comfortable using Korean than English until about a year ago. According to her, Joon began to use and learn more English since he entered kindergarten and attended school full time, compared to when he attended preschool part-time. Accordingly, the time of using and exposure to the English language might have felt him think that he was much more proficient in English than Korean. Yet, the mother admitted that Joon's English proficiency was getting improved faster than his Korean.

Accepting Joon's English but encouraging his use of Korean at home

Once Joon preferred speaking in English and began to use more English at home, the parents tried to encourage him to respond in Korean as much as possible at home. The mother shared that Joon used to have antipathy towards learning English when he was first exposed to English; however, since he became more confident in speaking English than Korean, he tended to show his antipathy toward speaking in Korean at home. Thus, the parents tried to encourage Joon to speak in Korean whenever they observed him speaking exclusively in English. However, the mother admitted that asking Joon to speak in Korean all the time or to use Korean to restate what he had said in English was difficult and even impossible. Accordingly, she and her husband recently accepted Joon's use of English. The mother added that she and her husband thought Joon's increased use of English was a natural development:

> I think that Joon's increased use of English is a natural phenomenon as most Korean-American children in the U.S. are commonly going through. Thus, we (she and her husband) have to accept and understand his increased use of English as time goes by.

Parents' negative attitude toward their own use of code-mixing

The mother stated that as Joon's use of English increased and her first child (Suji) became an English dominant speaker, she and her husband also tended to naturally insert English words or phrases into their Korean speech when they talked to their children. However, the mother thought that their use of code-mixing (word-level translanguaging) was not an appropriate habit for their children to learn Korean:

> I realized that we (her and her husband) recently inserted English words or phrases into our Korean speech when we responded to our children as their use of English increased. Yet, I do not think this is a good habit for our children to practice Korean. Thus, we decided to try not to mix up the languages and to keep our conversation only in

Korean so that our children could listen to complete Korean sentences from us.

Positive and negative impacts of learning two languages

Joon's mother thought that there was a positive impact on a child who learned two languages in the long run, such as more chance to have a better occupation. However, she pointed out that there might be possible negative impacts on children during their language emergent stage. The mother shared the moment when Joon was confused as he was exposed to the English language for the first time:

> When Joon was acquiring English for the first time, he was learning/ developing his Korean. I remember that Joon mumbled his speech ... and tended to stutter at the beginning of his speech. He showed that he had difficulty articulating his ideas. It looks like he was confused by the two different languages ... and I think he seemed to have speech disorders during his transition periods.

Joon's conscious use of Korean with his parents

According to the mother's journals, Joon tended to use more English than Korean with his older sister (Suji); however, when the parents joined the conversation, they mostly switched their language into Korean. The mother reported that when Joon knew that his parents were watching him and listening to his conversation, the amount of Korean that he used was increased although the parents did not ask him to speak in Korean.

One of the mother's journals displayed a concrete example of Joon's use of translanguaging at home, depending on his different interlocutors. The mother observed her children playing a video game at home. Joon presented his emotions and reactions to the game in English (e.g., "This is awesome"). When Joon spoke with his sister, Suji, English was the main language he used. Yet, when the mother interrupted their play to ask questions in Korean (e.g., "Aren't you guys hungry? How much longer will you play?"). Joon responded to his mother in Korean. This finding suggests that although the parents did not request that Joon speak in Korean all the time at home, Joon seemed to know that the home language was Korean and that he should use Korean when talking to his parents.

The mother's journal displayed another example of Joon's conscious use of Korean. According to the mother's report, Joon and Suji were fighting because they both wanted to take the same seat on the sofa while watching television. The mother asked them why they were fighting and who was at fault. Responding to his mother, Joon used English and made an excuse. However, after the mother scolded him in Korean, Joon switched his language to Korean and admitted that it was his fault. His mother thought that Joon's switch from English to Korean was a way to show his respect because of an extensive system of honorifics in the Korean language:

> Both Joon and Suji seemed to know that they have to be polite when we (she and her husband) teach them a lesson. When they feel that we are very mad at their bad behaviors, they tend to use Korean to express that they are sorry and to reflect on their wrongdoings. Because of the difference in honorific formality between English and Korean, if they reply in English ..., it is not easy to grasp whether they are taking our advice seriously and reflecting on their mistakes.

Considering his peers' language use and proficiency

According to his mother, Joon tended to use English more than Korean when talking to his friends who are second-generation Korean-Americans like him. He did this because he knew that they were more fluent in English than Korean. However, when he had a playdate with a Korean friend who came to the U.S. less than a year ago and had limited English proficiency, Joon predominantly used Korean with his friend. According to his mother's observation, Joon spoke 90% of the time in English and 10% of the time in Korean with his Korean-American peers, whereas, he spoke 90% of the time in Korean with the friend who recently arrived from Korea. When the mother asked Joon about his different language uses, he explained that "we (he and his friend) are speaking both Korean and English. But my Korean is better than his English. That's why I use Korean with him." His statement indicates that he was aware of his friends' different language proficiencies and adjusted his language use accordingly, which suggests that Joon is a bilingual speaker who can strategically manipulate or control his two languages.

The influence of context on Joon's language use

His mother's journals revealed that Joon's language use also was influenced by the context in which he interacted with his interlocutors. The language that the family members used during the dinnertime at home was mostly Korean because the parents often initiated the conversation. According to the mother's report, Joon primarily spoke in Korean although he sometimes incorporated English words or phrases in his Korean discourse when he was talking with his family.

On the other hand, the mother witnessed Joon's increased use of English when the family had a meal at a restaurant. The mother observed that Joon tended to use more English than Korean when they went out for lunch or dinner. For instance, while Joon was looking at the menu, he used English to talk and ask his parents about food items. In addition, when Joon heard his parents used English when ordering food to a waiter(ess), he began to use English exclusively with his parents. His mother believed that Joon's language use or choice was easily affected by the surrounding context or setting.

The mother shared another example that captures how Joon's language use was influenced by the context. The mother noticed that as soon as Joon came back home from his American school, he had difficulty speaking in Korean. According to her, he seemed to need time to retrieve Korean words to speak his ideas in Korean. The mother believed that it was difficult for Joon to switch to using Korean because he had been exposed to the English only context at the school and had been surrounded by English-speaking peers/teachers during all day.

Rena, the second-generation, female English dominant speaker

Rena's father and mother had moved to the U.S. 22 years ago when they entered a university in the U.S. After Rena's father found a job in the U.S., the family became permanent residents and planned to stay in the U.S. permanently. Rena and her two older brothers (5th- and 10th-graders each) were born in the U.S. and began their initial schooling in the U.S. During school breaks, the family has visited Korea once a year for a month. Rena's mother believed that visiting Korea was a good opportunity for Rena to learn about Korean culture and customs. According to the mother, learning about Korean culture and manner is more important than having fluent Korean proficiency for Rena since they did not plan to go back to Korea and permanently stay in the U.S. Thus, the parents' reason to send Rena to the Korean HL school was to provide Rena with an opportunity to be familiar with the Korean culture and manners/values. Since Rena's parents came to the U.S. during their teenage years, their English proficiencies were superior to those of other Korean parents in this study. It was reported that the parents often used English when communicating with Rena instead of asking Rena to use Korean.

"English is obligatory, but Korean is an extra language."

Rena's mother thought that learning the Korean language itself was not highly important for her child. From the mother's perspective, it was not mandatory for Rena to acquire perfect Korean proficiency. Rather, she viewed Korean as a tool that reflected Rena's cultural roots. The mother's following statements displayed her beliefs that she regarded Korean as an "additional" language because "extra" time and effort were needed to teach Korean in the U.S.:

Korean is an *additional* (my emphasis) language while living in the U.S. I believe that having the ability to speak perfect Korean is not mandatory while living in the U.S.... It is true that *extra* (my emphasis) time and effort are required when teaching Korean (to my children).

Flexible use of English at home thanks to the parents' fluent English

Rena's parents appeared to be liberal toward Rena's English use at home. The mother shared that when Rena replied in English to her parents' questions in Korean, they never asked her to respond in Korean again. The mother stated that the role of parents was not just teaching an HL; rather, she believed that flexible communication between the parents and children should be more important:

> If we (she and her husband) push Rena to speak in Korean whenever she says something to us, we would not have close interaction, which is not proper or ideal parenting from my perspective. Also, because my and my husband's English proficiency is better than Rena's Korean, we sometimes intentionally use English when we need to have deep conversations, such as when teaching a lesson or delivering important messages to our children.

Rena's mother further believed that the situation in her family was different from other Korean families when it comes to home language use and the parents' English proficiency. The mother added:

> I think that the situation in my family is different from other Korean families. Most Korean immigrant parents came to the U.S. at their older ages to pursue a higher degree at graduate school or to get a job. Thus, they tend to experience difficulty in communicating with their children ... because parents are not fluent in English, and children are not proficient in Korean. But we (she and her husband) did not go through this challenge.

As displayed, the mother appeared to believe that their fluent English worked as an advantage and a beneficial tool for communication in her family.

"My child's emotions and feelings are important."

Rena's mother strongly believed that parents in immigrant families should not push their children to learn Korean. She pointed out that before teaching Korean, it is important to identify whether their children were ready and interested in learning it. To corroborate her argument, she shared her recent experience in Korea.

During the data collection of this study, Rena's family visited Korea for a month, and the mother tried to send her children (Rena and her second child) to an elementary school in Korea as visiting students so that they could learn Korean in a formal school setting. But Rena did not want to go to the school because she was afraid of not being fluent in Korean when interacting with native Korean-speaking peers. The mother initially encouraged Rena to attend the school, but eventually ended up not forcing her. The mother considered Rena's emotions and feelings first rather than pushing her to attend the school in Korea against her will:

> I believe that educating HL should be decided based on my child's comfort level. There might be a negative impact on my child if she was forced to learn Korean. She might feel overwhelmed learning Korean with other native Korean-speaking peers.

Parents' negative attitude toward teaching two languages simultaneously

Rena's mother appeared to have a somewhat doubtful perspective when it comes to teaching young children two languages at the same time. In order to substantiate her argument, she shared her first and second children's language learning experiences. She sent her two older children to the Korean HL school when they became 3.5 years old. It was also the same time when they began to learn English in their American preschools. According to the mother, her two older children seemed to get confused with learning Korean in a school setting, explaining:

> My children's confusion was probably because we (she and her husband) used English by switching from Korean whenever our children did not understand what we said during our conversation. But, the teachers in the Korean language school used Korean only in the classroom. Thus, my children did not understand or learn much Korean and eventually refused to attend the school. I believe that they used to have a bad impression of learning Korean.

As she stated, her older children's negative emotional attitudes toward learning Korean led her to send Rena to the Korean HL school when she became 5 years old (1.5 years later than her older brothers). The mother mentioned that she could have sent Rena to the Korean HL school earlier (from preschool), but she was concerned that Rena would have the same experiences as her brothers did:

> I believe that it might be burdensome for Rena to learn two languages at the same time if she had not already acquired one of the languages. I think Rena was ready to attend the Korean language school from the

last semester (when she entered the first-grade class) since her English was somewhat established by that time; thus, I think that learning Korean would not impact her English negatively.

Nari, the second-generation, female balanced bilingual speaker

Nari's parents had been in the U.S. for 11 years since they came to the U.S. for her father to start his graduate study. After completion of his study, he started working as a researcher, and the parents became permanent residents in the U.S. Nari and her younger brother were born in the U.S. and began their initial schooling in the U.S. During school break, the family has visited Korea annually and stayed there for about a month each year. According to Nari's mother, Nari improved her Korean communicative skills while in Korea because she interacted with her grandparents and other relatives. The parents think that visiting Korea once in a while provided Nari with a great opportunity to learn about and practice Korean in a context where Korean was exclusively used. Nari identified herself as a balanced bilingual. But she felt a little more comfortable using Korean than English and was more confident when speaking Korean than English. She considered her Korean to be fluent and her English to be proficient.

"Teaching Korean is more important than English."

Nari's mother believed that learning Korean was significant for Nari since it was her HL, which she had to fully master as a Korean:

> Learning Korean and having fluent Korean proficiency are highly important for my children. I believe that they *must be* (my emphasis) fluent in Korean. It is a shame that my children do not speak Korean well. Accordingly, our role as parents is very important to our children. We are the only one who can stimulate them to use Korean. My children would not have much opportunity to use Korean unless they have our enforcement to use it. Thus, we are very important people for our children to teach Korean by using it and asking them to use it all the time at least at home.

As her response displays, Nari's parents not only greatly valued teaching Korean to their children but also believed that they have a strong responsibility to teach Korean. The mother also stated that it was important for them (she and her husband) to emphasize educating Nari in Korean because she would become an English dominant speaker in her future:

> It seems that Nari is more fluent in Korean than English right now, but I know that she will develop English at a faster rate .... Although we focus on the Korean language, she is going to be dominant in the

English language anyway as she lives in this English-speaking country and attends schools in the U.S. This is the reason why my husband and I are paying more attention to teaching Korean (than teaching English) to her.

Valuing literacy development beyond communicative skills

Nari's parents believed that both communicative and literacy skills were important when it comes to learning the HL. The mother mentioned that she tried to focus on Nari's Korean literacy learning beyond her Korean oral proficiency. According to her, the main reason for the parents to send Nari to the Korean HL school was to help Nari develop Korean literacy skills:

> Nari can learn and develop speaking and listening (in Korean) at home by interacting with us (her husband and her), but it is difficult for us to help her improve her literacy skills. We believe that reading and writing should be learned in a formal school setting in a more structured way.

The mother stated that she felt sorry for immigrant Korean children who barely read and write in Korean:

> I have seen many cases that second-generation Korean immigrant children eventually lost their HL. I think I understand the phenomenon, but I feel sorry and pity for them. Since literacy skills are a part of the important domain ....

Positive perspectives toward raising a child as bilingual

Nari's mother was the respondent who believed in the most advantages of raising her child as bilingual among the mothers of the first-grade students. The mother did not see any challenges or disadvantages when Nari was learning two languages simultaneously. She addressed:

> We are not worried or concerned about our child's language learning either in Korean or English. We know that it takes time. Instead of concerning Nari's different developmental stages for each language, we rather anticipate her future when she becomes full-fledged bilingual.

Nari's predominant use of Korean

The mother's journals reported that Nari used Korean 100% of the time at home when she communicated with family members and engaged in at-home activities. According to the mother's journals, Nari tended to have lots of conversations with her mother in the car on her way to or from her American school on weekdays. The mother mentioned that although Nari was engaged in school activities exclusively in English when she told her parents what happened at school, she always used Korean to describe the events in detail.

The mother's journals often showed how Nari utilized her Korean language repertoires when she was in an English context. For example, when the family went grocery shopping, the mother observed that Nari only used Korean to refer to the items that were displayed on the shelves with English labels in the store. One day, when the family went to the fruit section, the mother asked Nari which fruits she wanted to have, Nari answered "bananas" and "oranges" in Korean. The two words are English loanwords; thus, Korean adopted the same words from English but said them with Korean pronunciation (i.e., trans-enunciation). Although many Korean-American children tend to say English loanwords using the English pronunciation even in their Korean speech, Nari's mother observed that when Nari said the two words in her Korean speech, she did not follow the original Romanized pronunciation, but said them with Korean pronunciation.

Independent and proficient Korean reader

According to the mother's journals, Nari often chose to read Korean picture books by herself at home. The mother detected that Nari preferred reading Korean books to English ones by self-selecting from both English and Korean book options. During her independent reading, Nari often asked her mother for help when she found unknown Korean words. The mother usually explained the meanings of unknown words by providing synonyms or example sentences. But, once Nari's mother asked her whether she could conjecture the meaning of the unknown word by rereading the passage, Nari was able to determine the meaning of the unknown word. The mother reported that she usually asked Nari about to tell the stories when she finished reading them. According to the mother, Nari demonstrated her reading fluency and comprehension by retelling the stories accurately:

> Nari retells the story of the books using Korean only when she reads Korean books. When she was being asked to retell the story of English books, she is also able to retell the stories in Korean except for names of the characters and locations that were originally addressed in English in the books.

Self-aware of writing in Korean as much as possible

The mother's journals showed how Nari engaged in writing practices when she kept her diary entries in Korean for the Korean HL school homework.

According to one of the mother's journals, Nari asked her mother whether she was allowed to write her foreign friends' names in English while she was writing in her diary. Although the mother said it was okay to write their names in English, Nari momentarily stated that she could write them in Korean. As displayed and discussed earlier, Nari wrote her English name using Korean letters by engaging in transliteration. The mother reported that Nari checked with her mother to see if she transcribed her English name correctly by using Korean letters. The mother's journal substantiated the fact that Nari engaged in the cognitive process of thinking about how she should write English names using Korean letters.

Another example from the mother's journals displays Nari's consciousness about using Korean in her diary. Once Nari asked her mother about how to write the words "monkey bars" in Korean for her diary. Instead of transcribing the word in Korean by reflecting on the English phonetic sounds, as she did for her English names, Nari asked her mother for the corresponding word in Korean. According to the mother, Nari assumed that there was a word in Korean for the word "monkey bars" and wanted to write the Korean word in her diary. Indeed, her diary entry presents that she wrote the equivalent word in Korean.

Using Korean with family members but English to talk to herself

Nari's mother reported that Nari used Korean primarily when she talked to her parents and younger brother. The mother stated that Nari seemed to understand the appropriate language to use when she spoke to her interlocutors by considering their language uses and preferences. Once when Nari talked to her grandparents in Korean by using Skype, the grandmother asked her to sing a song that she had learned in her American school. Nari responded that she would sing a song that she had learned in the Korean HL school because her grandparents would not understand her if she sang a song in English. This example indicates that Nari identified her interlocutors (her grandparents) and their language use, which led her to decide to sing a song in the language that they could understand. Yet, Nari's mother sometimes heard Nari using English when she talked to herself or expressed emotions that she felt. The mother shared:

> Nari used Korean all the time when she talked to us, her younger brother, and her grandparents. Although she always used Korean, I occasionally overheard Nari was saying something to herself in English. When she expressed her feelings or emotions, she tended to instinctively use English.

This finding indicates that Nari, who used Korean predominantly when interacting with Korean speakers, sometimes thought and expressed herself in English as a proficient English speaker. As displayed in Figure 4.17, Nari employed Korean to avoid any disrespect to the teacher when expressing her emotion, but she translanguaged into English to talk to herself to express her honest emotion and discomfort freely. Nari's language in the example substantiates the mother's report about Nari's different language use depending on the interlocutors and/or setting.

Summary

This chapter illustrates the ways in which four 1st-grade Korean emergent bilingual students used Korean and English in their oral and written responses at a Korean HL School. Three students (Joon, Yuri, and Rena) identified themselves as English proficient, and one student (Nari) viewed herself as more proficient in Korean than English. The three English-proficient students often included English (speech that included all English or English word-level translanguaging) in their Korean discourse when they engaged in verbal interactions (85%, 79%, 79%, respectively). Yet, their use of English (written sentences that included all English or English word-level translanguaging) was less observed in their writing (23%, 26%, 42%, respectively) than their spoken language since they appeared to understand that writing was a more formal activity than speaking. In terms of the frequency and function of their translanguaging practices, it was found that the English-proficient students often engaged in translanguaging practices, and the four different functions—sociolinguistic knowledge, metalinguistic awareness, metacognitive insight, and sociocultural knowledge—were discovered in their oral and written language use.

In terms of the 1st-grade English-proficient students' oral language use, their translanguaging was most likely to function as sociolinguistic knowledge (49%, 48%, 57% for Joon, Yuri, and Rena, respectively), followed by metalinguistic awareness (32%, 36%, 27%), metacognitive insight (10%, 7%, 10%), and sociocultural knowledge (9%, 9%, 6%; see Appendix A). The English-proficient students' translanguaging functioned as their sociolinguistic knowledge when they flexibly chose the lexical items from their two languages, had quicker lexical access to a particular language, borrowed lexical items for unknown equivalent words, expressed bilingual identities, and varied their language use according to the interlocutors. Their translanguaging also demonstrated their metalinguistic awareness when creating a new word, elaborating on the concept, and controlling their language use. The findings further revealed that they engaged in translanguaging when they used their metacognitive insight through inner speech. Lastly, the students' translanguaging functioned as their sociocultural understanding when they incorporated culturally familiar or relevant Korean words in their English speech.

In terms of the English-proficient students' written language use, their translanguaging was most likely to function as sociolinguistic knowledge (50%, 64%, 70% for Joon, Yuri, and Rena, respectively), followed by metalinguistic awareness (41%, 30%, 25%), sociocultural knowledge (7%, 4%, 5%), and metacognitive insight (2%, 2%, 0%; see Appendix B). The English-proficient students' translanguaging in writing functioned as their sociolinguistic knowledge when they flexibly chose the lexical items from their two languages, had quicker lexical access to a particular language, borrowed lexical items for unknown equivalents or unsure spellings. The written translanguaging pattern was analyzed as the students' metalinguistic awareness when they identified their own language use and regulated their language choices for different places during compositions. Their translanguaging in writing also functioned as their metacognitive insight when they added the word from the other language when they engaged in an inner speech during the process of writing. The students' translanguaging in writing lastly functioned as sociocultural knowledge when they provided English sentences but incorporated Korean words or phrases to utilize their Korean cultural knowledge. In other words, the 1st-grade English proficient students flexibly utilized their language and linguistic repertoires from their two languages by engaging in translanguaging practices.

On the other hand, the 1st-grade Korean proficient student, Nari, consistently stayed in Korean when she spoke (93%) and wrote (99.5%), although she occasionally spoke English depending on the setting (e.g., during recess) and interlocutors (e.g., when responding to English-proficient peers). There was evidence of Nari's translanguaging for the four functions, but the pattern of her translanguaging was different from its use by the English-proficient students since Nari engaged in translanguaging only when she 1) repeated others' words that were in English (i.e., code alignment) and 2) spoke words that do not exist in Korean, including English proper nouns. However, Nari showed a different pattern in her oral language use during recess, and when she talked to herself; she predominantly spoke in Korean during the class discussions but chose to use English when communicating with other classmates during recess and engaged in self-talk. The different patterns of Nari's language use implies that Nari differentiated her use of language depending on the settings (in-class vs. out of class) and interlocutors (English dominant peers vs. Korean teacher).

In terms of her written translanguaging, only one sentence included an English word out of her 207 Korean sentences. Writing the English word appeared to be inevitable for Nari since she introduced her English name; however, she wrote it in Korean first by using Korean letters based on its English pronunciation and then provided it in English later within the parenthesis, which displayed her use of multimodal transliteration (Durán, 2017; García et al., 2017). In her other writing samples, Nari engaged in translanguaging that involved transliteration, in which she employed English phonology to write English words with Korean characters (for English proper nouns and English words that did not exist in Korean). Overall, Nari was aware that composition for the Korean HL school should be written in Korean, and she tried to use her Korean linguistic knowledge for the particular English words when writing. The examples suggest that Nari was able to utilize her sociolinguistic knowledge and metalinguistic awareness through translanguaging as she acknowledged her Korean audiences and then applied her linguistic knowledge by manipulating her written languages. Indeed, although Nari identified herself as more proficient in Korean than English, her language use findings indicate that she appeared to be becoming a competent bilingual in Korean and English.

The chapter also displays mini-case studies of three students (Joon, Rena, and Nari) to learn about their parents' attitudes and actions towards their child's language use as well as to provide other sociocultural influences on their language use. The finding indicates that there was a close relationship between the parents' attitudes and practices at home and the children's language use and learning. For instance, among the four 1st-grade parent participants, Nari's parents appeared to be the most supportive of their child's Korean language learning and believed that teaching HL to their child was of the greatest significance. Nari's parents also accepted their responsibility to teach Nari Korean as they had positive perspectives towards raising Nari as bilingual. In contrast, Rena's parents appeared to be the most supportive of Rena's English use by emphasizing her English language learning. For Rena's parents, learning English was obligatory, but Korean was an extra language; thus, it was not mandatory for Rena to acquire perfect Korean proficiency. Indeed, Nari was the student who mainly stayed in Korean and rarely translanguaged when speaking and writing in the classroom, but Rena was the most English-dominant student who presented her oral and written responses most often in English. Therefore, the findings suggest that parents' attitude towards HL learning was a significant factor in maintaining and developing children's HL (Guardado & Becker, 2015; Liang, 2018). It was further discovered that several sociocultural factors (e.g., family's immigration status and future residency, amount of interaction with other Korean relatives, the role of siblings) (Melo-Pfeifer, 2015) influenced the participating bilingual students' language use and learning.

References

Bialystok, E. (1991). Metalinguistic dimensions of bilingual language proficiency. In E. Bialystok (Ed.), *Language processing in bilingual children* (pp. 113–140). London, England: Cambridge University Press.

Busch, B. (2012). The linguistic repertoire revisited. *Applied Linguistics, 33*(5), 503–523.

Canale, M., & Swain, M. (1980). Theoretical bases of communicative approaches to second language teaching and testing. *Applied Linguistics, 1*, 1–47.

Durán, L. (2017). Audience and young bilingual writers: Building on strengths. *Journal of Literacy Research, 49*(1), 92–114.

Fogarty, R. (1994). *How to teach for metacognition.* Palatine, IL: IRI/Skylight Publishing.

García, O., Johnson, S., & Seltzer, K. (2017). *The translanguaging classroom. Leveraging student bilingualism for learning.* Philadelphia, PA: Caslon.

Grumperz, J. J. (1997). The retrieval of sociocultural knowledge in conversation. *Poetics Today, 1*(2), 273–286.

Guardado, M., & Becker, A. (2015). "Glued to the family" The role of familism in heritage language development. *Language, Culture and Curriculum, 27*(2), 163–181.

Halliday, M. A. K. (1973). *Explorations in the functions of language.* London: Edward Arnold.

Kress, G. (2015). "Literacy" in a multimodal environment of communication. In J. Flood, S. B. Heath, & D. Lapp (Eds.), *Handbook of research on teaching literacy through the communicative and visual arts* (Vol. 2, pp. 91–100). New York, NY: Routledge.

Liang, F. (2018). Parental perceptions toward and practices of heritage language maintenance: Focusing on the United States and Canada. *International Journal of Language Studies, 12*(2), 65–86.

Meichenbaum, D. (1985). Teaching thinking: A cognitive-behavioral perspective. In S. F. Chipman, J. W. Segal, & R. Glaser (Eds.), *Thinking and learning skills, Vol. 2: Research and open questions.* Hillsdale, NJ: Lawrence Erlbaum Associates.

Melo-Pfeifer, S. (2015). The role of the family in heritage language use and learning: Impact on heritage language policies. *International Journal of Bilingual Education and Bilingualism, 18*(1), 26–44.

Sayer, P. (2013). Translanguaging, TexMex, and bilingual pedagogy: Emergent bilinguals learning through the vernacular. *TESOL Quarterly, 47*(1), 63–88.

Swain, M. (2010). "Talking-it-through": Languaging as a source of learning. In R. Batstone (Ed.), *Sociocognitive perspectives on second language learning and use* (pp. 112–129). Oxford, England: Oxford University Press.

van Compernolle, R. A., & Williams, L. (2012). Reconceptualizing sociolinguistic competence as mediated action: Identity, meaning-making, agency. *Modern Language Journal, 96*(2), 234–250.

5 Oral and written language use and translanguaging functions of 3rd-grade Korean bilingual students

Third-graders' views of their language use, preferences, and proficiencies

Prior to the 3rd-graders' classroom language use, their home language use, language preferences, and self-reported language proficiencies were examined by conducting the interviews with each 3rd-grader. All the students answered that they primarily used Korean with their parents at home. The first three students—Toni, Julie, and Suji—were second-generation Korean-Americans who were born in the U.S., whereas Mina recently came to the U.S. from Korea for a temporary stay. The three Korean-American students (Toni, Julie, and Suji) preferred speaking in English to speaking in Korean and identified themselves as English dominant. In contrast, Mina preferred speaking in Korean and regarded herself as a Korean-dominant speaker.

In terms of their language proficiency, the three Korean-American students reported that their English skills were many times better than their Korean skills. Yet, they thought their Korean skills were acceptable for oral communication but limited for reading and writing in Korean. For instance, Toni stated, "My Korean is not really good, but it is okay to communicate with other Koreans. But, reading and writing in Korean are difficult." Julie also described her Korean reading and writing as limited, but thought her oral Korean was okay because she practiced it with her parents: "I am not good at Korean reading and writing, but speaking Korean is okay because I use Korean with my parents and practice it." On the other hand, Mina saw herself as a fluent Korean speaker but limited in English. Yet she believed that her English proficiency has been improved since she had stayed in the U.S.: "Korean is the language that I speak fluently. English is a little difficult for me although I learned it when I was very young in English kindergarten (in Korea). But I am getting better in English since I have lived in the U.S. for several months and have used English more."

According to the students' responses, there are differences in their language preferences and proficiencies between the second-generation Korean-Americans (Toni, Julie, and Suji) and the short-term visiting (for two years) Korean student (Mina). One reason for the difference in the students' language preferences and proficiencies might have been their immigration status. Similar to the 1st-graders' findings, the 3rd-graders' language use during the interviews corroborated their answers when they identified themselves as proficient English speakers (for Toni, Julie, and Suji) and as a fluent Korean speaker (for Mina). Accordingly, I refer to the first three students (Toni, Julie, and Suji) as English proficient and Mina as a Korean-proficient student throughout this paper. The following section displays the students' oral language use in their HL classroom and illustrates how their actual language use substantiates their views about their respective language proficiencies.

Third-graders' oral language use in the classroom

This section presents findings on how the 3rd-graders used their languages to orally communicate in an HL classroom. Although the students were encouraged to speak in Korean, they were allowed to use both languages (Korean and English). Table 5.1 shows the frequency of 3rd-graders' oral language use in English and Korean when they engaged in classroom interactions. It illustrates the pattern of language use by each student and his/her translanguaging practices.

As shown in Table 5.1, the three English-proficient students (Toni, Julie, and Suji) used more Korean (51%, 49%, 50%, respectively) than English (9%, 8%, 9%, respectively). Their overall language use indicates that they spoke in English less than 10% of the time. This is an unexpected finding because they all responded that they preferred speaking in English and identified themselves as English dominant. One reason why the English-proficient students might not have used much English during classroom interactions seemed to be that they were aware that they were supposed to use Korean in class. They often asked their teacher's (Mrs. Joen) approval to use English when they spoke. For instance, when Mrs. Joen asked Toni to provide additional information, he asked her permission to use English by saying (translated into English), "Then, I need to speak in English. Can I?" Similarly, Suji asked Mrs. Joen's permission about whether she and her classmates could use English during recess by asking (translated into English), "Can we speak in English now?" Although the three students rarely spoke completely in English, they still engaged in English word-level translanguaging in their Korean speech in the classroom (38%, 41%, 39%, respectively). In contrast, they tended to employ more English than Korean when they talked to one another during recess; the students' language use during recess displayed that they sometimes incorporated Korean words into their English discourse.

Meanwhile, Mina, who identified as Korean proficient, spoke in Korean 90% of the time in the classroom. On the other hand, she initiated her speech in English only 4% of the time, and it was often discovered when she interacted with her English-proficient peers during

Table 5.1 Third-graders' oral language use in the classroom

	Korean[a]	English[b]	Word-Level Translanguaging[c] (English Words in Korean Speech)	Word-Level Translanguaging[c] (Korean Words in English Speech)	Total	Frequency of Translanguaging at Sentence Level[d] (Korean to English)	Frequency of Translanguaging at Sentence Level[d] (English to Korean)
Toni	182 (51%)	32 (9%)	138 (38%)	8 (2%)	360 (100%)	19 times	11 times
Julie	196 (49%)	38 (8%)	170 (41%)	9 (2%)	413 (100%)	13 times	13 times
Suji	167 (50%)	29 (9%)	131 (39%)	11 (3%)	338 (100%)	21 times	9 times
Mina	332 (90%)	16 (4%)	22 (6%)	0 (0%)	370 (100%)	5 times	6 time

Note. The frequency of students' sentence-level translanguaging was provided, but the numbers were not counted in the total because the sentences were already included in the first two columns.

a. Spoke exclusively in Korean.
b. Spoke exclusively in English.
c. Intrasentential switching within a single utterance.
d. Intersentential switching between the utterances.

recess. Only 6% of her translanguaging was presented at the word level when she incorporated English words into her Korean discourse. In other words, there is a substantial amount of difference between the two groups in terms of their classroom language use and translanguaging incidence. In the section below, close analysis of the three English-proficient students' (Toni, Julie, and Suji) translanguaging in their spoken language is presented, followed by a close analysis of the Korean-proficient student's (Mina) translanguaging.

Functions of oral translanguaging among the English-proficient students

Close analysis of the three 3rd-grade English-proficient students' oral language use revealed that they engaged in translanguaging practices for 1) sociolinguistic knowledge, 2) metalinguistic awareness, 3) metacognitive insight, and 4) sociocultural understanding. Similar to the 1st-graders' findings, 3rd-grade English proficient students' oral translanguaging was primarily discovered in their Korean speech as they incorporated English words while speaking in Korean.

English-proficient students' sociolinguistic knowledge

The 3rd-grade English-proficient students' translanguaging was classified as demonstrating their sociolinguistic knowledge (Canale & Swain, 1980; van Compernolle & Williams, 2012) when 1) they flexibly used their dual lexicon, 2) they wanted to emphasize their meanings/ideas through translanguaging, and 3) they considered their different interlocutors. The sociolinguistic function characterized the majority of their oral translanguaging (63%, 61%, 60% for Toni, Julie, and Suji, respectively; see Appendix C).

Figure 5.1 shows that Suji engaged in translanguaging when she responded to Mrs. Joen's question based on the Korean folktale *The Rabbit's Liver* that the students read in class. Suji replied in Korean but inserted several English words ("turtle," "bunny," "right," and "lie") and the phrase ("to save his life") in her statements. During the interview, Suji demonstrated that she knew all the translanguaged words in Korean but added English words because she thought of them before she thought of the Korean words, stating "because I was able to quickly think about some words in English, then later in Korean." Indeed, in the subsequent statements, she spoke the translanguaged words ("turtle," "bunny," and "lie") and the phrase ("to save his life") in Korean as well (the italicized Korean word; turn 2 in Figure 5.1). This example illustrates that she employed her dual lexicon flexibly from her full language repertoires through translanguaging, which demonstrates her sociolinguistic competence. (English translations are provided within the brackets. Translanguaged words are underlined in the English translation.)

1. Mrs. Joen: 누가 나쁜 짓 을 한 거지? 토끼야 거북이야?

   [Who did a bad thing? The rabbit or turtle?]

2. Suji: Turtle 이 나빠요. 나는 bunny 가 right 한 거 같애. *토끼*는 lie 했는데 to save his

   life 한 거고. 그런데 *거북이*는 *살려고* 아니고, 용왕님 한테 잘 보일려고

   거짓말 한 거예요.

   [The <u>turtle</u> was bad. I think the <u>bunny</u> was <u>right</u> because he <u>lie</u>[d] <u>to save his life</u>.

   But the turtle did it to flatter the sea god, not to save his life.]

Figure 5.1 Flexible use of bilingual lexicon.

Figure 5.2 shows a similar example of translanguaging by another 3rd-grader, Julie. After reading the book *The Rabbit's Liver* in class, Julie stated her opinions about the characters' behaviors. As shown, she provided her statements in Korean, but her subsequent utterance includes several English words ("turtle," "lying," and "bad") in her Korean discourse. Yet, Julie had stated these English words in Korean in her prior statement (the italicized Korean word in Figure 5.1) the Korean words are italicized in Figure 5.2). Unlike the previous example by Suji, Julie exclusively spoke in Korean in her first two utterances and then later added the English words ("turtle," "lying," and "bad") that she had spoken in Korean. It appears that she purposefully selected the English language for the particular words ("turtle," "lying," and "bad"). Indeed, Julie stated in the interview that she decisively used English as she wanted to emphasize her personal opinion on the characters' behaviors from the book, explaining "I wanted to point out that the turtle's lying was [emphasized] *worse* than the rabbit's lying."

Julie: 토끼는 잘못 한 거요 왜냐하면 *거짓말* 자체가 *나쁜* 거니까. 근데 *거북이*는

   더 나빠요. Turtle 은 벼슬 받으려고 lying 한 거니까 엄청 bad 해요.

   [The rabbit did a bad thing because lying itself is bad. But the turtle did a worse

   thing. The <u>turtle</u> was <u>lying</u> to get a high prize, so he was extremely <u>bad.</u>]

Figure 5.2 Selecting the English language to highlight.

Figure 5.3 shows how two of the English proficient students employed translanguaging when they interacted with different interlocutors. When the class had pizza for a snack during recess, Julie exclusively spoke in English (turn 1). But when Mrs. Joen asked her a question in Korean (turn 2), Julie translanguaged into Korean to respond to her question (turn 3). Likewise, Toni reacted to Suji's statement using English (turn 4), but right afterward he translanguaged to speak to Mrs. Joen in Korean (turn 5). Julie and Toni's language uses in this example exhibits that they moved across their languages by considering their different interlocutors (Korean teacher vs. English proficient peers).

1. Julie: I don't like pineapple pizza. I want to eat pepperoni pizza.

2. Mrs. Joen: 왜 파인애플 싫어해?

   [Why do you hate pineapples?]

3. Julie: 파인애플 좋아하는데 근데 여기 피자에 있는 거는 싫어요.

   [I like pineapples, but do not like pineapples on pizza.]

4. Suji: I have allergy to pineapples. I can touch them but can't eat them.

5. Toni: Wow. Really? Allergy to pineapples? Hmm... 선생님, 갈릭 소스 더 주세요.

   [Teacher, can I have more garlic sauce?]

Figure 5.3 Interlocutor's influence on translanguaging.

English-proficient students' metalinguistic awareness

The metalinguistic functions of translanguaging (Bialystok, 1991) were displayed by the English proficient students when they 1) demonstrated their comparative linguistic knowledge of Korean and English, 2) ensured understanding of unknown words, 3) identified the language that is universally used, and 4) regulated their language use when making jokes (Jonsson, 2013). The English-proficient students' translanguaging sometimes functioned as metalinguistic awareness (31%, 33%, 32% for Toni, Julie, and Suji, respectively), and it was often observed at the word level rather than the sentence level (see Appendix C).

In Figure 5.4, the students engaged in translanguaging practices when they discussed the different language features between Korean and English. When Mrs. Joen asked the class to compare Korean and English, Julie utilized her knowledge of English and pointed out the specific language feature of English—intonations through translanguaging (turn 2). Toni then stated the difference in the written features between English and Korean by pointing out that English has capital letters (turn 5). Suji indicated that cursive writing is unique to the English language (turn 6). In their responses, they translanguaged into English to identity the specific language features ("intonation," "capitals," and "cursive") that exist only in English compared to Korean. Their use of translanguaging demon-strated that they were using their metalinguistic awareness by applying their prior knowledge about speaking and writing in the two languages.

1. Mrs. Joen: 한글과 영어의 다른 점 에 대하여 얘기 해볼래?

    [Can we discuss the differences between the Korean and English languages?]

2. Julie: 영어는 올라갔다 내려갔다 intonation 이 있어요.

    [English has up and down <u>intonation</u>.]

3. Toni: 쓰는 것도 달라요.

    [Writing is also different.]

4. Mrs. Joen: 그렇지 쓰는 것도 다르지. 한글 이랑 영어 쓰는게 어떻게 다르지?

    [Yes, you are right. How do the writing systems differ?]

5. Toni: 영어는 capital 로 시작하는데 한글은 그게 없어요.

    [English sentences should be initiated with <u>capital</u>[s], but Korean does not.]

6. Suji: 영어 cursive 하는 것도 있고 cursive 하는 거 저 진짜 좋아해요.

    [English has <u>cursive</u>. I like writing <u>cursive</u> a lot.]

Figure 5.4 Comparing the differences between Korean and English.

Figure 5.5 shows how Toni used translanguaging to ensure her understanding of an unknown Korean word. When Mrs. Joen asked the class a question about the Korean biography *Lee Whang* (turn 1), it appears that Toni was unsure of the Korean word "다짐" [pledge], so he asked a question to the teacher by adding its synonym both in Korean "결심" [decide] and English "decide" (turn 2). After Mrs. Joen con-firmed that his understanding was correct (turn 3), Toni answered her question in Korean by using the Korean word ("pledge") that he was uncertain about its meaning (turn 4). During the interview, Toni stated that he provided the synonym in Korean first and then in English later to ensure his understanding of the uncertain Korean word, explaining: "I added the English word because I am 100% sure the meaning of the word in English so I can check whether it [the Korean word "pledge"] has the same meaning." Toni's response indicates that he employed his linguistic resource from English to ensure his understanding of an uncertain Korean word, utilizing his metalinguistic awareness.

1. Mrs. Joen: 이황은 어떤 다짐을 했나요?

    [What did Lee Whang pledge?]

2. Toni: 다짐은...결심 이랑 같은 거예요? Like "decide"?

    [Pledge... Is it similar to the word "decide"? <u>Like "decide"?</u>]

3. Mrs. Joen: 응 맞아. 기억나?

    [Yes, correct. Do you remember?]

4. Toni: 오늘 배운 것은 오늘 다 익히자 라 고 다짐했어요.

    [He pledged that he would study what he learned on that day.]

Figure 5.5 Ensuring understanding of the unknown word.

Figure 5.6 displays Suji's use of translanguaging to identify the audience's language use. In line 2, Mina answered Mrs. Joen's question about the rabbit's trick in a Korean folktale, *The Rabbit and Tortoise*. After listening to Mina's response, Suji asked Mrs. Joen a question in Korean, but she translanguaged into English to speak to the rabbit (turn 3). Suji's translanguaging pattern in this example is interesting because her audience—the rabbit (the character in the book)—does not exist in reality, but she chose English to speak to the rabbit. During my interview, Suji explained the reason why she used English to speak to the rabbit by stating "I just pretended that the rabbit only speaks English and does not know Korean at all … because English is the worldwide language that almost everyone knows, but Korean is not." Her response indicates that she manipulated her languages as she was considering the language that is universally used.

1. Mrs. Joen: 토끼는 어떤 꾀를 부린 거지?

    [What trick did the rabbit do?]

2. Mina: 토끼가 간을 두고 왔다고 꾀를 부렸어요.

    [He said that he didn't bring his liver with him.]

3. Suji: 근데 선생님 토끼가 간을 어떻게 두고 다녀요? 토끼, you CAN'T just leave

    your liver.

    [But, teacher, how can the rabbit leave his liver? Rabbit, <u>you CAN'T just leave</u>

    <u>your liver.</u>]

Figure 5.6 Identifying the language that is universally used.

Figure 5.7 illustrates another example of Julie's use of translanguaging to illustrate her metalinguistic knowledge. In this example, Julie regulated her language use to make a joke. When Mrs. Joen heard a noise that the preschoolers were making in the hallway outside of the classroom, she mentioned that preschoolers were making noise because they were young (turn 1). In responding to Mrs. Joen, Julie added a sense of humor in her response through translanguaging (turn 2). Her translanguaging suggested that she used English to signal her joke rather than transmitting correct information. Suji seemed to intentionally choose English as she was playing with language to make a joke by exaggerating her statement, which suggests that her translanguaging functioned for adding a sense of humor.

1. Mrs. Joen: Preschooler 면 몇 살이지? 어리니까 시끄럽지.

   [How old are the <u>preschoolers</u>? They make noise since they are young.]

2. Julie: Preschooler 가 어려요? Preschooler 들은 20 years old and we are three years old.

   [Are <u>preschoolers</u> young? <u>Preschoolers</u> are <u>20 years old, and we are three years

   old.</u>]

Figure 5.7 Regulating her language use to make a joke.

English-proficient students' metacognitive insight

The English-proficient students' metacognitive skills were witnessed when they engaged in self-thinking processes through inner speech (Fogarty, 1994; Meichenbaum, 1985). However, since I was not the teacher for the 3rd-grade students, it was difficult to capture data on the 3rd-graders' inner speech from the audio-recordings of their class interactions. Hence, there was only one translanguaging example detected for this function in Toni's talk that revealed his metacognitive insight (1%) (see Appendix C). Figure 5.8 shows how Toni engaged in private speech through translanguaging. When Mrs. Joen complimented Mina's drawing (turn 1), Toni responded to Mrs. Joen in Korean (turn 2) but switched to English when talking to himself (turn 3). The example shows how Toni moved from interpersonal dialogues with Mrs. Joen to intrapersonal speech (to himself) by employing translanguaging. That is, Toni's use of Korean to respond to Mrs. Joen and the use of English for covert speech suggested that Toni utilized his metacognitive insight through translanguaging during the process of verbalization.

1. Mrs. Joen: 애들아, 미나 그림 그린 것 좀 봐. 진짜 잘 그렸지?

    [Look at Mina's drawing. Isn't it really great?]

2. Toni: 우와! 네. 진짜 같아요.

    [Yes, it is really great.]

3. Toni: (to himself, aloud) Oh, my gosh. She is so good at drawing. I am gonna steal your

    hands and draw (laughs).

Figure 5.8 Engaging in a private speech to himself.

English-proficient students' sociocultural understanding

The English-proficient 3rd-graders' translanguaging rarely functioned as sociocultural understanding (5%, 6%, 8% for Toni, Julie, and Suji, respectively; see Appendix C). The set of examples in Figure 5.9 shows how each student utilized his/her sociocultural knowledge (Gumperz, 1979; Halliday, 1973) by inserting culturally related Korean referents in their English discourse. (Bold fonts in English translations show the words that the students translanguaged in Korean.)

A. Suji: Do you have 색종이? I need a 색종이, the yellow one.

    [Do you have **origami papers**? I need a[n] **origami paper**, the yellow one.]

B. Toni: On New Year's Day, I did 세배 first thing in the morning.

    [On New Year's Day, I did **New Year's bows** (to elders in the family) first thing

    in the morning.

C. Julie: I have 한복, but it is too small for me now.

    [I have **hanbok** (traditional Korean clothes), but it is too small for me now.]

Figure 5.9 Inserting Korean words for culturally appropriate referents.

In line A, Suji asked the question in English but inserted the word for "origami paper" in Korean. In Korea, origami is a popular classroom activity. The Korean HL school provided colored origami papers to each class so that the students could play with them in class or during recess. Thus, Suji might have been familiar with the term in Korean. In line B, Toni added the Korean words "New Year's bows" and "rice cake soup" in his English responses. On New Year's Day in Korea, making bows to elder members of the family is a traditional custom. It appears that Toni was using his sociocultural knowledge by translanguaging the culturally specific term into Korean. Julie's statement in line C shows a similar pattern since she also inserted a culturally specific Korean word in her English utterance. The Korean word "hanbok" describes traditional Korean clothes that Korean people wear on holidays in Korea. Julie uttered this word in Korean when she saw the illustrations in a book that depicted Koreans wearing traditional clothes. Her use of this specific Korean word while speaking in English indicates that her translanguaging demonstrates her sociocultural knowledge from Korean.

Functions of translanguaging by the Korean-proficient student

Mina, who recently came to the U.S. from Korea, preferred to speak in Korean, indeed mainly used Korean (90%) and a minimum of English (4%). There were a few times when Mina used translanguaging in her oral speech (6%). Her use of translanguaging revealed when she inserted English words in her Korean utterances, and her translanguaging practices characterized three of the four functions: sociolinguistic knowledge (73%), metalinguistic awareness (24%), and sociocultural understanding (3%) (see Appendix C).

Korean-proficient bilingual student's sociolinguistic knowledge

Mina translanguaged the most for sociolinguistic purposes, accounting for 73% of her translanguaging. Close analysis revealed that Mina's translanguaging was found when she responded to her classmates who spoke in English. Figure 5.10 shows how Mina translanguaged into English when she interacted with her English-proficient peer, Suji. Mina asked a question to the class in Korean by translanguaging the word "cursive" in English. Suji replied in Korean but soon translanguaged into English in her subsequent response and when she asked Mina a question (turn 2). After listening to Suji's question in English, Mina switched her language to respond to Suji's question in English (turn 3). This example

1. Mina: 대문자 G 를 cursive 할 때 어떻게 써요?

    [How can I write <u>cursive</u> for the capital <u>G</u>?]

2. Suji: 나 알아. Let me give you a hand. Do you know how to write "s"?

    [I know. <u>Let me give you a hand. Do you know how to write "s"?</u>]

3. Mina: Yes. S is easy. I know how to write a lower-case s....

Figure 5.10 Response to interlocutor for code alignment.

implies that Mina was influenced by her peer, Suji, because Suji's translanguaging seemed to sanction her own. In other words, Mina conformed to a principle of *code alignment* (Sayer, 2013) as she responded to her interlocutor's language use by translanguaging.

Korean-proficient bilingual student's metalinguistic awareness

The second most frequent function for Mina was metalinguistic awareness, which characterized 24% of her translanguaging practices. Mina's language use during the class sessions displayed that she predominantly used Korean and rarely translanguaged into English. However, during recess, Mina used English to interact with her classmates who mainly spoke in English. Figure 5.11 shows how Mina spoke in English when she conversed with her English-proficient peers during recess. The students were randomly asking Siri funny questions. Mina successfully joined the conversation by following the language (English) that her classmates used. During the interview, Mina stated that she purposefully used English during recess as she knew that her classmates mainly spoke in English. This example shows that Mina was able to flexibly switch her languages according to the context (in-class versus during recess), which indicates that she was using her metalinguistic awareness.

1. Julie: How old are you?

2. Suji: Where are you at? Who are you?

3. Mina: Let me ask this. Are you a boy or a girl?

    …

4. Toni: Where is my mom right now?

5. Mina: That's a funny question. Where do I live?

Figure 5.11 Code alignment with interlocutors' language choice.

Korean-proficient bilingual student's sociocultural understanding

It was discovered that Mina translanguaged for sociocultural function when she employed culturally relevant Korean words in her English discourse. Since Mina rarely provided English discourse, inserting culturally relevant Korean words in her English utterances was a rare practice; thus, translanguaging for sociocultural function was characterized by only 3% of her translanguaging practices. Mina translanguaged in her English discourse when she referred to the Korean culturally specific referents. Figure 5.12 displays Mina's use of translanguaging into Korean in her English statement when she referred to the culturally specific referent, the Korean food item. On New Year's Day in Korea, having rice cake soup is a traditional custom. It appears that Mina was using her sociocultural knowledge by translanguaging the culturally specific term into Korean. (Bold fonts in English translations show the word that Mina translanguaged in Korean.)

Mina: On New Year's Day, we had 떡국 for breakfast.

             [On New Year's Day, we had **rice cake soup** for breakfast.]

Figure 5.12 Use of culturally specific referent in Korean.

Third-graders' language use when writing

The 3rd-graders' writing samples were analyzed focusing on their language use as well as the patterns and functions of their translanguaging. The students used much less translanguaging when writing than they did to orally communicate. Table 5.2 shows each student's written language use both from their in-class writings and their diary entries as homework.

As shown in Table 5.2, the three English-proficient 3rd-graders were more likely to stay in Korean when they wrote, compared to when they spoke. For Toni's case, he utilized much more Korean while writing (91% of the time) than speaking (51% of the time). Similarly, Julie and Suji employed more Korean when writing (88% and 85% of the time, respectively), compared to their use of Korean when speaking (49% and 50%). Although the students occasionally employed English lexical items in their Korean compositions, their use of translanguaging was at the word level, and the presence of sentence-level translanguaging was rarely observed (except for one case by Suji). In contrast, Mina, the Korean-proficient student, produced her written responses by using only Korean for her in-class writing. Yet, analysis of her diary writing samples showed the presence of English translanguaging at the word level (7%) as she inserted English proper nouns in her diaries.

Functions of written translanguaging among the English-proficient students

The 3rd-grade English-proficient students' use of translanguaging was less observed in their writing than their oral language data; however, they still occasionally demonstrated word-level translanguaging in their writing samples (9%, 12%, and 13% for Toni, Julie, and Suji, respectively). Their use of translanguaging in their writing was analyzed according to the following four categories: 1) sociolinguistic knowledge, 2) metalinguistic awareness, 3) metacognitive insight, and 4) sociocultural understanding.

Table 5.2 Third-graders' written language use from writing samples

	Total Number of Writing Samples	Korean-Only Sentences	English-Only Sentences	Word-Level Translanguaging (English Words in Korean Sentences)	Word-Level Translanguaging (Korean Words in English Sentences)	Total	Translanguaging at Sentence Level (Korean to English)[a]	Translanguaging at Sentence Level (English to Korean)[b]
Toni	34	276 (91%)	0	26 (9%)	0	302	0	0
Julie	31	253 (88%)	0	38 (12%)	0	291	0	0
Suji	32	265 (85%)	3 (1%)	46 (13%)	0	311	1	0
Mina	36	459 (93%)	0	31 (7%)	0	490	0	0

Note: The numbers of the students' written sentences were counted in the table.
a The frequency of the 3rd-graders' sentence-level translanguaging from Korean to English.
b The frequency of the 3rd-graders' sentence-level translanguaging from English to Korean.

English-proficient bilingual writers' sociolinguistic knowledge

Half or a bit more than half of the English proficient students' translanguaging in writing functioned as sociolinguistic knowledge (50%, 51%, 54% for Toni, Julie, and Suji, respectively; see Appendix D). There were two subcategories when the students translanguaged in this area while writing: 1) identifying linguistic features from both languages and 2) rewriting English words into Korean to ensure the Korean reader. The examples of their use of translanguaging to represent their sociolinguistic competence occurred when they flexibly operated their dual lexicon.

Figure 5.13 shows Julie's writing sample when she wrote about the differences between the Korean and English languages. As shown, Julie composed her texts using Korean only. Yet, close analysis of the drawing space shows the presence of her translanguaging. Before the text, Julie wrote English alphabets (a, b, c, d …) on the left side and Korean letters (가, 나, 다 …)

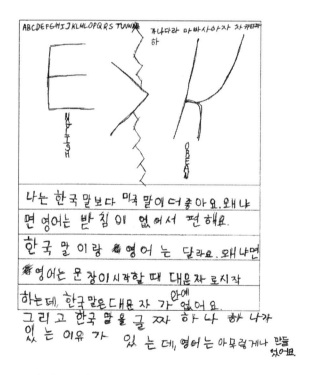

I prefer the English language to the Korean language. English is easy because it does not have batchips [Korean final consonants placed under the vowels]. Korean and English are different. English has capital letters, but Korean does not have them. And Korean has individual meaning in each letter, but English words can be made by combining letters.

Figure 5.13 Using linguistic features from both languages (dual lexicons).

on the right side. Under each letter, Julie wrote the word "English" and the word "Korean" and drew the line between the two words to separate the spaces for each language. Then she presented the symbol (>) to indicate that she liked English more than Korean. This writing sample reveals that her translanguaging was multimodal and semiotic since she used all the linguistic resources (by writing, drawing, providing text labels with an associated symbol) available to her during the processes of her writing.

Julie's translanguaging illustrates how she utilized her linguistic knowledge by identifying different linguistic features from the two languages, which demonstrates her sociolinguistic knowledge. (English translations of the students' Korean writing samples are provided above the end of the Figures. The words or sentences that students wrote in English are underlined in the English translation.)

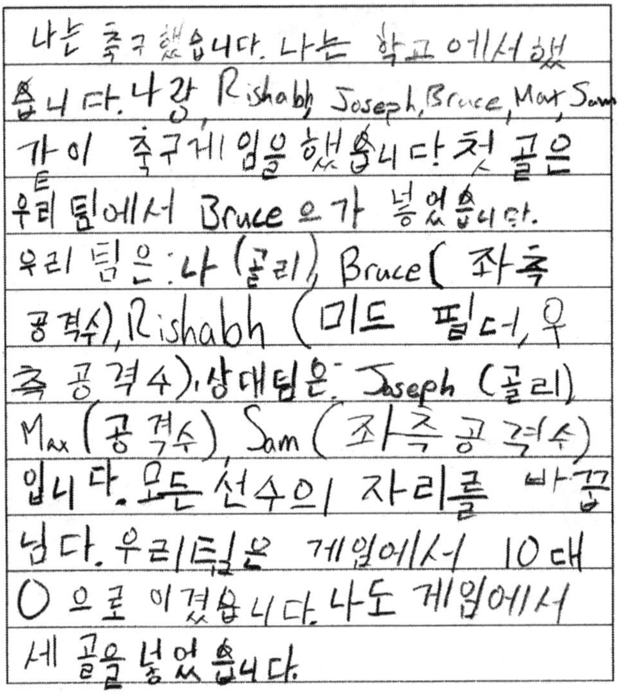
나는 축구 했습니다. 나는 학교에서 했
습니다. 나랑 Rishabh, Joseph, Bruce, Mat, Sam
같이 축구게임을 했습니다. 첫 골은
우리 팀에서 Bruce 으가 넣었습니다.
우리 팀은: 나 (골리), Bruce (좌측
공격수), Rishabh (미드 필더, 우
측 공격4), 상대팀은: Joseph (골리)
Max (공격수), Sam (좌측 공격수)
입니다. 모든 선수의 자리를 바꿉
닙다. 우리팀은 게임에서 10대
0으로 이겼습니다. 나도 게임에서
세 골을 넣었습니다.

I played soccer. I played it at school with Rishabh, Joseph, Bruce, Mat, and Sam. Bruce from my team got the first goal. My team members were me (goalie), Bruce (left-forward), and Rishabh (mid-fielder; rightforward). The opponents' team consisted of Joseph (goalie), Max (forward), and Sam (left-forward). Each player switched his position each game. My team won the game by a score of 10 to 0. I got three goals.

Figure 5.14 Reproducing the word in Korean for the Korean reader.

Figure 5.14 shows Toni's diary entry, in which he revealed that he was using his sociolinguistic knowledge when translanguaging. In his diary, Toni wrote about when he played soccer with his friends and explained the positions for each player. Close analysis indicated that he wrote his friends' names in English, which seems inevitable for Toni to write them in English as his friends used English names. However, when he provided each player's soccer position, he wrote them all in Korean. In fact, there is a trace that Toni wrote the word "left" in English for the position "left forward," but he erased it and rewrote its referent in Korean. The same practices were found when he wrote the words for mid-fielder and goalie. During the interview, Toni stated that he was thinking about his Korean teacher as the reader of his diary entry and tried to write all the words in Korean, explaining "I knew that this [his diary entry] would be read by my Korean teacher, so I rewrote the word [left forward] in Korean for her to read and understand what I wrote." His response from the interview implies that Toni utilized his sociolinguistic knowledge by appropriately employing translanguaging while writing according to the perceived audience (Halliday & Hasan, 1989).

English-proficient bilingual writers' metalinguistic awareness

Out of the four functions, metalinguistic awareness was characterized the second most frequent function throughout the three English-proficient students' translanguaging practices (42%, 40%, 37% for Toni, Julie, and Suji, respectively; see Appendix D) and was found at the word-level, except for one incidence of sentence-level translanguaging by Suji. There were two subcategories when the students translanguaged in this area while writing: 1) distinguishing spaces for texts (in Korean) and drawing (in English) and 2) using metalinguistic insight when writing proper nouns. Similar to the 1st-graders' findings in the earlier chapter, the 3rd-graders' writing samples displayed that they mainly used Korean when they composed the texts in the body but often used English in drawing spaces.

The 3rd-graders' use of Korean and English in their texts versus drawing spaces was analyzed. As displayed by the 1st-grade students' findings, the 3rd-grade English-proficient students also used translanguaging when they wrote in the drawing spaces (44%, 52%, 60% for Toni, Julie, and Suji, respectively), whereas their use of translanguaging was less observed in the body of their writing (18%, 13%, and 9%, respectively). In addition, the 3rd-graders composed all in Korean (the body of texts and captions) without utilizing the translanguaging strategy in their writing (38%, 35%, and 31%, respectively). This translanguaging pattern exemplified the students' metalinguistic understanding since they were able to identify their own language use and regulate their language choices for different spaces in their compositions.

The English-proficient students' responses during the interviews explained the reason why they tended to write the text in Korean but often used English in the drawing spaces. For example, Toni explained that writing at the Korean HL school should be done in Korean because "[his] writing is read by the Korean teacher thus it should be written in Korean," but he understood that he could use English when he described his drawing by providing text labels in English. Similarly, Julie stated that she consciously used Korean while writing in the texts, but she purposefully chose English in the drawing spaces, explaining "I know that I chose Korean when I was writing because this is writing for my Korean school, but I also deliberately chose English when I talked about my drawings."

Figure 5.15 displays Suji's writing sample when she differentiated her language use for the main text versus drawing. Suji wrote her diary entirely in Korean, whereas, all the text labels around her drawings were written in English. However, in her Korean sentences, she included English proper nouns ("Rockefeller center" and "Legos") and English loanwords ("skates") by using Korean letters. The example of Suji's translanguaging indicates her use of transliteration—in which bilinguals employ their phonological understanding from one language to write letters in the other language (García, Johnson, & Seltzer, 2017). In other words, when she wrote "Rockefeller center," "skates!" and "Legos," she converted English phonetics to Korean pronunciation with Korean characters. Yet, she had written these words in English when she provided the text labels to depict her

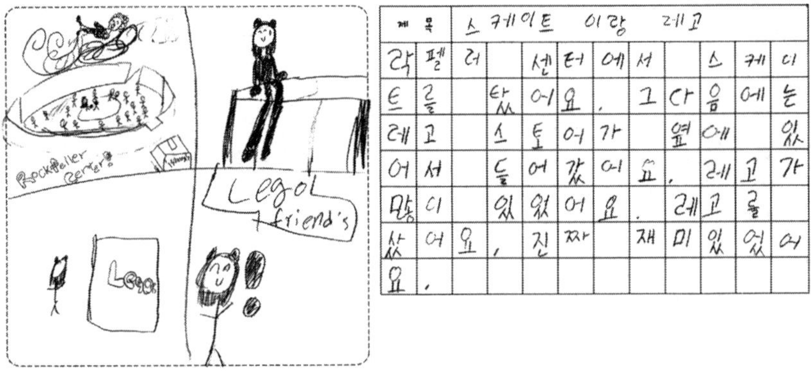

Title: Ice skating and Legos

I ice skated at the Rockefeller Center. There was a Lego store next to the center, so we went there. There were a lot of Legos. I bought Legos. It was very exciting.

Text labels: Rockefeller Center, Skates, Lego friend's, Legos

Figure 5.15 Selecting different languages for the main texts versus drawing spaces.

drawings. Suji consciously distinguished her language uses for official versus unofficial communication, which demonstrates her metalinguistic awareness.

A similar finding was observed in Toni's diary entry in Figure 5.16. As shown, Toni wrote his diary in Korean except for two English words: "Target" and "Black Dog." Close analysis revealed that he engaged in transliteration (García et al., 2017) for the English words "barbeque ribs" and "catfish sandwich." Similar to what Suji did in the previous example, Toni utilized the English phonology of the words to write them with Korean letters. For his direct English translanguaged words, "Target" is the name of a store in the U.S., and "Black Dog" is the name of a restaurant in the town; both are proper nouns. It was interesting to see that he translanguaged into English for the proper nouns and transliterated for the common nouns. In the interview, Toni explained that the proper nouns ("Target" and "Black Dog") did not represent their literal meanings. In contrast, the common nouns ("barbeque ribs" and "catfish sandwich") were names of particular food items, and their meanings would not change when written in the two languages. Toni explained that "I wrote them in English because if I wrote them in Korean, the meaning could be different … black dog would be a totally different meaning. And target, too. But the rest of the words would be the same even if they were written in Korean because there is only one

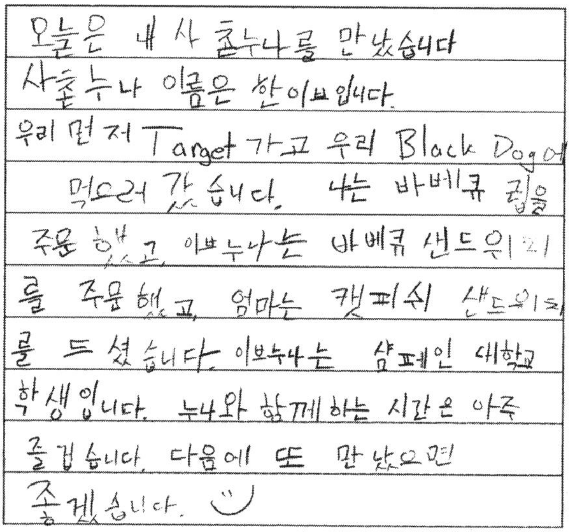
오늘은 내 사촌누나를 만났습니다
사촌누나 이름은 한이브입니다.
우리 먼저 Target 가고 우리 Black Dog에
먹으러 갔습니다. 나는 바베큐 립을
주문 했고, 이브누나는 바베큐 샌드위치
를 주문했고, 엄마는 캣피쉬 샌드위치
를 드셨습니다. 이브누나는 샴페인 대학교
학생입니다. 누나와 함께하는 시간은 아주
즐겁습니다. 다음에 또 만났으면
좋겠습니다. :)

I met my cousin today. Her name is Eve Han. We went to the Target store and the Black Dog [restaurant]. I ordered Barbeque rib and my cousin ordered a barbeque sandwich. My mom ate a catfish sandwich. My cousin is a college student. I enjoyed spending time with her. I would like to see her soon again.

Figure 5.16 Choosing English purposefully for particular proper nouns.

meaning for those words." Toni's explanation indicates that he understood that the meanings of some English words would be comprehensible when they are written with Korean characters, but others would not. His explanation about his language choice suggests that his use of translanguaging was purposeful, and it further demonstrates his metalinguistic awareness about his written language use.

English-proficient bilingual writers' metacognitive insight

The students' metacognitive skills were witnessed when they engaged in self-thinking processes for their writing through inner speech. However, as stated earlier, since I was not the teacher for the 3rd-grade students, it was difficult to capture data on the students' self-talk from the audio-recordings of their class interactions. However, there was one example of Toni's use of translanguaging in his thinking and self-directed talk that revealed his metacognitive insight (4% for Toni; see Appendix D).

In Figure 5.17, Toni introduced his cousin's names both in English and Korean at the beginning of the entry, but he only used his cousin's

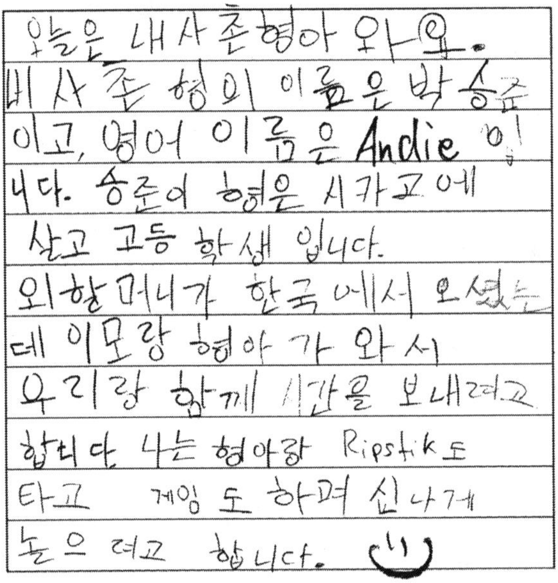

My cousin will visit my house today. My cousin's name is Seung-joon Park, and his English name is <u>Andie</u>. Seungjoon lives in Chi-cago, and he is a high school student. Since my grandmother came to see us from Korea, we will have a great time with my aunt and Seungjoon. I will ride a <u>Ripstik</u> and play games with Seungjoon, and we will have a fun time together.

Figure 5.17 Manipulating cognitive thinking through inner speech.

Korean name when he referred to him in the rest of his diary. Indeed, after introducing both names (in English and Korean), there was a trace of his using the English name, which Toni erased, later replacing it with the Korean name. During the interview, Toni explained: (translated into English) "I came up with the English name first because I call him by his English name, but I erased it and rewrote it with his Korean name because I knew that this was my Korean diary homework, so I talked to myself that I should write it in Korean." When Toni switched his cousin's name from English to Korean, it appeared that he was using his metacognitive insight as he was monitoring and controlling his language use. Toni's statement during the interview suggested that he understood that he *had to* use Korean for his cousin's name by recognizing that he was writing his diary in Korean. This example demonstrates that Toni was able to manipulate his cognitive process and thinking through translanguaging, which implies that he was using his metacognitive skills.

English-proficient writers' sociocultural understanding

The 3rd-grade English-proficient students' use of translanguaging for the sociocultural function occurred when they used culturally familiar or relevant Korean words. Since the students did not produce any main texts in English (except for one case by Suji; see Figure 5.14), only a few written translanguaging examples were found for this function (4%, 9%, 9% for Toni, Julie, and Suji, respectively; see Appendix D). Their translanguaging for this function was observed in their drawings when they inserted culturally relevant Korean words among other English text labels. The students chose to write the words in Korean if they were specific to the Korean culture and customs, which demonstrated their cultural knowledge and understanding in Korean.

Figure 5.18 displays Suji's use of translanguaging to demonstrate her sociocultural knowledge when she provided text labels to her drawings both in Korean and English. Suji wrote her diary entry entirely in Korean but chose to use both languages when adding text labels to describe her drawings. She provided several text labels in English ("School event," "fun," and "Yay") but added text labels in Korean for the words that are related to Korean culture ("Korean New Year's Day," "Korean food"). She further translanguaged for the English phrases by incorporating Korean words (italicized) that have cultural references ("making *lucky bag*" [symbols of luck in Korean], "wearing *Hanbok*" [Korean traditional clothes], and "making *Jegi*" [Korean traditional game]). The translanguaged phrases that included culturally specific Korean words

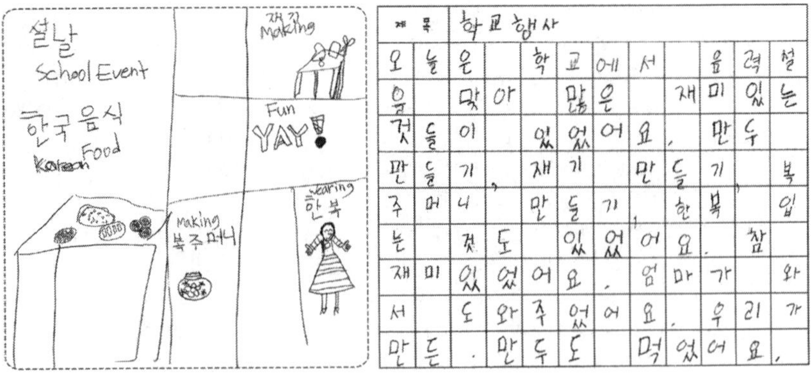

Title: *School Event*

Today we celebrated the Korean New Year's Day at my school. There were many interesting things—making dumplings, making Jegi [the tool for Korean traditional game], making lucky bag [symbol of luck in Korean], and wearing Hanbok [traditional Korean clothes]. It was very fun. My mom came to help us. We ate the dumplings that we made together.

Text labels: 설날 *[Korean New Year's Day],* School event, 한국 음 식 *[Korean food],* Korean Food, 제기 *[Jegi; the tool for Korean traditional game]* making, making 복주머니 *[lucky bag; symbols of luck in Korean],* wearing 한복 *[traditional Korean clothes],* Fun, Yay!

Figure 5.18 Inserting culturally relevant words using Korean.

indicated that Suji employed her sociocultural knowledge to describe each of the items in her drawings.

Figure 5.19 exhibits a similar translanguaging pattern in Julie's diary writing. As shown, Julie added text labels to her drawings in English for the places in the U.S. (i.e., Chicago trip, museum, shopping center, hotel, and inside the restaurant), but she chose to write her family members ("mom," "dad," and "younger sister") in Korean. Julie's explanation of her language use showed that she selected Korean to refer to her family because Korean represented her sociocultural upbringing: (translated into English) "I prefer to call mom and dad in Korean. Because … if I call mom and dad (in English), I feel like I am not that close to them."

My family went to Chicago. I went to a museum with my mom,
dad, and younger sister, and we saw many things there.
We ate pizza and salad at the restaurant. I was full because I ate
a lot. I went shopping with my mom. My mom bought pretty
clothes for me. We went to the hotel and stayed a night there.

Text labels: *Chicago Trip*, *Museum*, 엄마 [Mom], 아빠 [Dad],
동생 [Younger Sister], 나 [Me], *Shopping center*, *Hotel*, *Inside the
restaurant*

Figure 5.19 Selecting Korean words when referring to family members.

Functions of written translanguaging by the Korean-proficient student

Mina's language use in her writing samples was presented in Table 5.2.
Mina mainly composed in Korean (459 out of 490 sentences; 93%) when
she engaged in in-class writing and diary entries. Only 7% of her sentences
included English words (31 out of 490 sentences) throughout her writing
samples. In other words, Mina occasionally used English word-level

translanguaging in her Korean writing. Yet, unlike the English-proficient students, all of Mina's translanguaged English words were proper nouns that were influenced by the U.S. context (e.g., the name of her foreign friends, landmarks or places to go, book or movie titles). Mina seemed to understand that she could use English words while writing in Korean if the words only existed in English. Overall, Mina's translanguaging mainly functioned as metalinguistic awareness (68%) and sometimes functioned as sociolinguistic knowledge (32%) (see Appendix D). It is important to note that Mina, who recently came to the U.S. from Korea, showed more advanced writing skills throughout her overall writing samples, such as sentence complexity, word choices, the length of writings, handwriting, than the other English-proficient 3rd-graders.

Figure 5.20 shows Mina's writing sample where she incorporated English words in her Korean sentences. Mina used English words for the titles of English books that she had thought about buying for her friend as a birthday gift. During the interview with Mina, she explained that she wrote the English titles because they originally were in English, and she was worried that she would change their meanings if she translated them into Korean: "I wrote them (the list of books) in English because they are originally written in English. And I know that sometimes if I translate them, the original meanings are easily changed." From her response, Mina seemed to understand that translanguaging into English while writing in Korean is acceptable if 1) the writer is using words that are originally written in English and 2) when the translation into Korean does not maintain the original meaning. Mina's use of English in this example demonstrated her sociolinguistic knowledge as she appropriately employed translanguaging while writing according to the word choice or topic (Halliday & Hasan, 1989).

Below the entry, Mina provided a text label in English after drawing the heart shape (writing "books" inside of the heart shape), but she had provided the word in Korean in her main text. This indicates that Mina appeared to understand that she had to write the main texts in Korean, but the text labels could be written in English. As the other 3rd-grade English-proficient students showed, Mina's translanguaging demonstrated her metalinguistic awareness when she differentiated her language use for official (main texts) and unofficial (drawing spaces) communication.

Figure 5.21 displays Mina's use of multimodality (Korean, English, and visuals) as a type of translanguaging practices. Mina wrote a diary entry about when she made a bracelet and used Korean to describe how to make the bracelet. Then she provided text labels in English to describe her drawings ("step 1," "step 2," "step 3," "pull," and "I ♥ making bracelets"). Mina connected her written texts and drawings by using the arrow symbol. During the interview, Mina pointed out that she drew the illustrations to help Mrs. Joen, who would read her diary, understand how to make the bracelet from her writing: "Making the bracelet was difficult to explain in writing. So, I drew the pictures to help my teacher understand

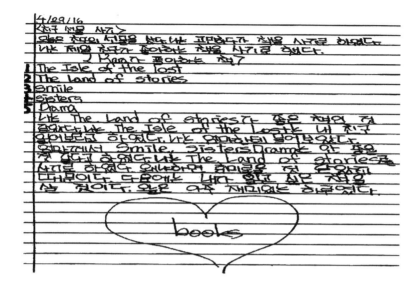

Title: *Buying a birthday present for my friend.*

I bought a birthday gift for my friend. I decided to buy a book for her. I wanted to buy a book that she liked the most.

<The book that <u>Kara</u> likes>
1. <u>The Isle of the Lost</u>
2. <u>The Land of Stories</u>
3. <u>Smile</u>
4. <u>Sisters</u>
5. <u>Drama</u>

I thought that The Land of Stories is the best. I asked her to read The Isle of the Lost. I asked my mom and she told me that <u>Smile</u>, <u>Sisters</u>, and <u>Drama</u> are the good ones. I decided to purchase The <u>Land of Stories</u> because it looked interesting to read. I will buy a book that I want to read for the next time. Today was a very interesting day.

Text label: <u>books</u> (inside her drawing of the heart shape)

Figure 5.20 Translanguaging for words that are originally in English and for the text label.

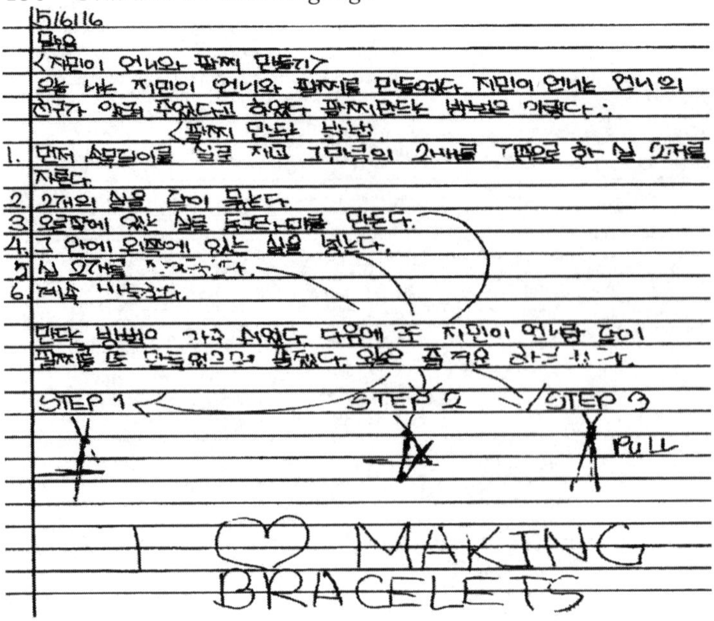

5/6/16
제목
〈지민이 언니와 팔찌 만들기〉
오늘 나 지민이 언니와 팔찌를 만들었다. 지민이 언니는 친구의
언니 언제 주었다고 한다. 팔찌만드는 방법은 이렇다.:
〈팔찌 만드는 방법〉
1. 먼저 손목이를 실로 재고 그만큼의 2배를 가지고 한 실 2개를
   가진다.
2. 2개의 실을 묶어 준다.
3. 오른쪽에 있는 실을 동그라미를 만든다.
4. 그 다음에 왼쪽에 있는 실을 넣는다.
5. 두 실을 "잡아당긴다."
6. 계속 반복한다.

계속 반복이 가장 쉬웠다. 다음에 또 지민이 언니랑 같이
팔찌를 또 만들었으면 좋겠다. 오늘 좋은 경험 하는 날이다.

STEP 1   STEP 2   STEP 3

                     ✗   PULL

I ♡ MAKING BRACELETS

Title: *Making bracelets with Jimin*

Today I made bracelets with Jimin. She told me that she learned
how to make bracelets from her friend. This is how to make a
bracelet.

<How to make a bracelet>
1. Measure your wrist using a string and prepare two threads that
are double the length of your wrist.
2. Tie the two threads to each other.
3. Make a circle using the right thread.
4. Put the left thread in the right circle-shaped thread.
5. Pull the two threads.
6. Repeat several more times.

Making a bracelet was easy. I want to make it again with her.
I had a great time.

Text labels: STEP 1, STEP 2, STEP 3, PULL, I ♥ MAKING
BRACELETS

Figure 5.21 Using multimodality to make meaning.

what I wrote and how to actually make the bracelet." Mina's statement illustrates that she believed her drawing could assist her writing.

She further used the heart symbol in her English text labels instead of writing "love" because she wanted to highlight how much she loved making bracelets. This example illustrates that Mina used multimodal semiotic resources (drawing and symbol) beyond writing with dual languages (Korean and English) when she delivered her messages in a written form. Overall, Mina's use of translanguaging was multimodal and semiotic (Busch, 2012; Durán, 2017; Kress, 2015) as she used all the linguistic resources available (by writing the main texts in Korean, providing text labels in English, and including related symbols and numbers), which contributed to her meaning-making processes in writing.

Summary

This chapter presents findings of four 3rd-grade Korean bilingual students' Korean and English language use when they spoke and wrote at a Korean HL School. There were three students (Toni, Julie, and Suji) who identified themselves as English proficient, and one student (Mina) viewed herself as Korean proficient. The three 3rd-grade English-proficient students included English (speech that included all English or English word-level translanguaging) when they engaged in verbal interactions (51%, 49%, 50%, for Toni, Julie, and Suji, respectively) in the Korean language classroom. They also included English (written sentences that included all English or English word-level translanguaging) when engaging in writing tasks (9%, 12%, 13%, respectively). Similar to the 1st-graders' language use findings, the 3rd-graders' use of English was less observed in their writing than their spoken language. Close analysis of their oral and written language use further displayed that the 3rd-graders engaged in less translanguaging practices than the 1st-graders did. The older grade students seemed to be more cognizant of their language use and tried to meet their teacher's expectations by using Korean in the classroom. It is possible that the 3rd-graders were more likely to stay in Korean when speaking to the teacher at the Korean HL school because they understood that the Korean language required honorifics, which could not be expressed in English. Yet, they still engaged in translanguaging practices occasionally, and three out of the four different functions—sociolinguistic knowledge, metalinguistic awareness, and sociocultural understanding—were discovered in their oral and written language use (metacognitive function was discovered in Toni's oral and written translanguaging only).

In terms of the 3rd-grade English proficient students' oral language use, their translanguaging was most likely to function as sociolinguistic knowledge (63%, 61%, 60% for Toni, Julie, and Suji, respectively), followed by metalinguistic awareness (31%, 33%, 32%), sociocultural understanding (5%, 6%, 8%), and metacognitive insight (1% for Toni only; see Appendix C). The 3rd-grade English-proficient students' translanguaging functioned as their sociolinguistic knowledge when they flexibly used their dual lexicon, had quicker lexical access to a particular language, and considered their different interlocutors. The students' translanguaging also demonstrated their metalinguistic awareness when they exhibited their comparative linguistic knowledge of Korean and English, ensured understanding of unknown words, identified the language that is used universally, and controlled their own language use. The findings further revealed that their translanguaging functioned as their sociocultural understanding when they incorporated culturally familiar or relevant Korean words in their English discourse. Lastly, there was only one example of translanguaging by Toni demonstrated his metacognitive insight through inner speech.

Regarding the 3rd-grade English-proficient students' written language use, their translanguaging practices were most likely to be functioned as sociolinguistic knowledge (50%, 51%, 54% for Toni, Julie, and Suji, respectively), followed by metalinguistic awareness (42%, 40%, 37%), sociocultural understanding (4%, 9%, 9%), and metacognitive insight (4% for Toni only; see Appendix D). The students' translanguaging in writing functioned as their sociolinguistic knowledge when they utilized their linguistic resources across both languages and flexibly operated their dual lexicon. The students' written translanguaging practice was analyzed as their metalinguistic awareness when they identified their own language use and regulated their language choices for different places during compositions. Their translanguaging in writing also functioned as sociocultural when they inserted Korean words or phrases for cultural purposes during their compositions in English. Lastly, only one translanguaging example by Toni performed as metacognitive function; Toni demonstrated his metacognitive insight when he identified and regulated his language use after engaging in a self-directed talk during composition. Overall, the 3rd-grade English-proficient students did not often engage in translanguaging, especially when writing, but when they did so, they flexibly utilized their language and linguistic resources from their two languages through translanguaging.

On the other hand, the 3rd-grade Korean-proficient student, Mina, primarily used Korean when she engaged in speaking (90%) and writing (93%), but her intermittent translanguaging was detected. Throughout her spoken language, Mina translanguaged into English to speak with her English-proficient peers during recess. Mina's oral translanguaging demonstrated that she conformed to a principle of *code alignment* (Sayer, 2013) by utilizing English, which indicates that she was metalinguistically aware of other classmates' language preferences and also was able to communicate fully in English with them. This finding is similar to what the 1st-grade Korean-proficient student (Nari) displayed in her classroom language use (see Chapter 4). In terms of her translanguaging in writing, Mina engaged in translanguaging by incorporating English words in her Korean sentences (7%; 31 out of 490 sentences), and all of her English translanguaged words were influenced by the U.S. context (e.g., names of her foreign friends, book or movie titles). In other words, Mina understood that she could write English words during her Korean compositions if they only existed in English (e.g., English proper nouns). This is different from Nari's (the 1st-grade Korean-proficient student) written translanguaging findings that involved transliteration (i.e., writing English words using Korean characters) as she was aware that composition should be written in Korean for the Korean HL school. Although Mina, who recently came from Korea, identified herself as Korean dominant and limited in English, her language use findings suggest that she was able to strategically utilize more appropriate language from her bilingual repertoires considering different purposes, settings, and inter-locutors, which implies that she was becoming a sociolinguistically competent and metalinguistically cognizant bilingual learner.

References

Bialystok, E. (1991). Metalinguistic dimensions of bilingual language proficiency. In E. Bialystok (Ed.), *Language processing in bilingual children* (pp. 113–140). London, England: Cambridge University Press.

Busch, B. (2012). The linguistic repertoire revisited. *Applied Linguistics, 33*(5), 503–523.

Canale, M., & Swain, M. (1980). Theoretical bases of communicative approaches to second language teaching and testing. *Applied Linguistics, 1*, 1–47.

Durán, L. (2017). Audience and young bilingual writers: Building on strengths. *Journal of Literacy Research, 49*(1), 92–114.

Fogarty, R. (1994). *How to teach for metacognition.* Palatine, IL: IRI/Skylight Publishing.

García, O., Johnson, S., & Seltzer, K. (2017). *The translanguaging classroom. Leveraging student bilingualism for learning.* Philadelphia, PA: Caslon.

Gumperz, J. J. (1979). The retrieval of sociocultural knowledge in conversation. *Poetics Today, 1*(2): 273–286.

Halliday, M. A. K. (1973). *Explorations in the functions of language.* London: Edward Arnold.

Halliday, M. A. K., & Hasan, R. (1989). *Language, context and text: Aspects of language in a social-semiotic perspective* (2nd ed.). Oxford: Oxford University Press.

Jonsson, K. (2013). Translanguaging and multilingual literacies: Diary-based case studies of adolescents in an international school. *International Journal of the Sociology of Language, 224*, 85–117.

Kress, G. (2015). *"Literacy" in a multimodal environment of communication.* In J. Flood, S. B. Heath, & D. Lapp (Eds.), *Handbook of research on teaching literacy through the communicative and visual arts* (Vol. 2, pp. 91–100). New York, NY: Routledge.

Meichenbaum, D. (1985). Teaching thinking: A cognitive-behavioral perspective. In S. F. Chipman, J. W. Segal, & R. Glaser (Eds.), *Thinking and learning skills, Vol. 2: Research and open questions.* Hillsdale, NJ: Lawrence Erlbaum Associates.

Sayer, P. (2013). Translanguaging, TexMex, and bilingual pedagogy: Emergent bilinguals learning through the vernacular. *TESOL Quarterly, 47*(1), 63–88.

van Compernolle, R. A., & Williams, L. (2012). Reconceptualizing sociolinguistic competence as mediated action: Identity, meaning-making, agency. *Modern Language Journal, 96*(2), 234–250.

6 A longitudinal study

Focal students' bilingual language
use over time and the sociocultural
influences on HL development

Characteristics of the two focal students

Out of four 3rd-graders who participated in this study, Toni and Julie were identified as focal students. Both Toni and Julie were former participants as 1st-graders in the pilot study that was conducted in the 1st-grade classroom at the same Korean HL school in Spring 2014.

Toni, the second-generation, male 3rd-grader

Toni was born in the U.S. and considered himself to be English proficient. Toni's parents had lived in the U.S. for 14 years as permanent residents. During school breaks, the family visited Korea on an annual basis and stayed there for about a month each year. Toni's mother believed that Toni was able to improve his Korean communicative skills while staying in Korea for a month every year because he had opportunities to meet and talk with his relatives and other Koreans.

Julie, the second-generation, female 3rd-grader

Julie was also born in the U.S. and considered herself to be English proficient. Julie's parents had lived in the U.S. for 9 years. Julie's parents were obtaining their Ph.D. degrees and planned to get jobs in the U.S. Similar to Toni's family, Julie's family visited Korea on an annual basis during school breaks. Julie's mother stated that visiting Korea provided Julie with a good opportunity to improve her Korean communicative skills and learn about her heritage culture.

Comparison of two focal students' oral language use between 1st and 3rd grade

Table 6.1 compares Toni and Julie's language use during classroom interactions when they were 1st- and 3rd-graders. The table displays how often Toni and Julie used Korean, English, and translanguaging when they spoke in both grades.

Table 6.1 Comparison of Toni and Julie's oral language use between 1st and 3rd grade

	Only Korean	Only English	Word-Level Translanguaging[a] (English Words in Korean Speech)	Word-Level Translanguaging[b] (Korean Words in English Speech)	Frequency of TL at Sentence-Level (Korean to English and vice versa)
1st grade (Spring 2014) Toni	36 (12%)	122 (41%)	138 (46%)	4 (1%)	91 times
Julie	41 (13%)	98 (32%)	163 (53%)	6 (2%)	87 times
3rd grade (Spring 2016) Toni	182 (51%)	32 (9%)	138 (38%)	8 (2%)	30 times
Julie	196 (49%)	38 (8%)	170 (41%)	9 (2%)	26 times

Notes
a Intrasentential switching within a single utterance when the students inserted English words as they spoke in Korean.
b Intrasentential switching within a single utterance when the students inserted Korean words as they spoke in English.
c Intersentential switching between the utterances (Korean to English and vice versa).

Increased use of Korean when speaking in 3rd grade

As shown in Table 6.1, when Toni and Julie were in 1st grade, they both spoke more in English than in Korean (41% in English vs. 12% in Korean for Toni; 32% in English vs. 13% in Korean for Julie). Conversely, their 3rd-grade language use revealed that they spoke more in Korean than in English (51% in Korean vs. 9% in English for Toni; 49% in Korean vs. 8% in English for Julie). Both Toni and Julie still engaged in word-level translanguaging when they were in 3rd grade, but the frequency of inserting English words when they spoke in Korean decreased (from 46% to 38% for Toni; from 53% to 41% for Julie). The frequency of their sentence-level switching (from Korean to English and vice versa) was also less observed in their 3rd-grade classroom (from 91 to 30 times for Toni; from 87 to 26 times for Julie). In other words, there was an increased use of Korean and a decrease in their use of English when they were in 3rd grade compared to when they were in 1st grade.

Development of vocabulary knowledge in Korean

The focal students' increased vocabulary knowledge in Korean appeared to play a role in their increased use of Korean as 3rd-graders. Comparison of Julie's language use in Figure 6.1 (as a 1st-grader) and Figure 6.2 (as a 3rd-grader) display that when Julie was a 1st-grader, she translanguaged into English as she did not know the equivalent words in Korean, but by 3rd grade, she had acquired knowledge of the same words and uttered them in Korean. As shown in Figure 6.1, Julie (1st-grader) translanguaged into English for the words "story" and "remember" (turn 2) when she responded to the question about the book that the class read. When she was asked how to say the translanguaged words in Korean, she stated that she did not remember the word "story" in Korean and did not know the corresponding word for "remember" in Korean. The example indicates that Julie translanguaged into English for unknown words to complete her response, which functioned as a communicative purpose. (English translations are provided within the brackets. Translanguaged words are underlined in the English translation.)

    1. T: 윤이 이름을 영어로 어떻게 썼지?

               [How did Yoon write her name in English?]

    2. Julie: 나 그 story remember 해요.

               [I remember the story.]

Figure 6.1 Julie's (1st-grade) employment of English for uncertain Korean words.

On the other hand, Julie's 3rd-grade language use in Figure 6.2 demonstrated that she had acquired the two Korean words ("story" and "remember") that she did not know in 1st grade. Julie's answer to Mrs. Joen's question included the Korean words for "story" and "remember" (the bold and italicized Korean word; turn 2). Despite evidence of her vocabulary gain, Julie translanguaged the word "story" into English in her Korean subsequent statement (turn 3). That is, Julie spoke the English word after saying it in Korean by employing her vocabulary knowledge from English. In the interview, Julie stated that (translated into Korean) "I think I spoke it English because I know the word in English as well." Julie's 3rd-grade language use example displays not only her Korean vocabulary gain but also her flexible use of dual lexicon through translanguaging as a bilingual speaker's communicative strategy.

1. Mrs. Jeon: 우리 지난주에 읽은 동화책 내용 누가 발표해 볼래? 줄리 해볼래?

    [Who wants to tell the story of the book that we read in class last week? Julie, can

    you try?]

2. Julie: 어...그 책 *이야기* 저 *기억나*는 거 같아요.

    [Umm... I think I remember the story of the book.]

3. Julie: 근데 저 story 제대로 다는 기억 못할 수도 있어요.

    [But I might not remember the whole <u>story</u> correctly.]

Figure 6.2 Julie's (3rd-grade) demonstration of Korean vocabulary gain and flexible use of dual lexicons.

Comparing Toni's language use in Figure 6.3 (in 1st grade) and Figure 6.4 (in 3rd grade) also shows evidence of his vocabulary gain in Korean. In Figure 6.3, Toni as a 1st-grader responded to the teacher's question by translanguaging the words "favorite part" (turn 2). When

1. T: 너네 은혜 반 친구들이 이름이 담긴 병 만든 거 기억해?

    [Do you all remember the part when the classmates created the name jar for

    Unhei?]

2. Toni: 네, 그거 내 favorite part 에요.

    [Yes, that was my <u>favorite part</u>.]

Figure 6.3 Toni's (1st-grade) translanguaging for unknown Korean words.

Toni was asked how to say the words in Korean, he stated that he knew how to say "like" but did not know the word "favorite" in Korean. Similar to the previous example by Julie, Toni (as a 1st-grader) also translanguaged into English for unknown words to complete his response, which performed as a communicative purpose.

Analysis of Toni's 3rd-grade language use in Figure 6.4 demonstrated that he had acquired the word ("favorite") in Korean. Toni's response to Julie's question included the Korean word (the bold and italicized Korean word; turn 2) for "favorite" (turn 2). Yet, Toni later incorporated the word "favorite" in English in his Korean utterance (turn 4). It seemed that Toni spoke the word in English instinctively (turn 4) as he responded to Julie's praise (turn 3). In the interview, Toni explained that he sometimes used English because speaking in English is natural behavior as a bilingual, stating "I used English because sometimes I naturally spoke in English without knowing or realizing because I speak both Korean and English when talking to other bilinguals." Like the previous example by Julie, Toni's 3rd-grade language use example indicates that he had developed his Korean vocabulary knowledge but drew from his dual lexicon (bilingual vocabulary) to communicate with his bilingual audience.

1. Julie: 누가 이거 할래?

             [Who wants to do this game?]

2. Toni: 나 할래. 이거 내가 *제일 좋아하는* 게임이야.

             [I will do it. That is my favorite game.]

3. Julie: 엄청 잘한다.

             [You are so good at this.]

4. Toni: 내가 말했지? 내 favorite 이라고!

             [I told you that it was my favorite!]

Figure 6.4 Toni's (3rd-grade) demonstration of Korean vocabulary gain and flexible use of dual lexicon.

Figure 6.5 shows a similar pattern when comparing the two students' language use between 1st and 3rd grades. In Figure 6.5, Julie translanguaged into English for the words "shy" and "nervous" (turn 2) when responding to the question (turn 1). When she was asked how to say the words in Korean, she described the characteristics of being shy and nervous by using the English words ("face red" and "heartbeat" for the word "shy" and "worry" for the word "nervous") but stated that she did not know the corresponding

1. T: 처음 미국학교 갔을 때 어땠어?

   [How did you feel when you went to the school for the first time?]

2. Julie: 저 학교 처음 갔을 때 많이 shy 하고 nervous 했어요.

   [When I went to the school for the first time, I was very <u>shy</u> and <u>nervous</u>.]

3. T: Shy 랑 nervous 한 거 어떻게 한국말로 할 수 있지?

   [How can you describe being <u>shy</u> and <u>nervous</u> in Korean?]

4. Julie: Shy 는 face red 하는 거고, nervous 는 heart beat 돼요 왜냐면 worry 많이 해서.

   Korean 으로는 잘 몰라요.

   [Being <u>shy</u> is when someone's <u>face</u> becomes <u>red</u>, and if you feel nervous, your

   <u>heart</u> is <u>beat</u>[ing] because you <u>worry</u> a lot. I do not know them in <u>Korean</u>.]

Figure 6.5 Julie's (1st-grade) translanguaging to sustain communication.

words in Korean (turn 4). Julie's response in turn 4 indicates that she was able to explain the definitions of the unknown Korean words using English. In other words, Julie employed the vocabulary knowledge from English for the unknown Korean words to complete her response.

On the other hand, Julie's 3rd-grade language use in Figure 6.6 demonstrated that she had acquired the Korean words that she had not known in first grade. Julie's answer to Mrs. Joen's question included the Korean words for "shy" and "nervous" (the bold and italicized Korean words; turn 2). However, although Julie demonstrated her vocabulary gain in Korean, she still incorporated the English word "nervous" in her Korean discourse (turn 4). Close analysis revealed that she uttered the word in Korean first and then translanguaged to repeat the word

1. Julie: 에르반이 *부끄러워서* 귀가 빨개졌어요. *떨리고* 겁이 났어요 실수할까봐.

   [Erevan's ears became red because he was shy. And he felt nervous and anxious.]

2. Julie: 왜냐면 수학문제 푸는데 실수할까봐 *떨렸어요* nervous 했어요.

   [Erevan was nervous <u>nervous</u> (repeated the word); he was afraid of making

   mistakes when he solved the mathematics problem.]

Figure 6.6 Julie's (3rd-grade) employment of translanguaging to emphasize.

in English. In the interview, Julie explained that she repeated the word in English to emphasize its meaning in her response. Julie stated, "I said the word 'nervous' again in English because I wanted to emphasize how much Erevan (the character in the book) was nervous." A similar translanguaging incidence was appeared in her other Korean discourse and discussed in the prior chapter (see Figure 5.2 in Chapter 5). In the earlier example, Julie translanguaged into English when she wanted to highlight her opinion. Her translanguaging in this example also was to emphasize her intended meaning by repeating the word in English. Julie's translanguaging is similar to the concept of bilingual re-voicing (Gort & Sembiante, 2015).

Another comparison of Toni's language use in Figure 6.7 (in 1st grade) and Figure 6.8 (in 3rd grade) also displays evidence of Toni's vocabulary growth in Korean. In Figure 6.7, Toni as a 1st-grader did not seem to know the Korean word "뜻 [*Ttuet*; meaning]" when he was asked its meaning in Korean (turn 2). Yet, after the teacher provided the example from the book to show how the word is used (turn 3), Toni understood the meaning of the word and successfully answered to the teacher's question in Korean. Nevertheless, he still uttered the word ("meaning") in English when he provided his answer in Korean (turn 4).

1. T: 너네는 모두 너네 이름에 담긴 뜻을 알아?

[Do you all know the meanings in your names?]

2. Toni: 뜻? 그게 뭐예요?

["*Ttuet*" (meaning)? What is that?]

3. T: 예를 들어... 책에서 윤은 이름의 뜻이 지혜 였잖아. 영어로 shining wisdom.

너네들은 뭔지 알고 있어?

[For example, the meaning in Yoon's name in the book was shining wisdom. It is

in English. Do you all know about yours?]

4. Toni: 아 나 이름에 meaning. 나 엄마가 알려줬는데, 힘세고 강한 거가 meaning

이래요.

[Oh, the <u>meaning</u> in my name. My mom told me that the <u>meaning</u> is strong and

tough.]

Figure 6.7 Toni's (1st-grade) translanguaging to provide the answer to the question.

On the other hand, Toni's 3rd-grade responses in Figure 6.8 exhibit that he said the word "meaning" in Korean (the bold and italicized Korean word; turn 2) in responding to Mrs. Joen's question (turn 2). When Mrs. Joen asked the class whether they knew the Korean word "officialdom" (turn 1), Toni answered her question by using the word "meaning" in Korean. However, similar to what Julie did in the previous example, Toni also spoke the acquired Korean word ("meaning") in English later (turn 4). It appeared that Toni spoke the word "meaning" in English instinctively as he was thinking about the meaning of the English word for "officialdom" (turn 4). During the interview, Toni explained, "I was thinking about the meaning of the word (officialdom) in English, so I think I said the word ('meaning') in English automatically." His response indicates that Toni presented his bilingual identity by intuitively using English since he knew the word in both languages. That is, Toni as a bilingual speaker was able to move across the languages flexibly by selecting his dual lexicon from his bilingual resources.

1. Mrs. Joen: 벼슬이라고 했는데 벼슬이 뭐지?

    [The book says *"byeoseul"* (officialdom), do you know the meaning of the word?]

2. Toni: 벼슬... 그 **뜻** 뭐지...? 아 그거 부자 되고 상 받는거요.

    [Byeoseul...what is the meaning of it? Oh, it is.... To become rich and get prize.]

3. Mrs. Joen: 그렇지. 높은 지위를 갖는 거를 벼슬이라고 해.

    [Right. It indicates getting a higher status in the position.]

4. Toni: 근데 벼슬 영어로 바꾸면 그 meaning 이 변해요?

    [But, does the <u>meaning</u> change if I translated the word in English?]

Figure 6.8 Toni's (3rd-grade) flexible use of dual lexicons through translanguaging.

Development of Korean honorifics

A comparison of Toni and Julie's oral language use between 1st and 3rd grade showed that their use of honorifics (a formal and humble form of speaking) has been firmly established. It is important to note that using honorifics is required practice in the Korean language when speaking to elders as a way of expressing politeness, courtesy, or respect when addressing or referring to them (Brown, 2011; Lee, 2005). Since young Korean children seldom use it with their parents in the home setting to express intimacy, school is the primary setting where young Korean children learn how to use it properly with the teacher.

When Toni and Julie were in 1st grade, Julie was the student who did not use honorifics to communicate with me (her 1st-grade teacher). On the other hand, analysis of the students' oral language use in 3rd grade showed that Julie used honorifics appropriately when responding to Mrs. Joen. In addition, Julie also appropriately used honorifics during the interviews with me, and when she met other Korean teachers in the school building.

For Toni's case, although he was more likely to use Korean honorifics to address me in his 1st-grade class, he did not always use them appropriately. There are different levels of Korean honorifics depending on the level of politeness. For instance, to make honorifics, Korean speakers not only have to add a suffix to the end of verbs but also switch the verbs to suppletive forms to connote being humble. In 1st grade, Toni often correctly added suffixes to the end of verbs but rarely used the polite form of verbs. However, his 3rd-grade speech displayed that he used honorifics appropriately and correctly with Mrs. Joen in his 3rd-grade classroom and with me during the interviews. Overall, it was revealed that both Toni and Julie used Korean honorifics appropriately throughout their 3rd-grade language use data when they talked to their teacher (Mrs. Joen) and to me during the interview.

Comparison of focal students' writing between 1st and 3rd grade

Table 6.2 shows a comparison of Toni and Julie's written language use in 1st and 3rd grades. The table displays how often Toni and Julie used Korean, English, and translanguaging when they engaged in writing practices in both grades.

As shown in Table 6.2, when Toni and Julie were in 1st grade, they produced English-only sentences (21% and 26%, respectively) and added English words while composing in Korean (36% and 28%, respectively); thus, more than half of their writing included English words or sentences (57% and 54% in Toni's and Julie's writing samples). However, analysis of their writing samples in 3rd grade revealed that they predominantly wrote in Korean (91% and 92%, respectively) and did not provide any sentences written entirely in English (see Chapter 5 for the details). In addition, the frequency of their word-level translanguaging (inserting English words into their Korean sentences) decreased when they became 3rd graders (from 36% to 9% for Toni; from 28% to 8% for Julie). Similar to the comparison found in their oral language use, there was an increase of Korean and a decrease of English in their written language use as they got older.

Increased use of Korean when writing in 3rd grade

Toni, who mainly composed in Korean as a 3rd grader, frequently used English in his 1st-grade writing samples. Figure 6.9 shows one of Toni's

Table 6.2 Comparison of Toni and Julie's written language use between 1st and 3rd grade

		Korean-Only Sentences	English-Only Sentences	Word-Level Translanguaging[a] (English Words in Korean Sentences)	Word-Level Translanguaging[b] (Korean Words in English Sentences)	Frequency of TL at Sentence-Level (Korean to English or vice versa)
1st grade (Spring 2014)	Toni	45 (43%)	22 (21%)	38 (36%)	0	12 times
	Julie	51 (46%)	28 (26%)	31 (28%)	0	17 times
3rd grade (Spring 2016)	Toni	276 (91%)	0	26 (9%)	0	0 times
	Julie	253 (92%)	0	23 (8%)	0	0 times

Notes
[a] The frequency of the students' English word-level translanguaging in Korean sentences.
[b] The frequency of the students' Korean word-level translanguaging in English sentences.
[c] The frequency of the students' sentence-level translanguaging from Korean to English or vice versa.

1st-grade writing samples in which he drew and wrote about a favorite scene from the picture book *The Name Jar* that the class read together. As shown, although Toni did not provide complete sentences in his writing, he used English when he wrote the phrase ("English name practice") and words ("smile" and "Unhei"—the main character's name) to explain what he drew. On the other hand, Toni did not provide any sentence in English throughout his 3rd-grade writing samples, and 91% of his writing was in Korean exclusively. He incorporated English words in his Korean sentences 9% of the time only (see Chapter 5 for Toni's 3rd-grade writing samples).

Text labels: *English Name practice*, *smile*,
Unhei [the name of a character from the book]

Figure 6.9 Toni's (1st-grade) use of English to describe his drawing.

A similar pattern was observed in a comparison of Julie's 1st- and 3rd-grade writing samples. Figure 6.10 displayed Julie's 1st-grade writing sample, which also illustrates her favorite scene from the same book *The Name Jar*. As shown, Julie wrote a sentence in English to describe the scene that she drew. The text labels around her drawings also show that she employed English to describe what she drew and for the speech bubbles (i.e., "Korean airline," "Take care," "BYE!" and "sad"). Yet, she provided two text labels in Korean ("grandmother" and "Korean traditional lucky bag"), which are considered as culturally relevant Korean words. This pattern of translanguaging was also discovered in her 3rd-grade writing. Julie, as a 3rd-grader, employed English to indicate places in the U.S. (e.g., Chicago trip, museum, shopping center, hotel, and inside the restaurant) but used Korean to refer to her family members (mom, dad, and younger sister) (see Figure 5.18 in Chapter 5 for Julie's 3rd-grade writing sample). Although Julie occasionally employed Korean when she provided culturally relevant words, most of her writing was completed in English when she was in 1st grade. Contrariwise, Julie's 3rd-grade writing samples showed that 92% of her sentences were

The grandmother gave Unhei her lucky bag.

Text labels: Korean Airline, Take Care, 할머니 *[Grandmother],*
복주머니 *[Lucky Bag], Bye! Sad*

Figure 6.10 Julie's (1st-grade) employment of English and Korean to describe
her drawing.

completely written in Korean, and only 8% of her writing included
English words in her Korean sentences (see Table 6.2).

The overall findings from Toni's and Julie's writing samples showed
that there had been increased use of Korean and a decrease of English
throughout their compositions. Regarding the increased use of Korean
in their writing in 3rd grade, they both seemed to understand that they
were supposed to use Korean for their formal writing at the Korean HL
school. Yet, since Toni and Julie in 3rd grade still engaged in translanguaging at the word-level by incorporating English words in their
Korean sentences, I sought to find any observed different patterns in their
word-level translanguaging between 1st- and 3rd-grade writing samples.

Comparison of different types of word-level translanguaging

A comparison of Toni and Julie's word-level translanguaging between their
1st- and 3rd-grade writing samples revealed that there were different
grammatical patterns in their translanguaged words. Table 6.3 presents

Table 6.3 Focal students' word-level translanguaging (English word insertion in Korean sentence)

Translanguaging Pattern	Toni		Julie	
	1st Grade	3rd Grade	1st Grade	3rd Grade
Common nouns that exist in both languages (e.g., friend, school, food)	14 (37%)	0	12 (39%)	0
Proper nouns that exist in English only (e.g., people's names, names for places)	10 (26%)	23 (88%)	9 (29%)	21 (91%)
English loan words (e.g., banana, pizza)	7 (16%)	3 (12%)	6 (19%)	2 (9%)
Adjectives that exist in both languages (e.g., pretty, delicious)	3 (8%)	0	2 (6%)	0
Verbs that exist in both languages (e.g., invite, tease)	4 (8%)	0	2 (6%)	0
Total	38 (100%)	26 (100%)	31 (100%)	23 (100%)

when and how Toni and Julie translanguaged at the word level in both grades as they were inserting English lexical items in their Korean sentences.

As shown in Table 6.3, when Toni and Julie were in 1st grade, they most frequently translanguaged into English for common nouns that exist both in Korean and English. For example, Toni inserted the English words "swimming pool" and "slides" in his diary writing, when he wrote, "나는 swimming pool 가고 slides 탔어요" [I went to swimming pool and rode slides], even though there were equivalent words in Korean. Similarly, Julie inserted the English word "cartoon" into a Korean sentence when she wrote, "나는 동생이랑 오늘 cartoon 봤어요." [Today I watched a cartoon with my younger sister] although the corresponding word for "cartoon" exists in Korean. When they were asked whether they knew the translanguaged words in Korean during the interviews, Toni answered that he did not know the equivalent words for "swimming pool" and "slides" in Korean. Julie stated that she knew the word for "cartoon" in Korean but wrote it in English because she did not know the correct spelling of it in Korean.

The students' writing samples in first grade showed their occasional translanguaging into English for adjectives and verbs as well. For example, Julie incorporated the adjective "pretty" in her Korean sentence "내 영어 이름이 pretty 해요" [My English name is pretty]. Similarly, Toni inserted the verb "invite" while writing in Korean "내 친구가 생일파티 invite 해서요" [My friend invited me to his birthday party]. In both cases, the equivalent words exist in Korean. During the interview, Toni stated that he did not know the Korean word for "invite." Although Julie answered that she knew the Korean adjective for the word "pretty," she admitted that she wrote it in English because she was unsure about the correct spelling of it in Korean.

Analysis of their 1st-grade writing samples indicated that they appeared to borrow their linguistic resources from English to complete their Korean writing because they did not know the equivalent words or correct spellings of the words in Korean. On the other hand, in their 3rd-grade writing samples, they did not translanguage for words (common nouns, adjectives, and verbs) that exist in both languages; rather, their translanguaging mainly occurred when they wrote English proper nouns in their diary entries (88% for Toni and 91% for Julie). For instance, Toni often mentioned his foreign friends' names in his diary entries (e.g., 나는 Mike 와 축구를 했습니다 [I played soccer with <u>Mike</u>]), and Julie often stated the places where she went (e.g., 나는 오늘 엄마랑 TJ Max 에 갔습니다 [I went to TJ Max with my mom today]). Since the words only exist in English, it seemed reasonable for them to write the proper nouns using English.

In both grades, Toni and Julie sometimes added English loan words while composing in Korean. However, the presence of English for English loan words decreased when they were in 3rd grade (from 7 times to 3 times in Toni's writing and from 6 times to 2 times in Julie's writing). Close analysis revealed that they had transliterated the English loan words using Korean letters in their 3rd-grade writing. For example, in their diary entries, Toni wrote "샌드위치" [sandwich] and Julie wrote "스케이트" [skate] using Korean characters based on how the words are pronounced in English. Hence, Toni's and Julie's use of direct translanguaging into English was less detected in their 3rd-grade writing samples. Because their transliterated words did not contain English letters, the incidences were not counted as word-level translanguaging in Table 6.3.

Translanguaging across receptive and productive skills of language

When Toni and Julie were in 1st grade, they were asked to retell a story in a written form after reading a passage in Korean that illustrates the importance of keeping a promise. For this particular writing task, they were allowed to use both languages to provide their written responses. Although Toni and Julie had read the story in Korean, they primarily wrote their retellings in English and then provided their summary in Korean, which suggests that they engaged in translanguaging practices across their receptive (reading) and productive (writing) skills of their languages.

Figure 6.11 displays Toni's written retelling of the Korean story. Analysis of Toni's writing indicates that although he made spelling mistakes for several English words (i.e., "waeting" for "waiting," "firend" for "friend," "mishon" for "mission," "supr" for "super," and "made" for "mad"), he successfully retold the story using English. The finding displays that Toni moved across the languages for reading versus writing, and his translanguaging into English for his productive skills of writing demonstrates his receptive skills of reading and comprehending the text in Korean. Although Toni included his Korean writing, he provided only one sentence in Korean and it did not recount the story; rather, he stated how he would feel if he were the main character in the book. In the interview, Toni stated, "I wrote about the story in English first because I thought that I could write better in English, then I wrote something in Korean because I knew that I had to write in Korean as well." The comparison of his writing in the two languages indicates that his English writing was much advanced than his Korean writing in terms of the purpose of writing, use of convention, sentence fluency including the length of writing. The findings imply that Toni might have developed his writing skills more in English than Korean, which led him to feel more confident in writing in English than Korean. (English translations of the students' Korean writing samples are provided at the end of the figures.)

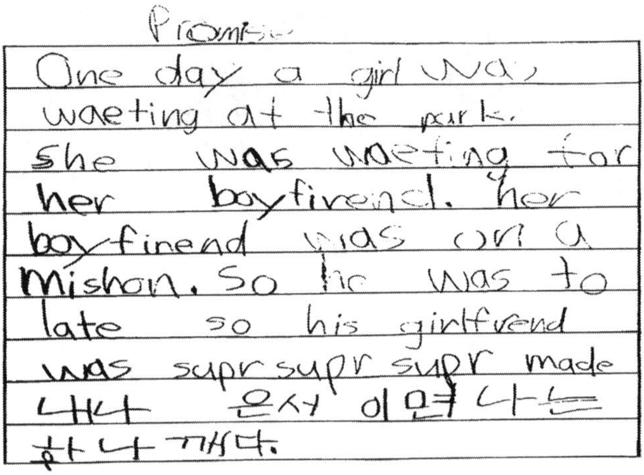

Translation for Korean writing:
If I were Eunseo, I would be mad at him.

Figure 6.11 Toni's (1st-grade) writing sample in both English and Korean.

Figure 6.12 displays Julie's written retelling of the Korean story both in English and Korean. As shown, Julie also initiated her written retelling in English and then completed it in Korean. Similar to Toni's finding, Julie also chose English first to provide her productive skills of writing through translanguaging, which demonstrates her receptive skills of reading and comprehending the text in Korean. Comparing her compositions in English and Korean indicates that Julie provided clear ideas when retelling the story in both languages, and her writing skills (such as sentence structure and fluency, convention) appear to be established equivalently both in English and Korean.

		Promise		
A	girl	went	to	the
park	because	a	boy	was
coming	to	the	to	play
with	the	girl. The	boy	
calmed	30	minutes	late	
so,	the	girl	was	
mad. The	next	day	she	
asked	him	to	come	on
3	oclock	and	he	
came	in	30	m\inuts	
late	again	so	she	was
mad	again.			
어슨산	은 서가	재민이를		
공원에	오라고	헸어요. 그러		
데	재민이가	30은	늦었	
습니다.	은 서 가	하ㄴ겠습니		
다.				

Translation for Korean writing:
One day, Eunseo asked Jaemin to come to the park. But Jaemin
was 30 minutes late. Eunseo was mad at him.

Figure 6.12 Julie's (1st-grade) writing sample in both English and Korean.

Yet, during the interview, Julie stated, "I wrote it in English first because it is easier to write [in English], and then I wrote in Korean. But I copied some [of my English writing] for my Korean writing." Her response indicates that she presented the full summary of the story in English from the text, whereas her Korean writing is a translated summary of her English retelling. Indeed, her English retelling provides more detailed information than her Korean writing. That is, Julie used a translating strategy when she composed in Korean from what she wrote in English. Similar to Toni's findings, Julie appeared to be felt more comfortable and confident in writing in English than Korean.

Since both Toni and Julie read the story in Korean, it is interesting to see that they chose to write the story in English first. In addition, their responses from the interviews show that they preferred to write in English, which indicates that they felt more comfortable using English when they had an option to choose their language for the writing task no matter in what language they received the information. In other words, Toni and Julie had read and comprehended the text in Korean but provided their written responses using English, which shows evidence of their translanguaging into a stronger language (English) for their productive skill of language. Indeed, throughout their 1st-grade writing samples, they were more likely to employ English for their written work. On the other hand, analysis of their 3rd-grade writing samples, as shown in Chapter 5, exhibits that Toni and Julie delivered their thoughts and ideas by consistently writing in Korean when they engaged in in-class writing and kept their diary entries. The focal students' 3rd-grade overall language use reveals that they were more likely to stay in Korean when speaking and writing in the Korean HL school than they did in 1st grade. Interviews with the students and their mothers provided reasons why and how they were able to increase their use of Korean and even develop their Korean (vocabulary growth and use of honorifics) and over the years.

Sociocultural influences on the focal students' HL development

Parents' influence and home language policy

When Toni and Julie were 1st-graders, they said that they were more likely to use English than Korean at home even when interacting with their parents. Although their parents asked them questions in Korean, they stated that they mostly replied in English. In other words, when Toni and Julie were 1st-graders, their primary language at home was English, according to their 1st-grade interview results.

Yet, it was interesting to find that their language use at home in 3rd grade had shifted. Toni, as a 3rd-grader, stated that he was required to speak in Korean at home upon his father's request, explaining:

> I have to speak in Korean with my parents. My dad gets mad when I reply back in English during our conversation. He really wants me to use Korean all the time at home. When my dad is not at home, I can use English for my mom. But when there is my dad, I always have to use Korean.

Toni's mother provided a more concrete answer to explain why her husband became strict about Toni's language use. His mother stated that the parents were generous about Toni's English use at home when he was in 1st grade. However, when they observed that Toni exclusively used English with them, the father forced Toni to use Korean:

When Toni was in the first grade, we did not push him to use Korean at home because we believed that it was a transition time for him from using more Korean to more English. But, after a certain period, we witnessed that Toni used English predominantly even with us at home. Thus, my husband strictly told Toni that he had to speak in Korean whenever he says something to us.

Similarly, Julie stated that it was acceptable for her to use English at home when she was a 1st-grader, but by the time she became a 3rd-grader, her parents made a Korean-speaking-only rule at home. She shared:

> Korean is the language that my family has to use at home. It was okay to use English when I was young, and I used English all the time. But nowadays my parents keep asking me to speak only Korean at home. We have a Korean-speaking only rule (at home).

Julie's mother shared that Julie used to be outgoing and talkative when she interacted with others in Korean, which had led her to learn Korean quickly. Yet, once Julie entered a kindergarten, she had difficulty interacting with peers in her American school because of her limited English proficiency. Therefore, her parents considered English learning to be an important issue for Julie at that time. Her mother explained,

> When we saw that Julie often felt depressed, we thought that teaching English should be the first step for Julie so that she would feel confident in her American school. That's why there had been a time when we provided educational resources more in English than in Korean. For instance, we provided English songs, videos, and books at home.

As Julie became proficient in English, her parents observed that she tended to speak only in English and rarely used Korean. Her mother explained that this was the reason why they initiated a Korean-only rule at home: "We were concerned about her not using Korean, so we decided to make a Korean-language-only rule at home."

Parents' instructional focus on Korean literacy learning

Interviews with the focal 3rd-graders' mothers and their journal reports documented their practices at home for improving their children's reading and writing in Korean. Both mothers stated that they already regarded their children as English dominant and would become more English dominant and losing their Korean in the future. The mothers indicated that they were concerned about their children's literacy development in Korean because of the limited opportunities and resources for HL literacy learning. Thus, both Toni and Julie's parents had engaged in their children's literacy learning on a regular basis by providing instruction for Korean reading and writing at home.

Korean book reading time

Both the mothers' interview results and journal reports showed that they spent a Korean book reading time with their children on a regular basis at home. Julie's mother pointed out that she felt Julie was a slow reader when she read Korean books, compared to when she read English books in 1st grade. Once the mother noticed that Julie was a slower reader in Korean than in English, she had held Korean book reading time with Julie every night until now. She asked Julie to read a Korean picture book aloud, and she helped her with difficult Korean words or phrases, along with their pronunciations and meanings. According to the mother, although Julie sometimes asked her mother for help when she found unknown Korean words, she was able to become an independent reader when reading Korean books by the time that she was a 3rd-grader.

In Toni's case, Toni's mother stated that Toni was an avid reader when it came to the fantasy fiction genre. According to his mother, Toni began to read the *Harry Potter* series in English in 2nd grade. When Toni's grandparents from Korea visited his home during the break between 2nd and 3rd grade, they brought the *Harry Potter* series written in Korean. Toni began to read the Korean version of the books independently in 3rd grade. Toni often told his mother that there were many unknown Korean words, which she usually explained by providing synonyms or example sentences. The mother believed that this practice (his independent reading with her assistance) had helped Toni to improve his oral and reading fluency in Korean as well as to develop his Korean vocabulary.

Both mothers acknowledged that they had focused on their children's Korean reading comprehension beyond their decoding skills in Korean. Toni's mother stated that although Toni read Korean books relatively fast, sometimes he did not understand the stories of the books that he read. The mother reported that she usually checked Toni's reading comprehension by asking Toni to retell the stories when he finished reading Korean books, explaining:

> Whenever Toni told me he was done reading Korean books, I asked him to retell the story of the books, but he often said that I don't know or I don't remember; thus, I usually provided guided questions about the character or scene so that he could tell me about the story.

Similarly, Julie's mother mentioned that she often asked Julie to retell the story of Korean books. According to her mother, Julie sometimes provided the retelling of Korean storybooks in English, but her English retelling indicated that she comprehended the stories accurately. She explained:

Julie sometimes told me her retelling story in English although she read the book in Korean. But I was able to see that she understood the story. Whenever she answered in English, I encouraged her to retell the story in Korean again.

Korean dictation tests for vocabulary learning

In terms of the students' improved Korean vocabulary, both mothers explained that they held Korean dictation practices with their children three to five times per week. Because Korean is a shallow orthography system, which has one-to-one phoneme (sound) and grapheme (spelling) correspondence (Wang, Park, & Lee, 2006), it is important for a Korean child to learn how each phoneme represents a particular grapheme. Both Toni's and Julie's mother stated that they prepared 10 to 15 Korean words, phrases, or sentences from the Korean books that their children read, and then the mothers read them aloud for their children to write them down. Although the Korean HL school provided a Korean dictation test every week, the mothers spent additional time on their children's Korean vocabulary learning by having them take Korean dictation practices at home. Both mothers thought that the Korean dictation tests helped their children to develop their Korean vocabulary knowledge with the correct spelling. Toni's mother additionally stated that she always made sure that Toni understood the meaning of the words or phrases that were on the dictation tests. For instance, the mother often provided example sentences that included the target vocabulary or phrases after Toni wrote the word during his Korean dictation tests so that he could learn about how to use the words in different or diverse contexts.

The mothers' interview and journal responses indicated that they had spent more time on their children's Korean literacy learning than on their Korean oral proficiency. According to Toni's mother, there was a relatively small amount of time for Toni to develop his Korean literacy skills, explaining:

> Toni had more opportunities to learn and develop his speaking and listening in Korean by interacting with us (her husband and her), his Korean relatives, his Korean friends, etc., but he learned Korean reading and writing at the Korean language school only. Thus, we (her husband and her) have tried to provide more opportunities and resources for Toni to improve his literacy skills in Korean at home.

Similarly, Julie's mother pointed out that she and her husband wanted Julie to be competent in Korean reading and writing beyond her communicative skills in Korean. The mother also conjectured that because Julie would develop English at a faster rate in her near future, she believed that it was important for them (her husband and her) to emphasize Korean language learning for Julie by engaging in Korean literacy practices at home:

We know that Julie will develop English at a faster rate…. Although we focus on the Korean language, she is going to be dominant in the English language as she lives here (U.S.) and interacts with English-speaking people. Thus, we tried to spend time teaching her Korean and provide educational resources in Korean as much as possible at home. We really want Julie to be competent not only in her communicative skills but also in her literacy skills in Korean.

Relatives' influence

The focal mothers' journals showed that their relatives also influenced their children's Korean language learning. In Toni's case, his Korean grandparents visited Toni's house in the U.S. and stayed there for a month during part of the data collection. Because Toni's grandparents did not speak any English, the language that Toni had to use with them was Korean, which eventually resulted in Toni practicing more Korean. One of the mother's journal entries indicated that Toni had learned how to play a Korean traditional game "Yutnori" from his grandmother. The mother believed that learning a traditional game from the grandmother had not only provided a good opportunity for Toni to learn about the cultural aspect of Korea but also had helped Toni improve his listening and speaking in Korean because Korean is the only language that Toni could use with his grandmother. The mother observed that Toni always paid close attention to his grandmother to understand what she said, explaining:

> When we explained something to Toni in Korean, but he did not get it, he often asked us to say it again in English, since he knew that we could speak in English. But during the conversation with his grandparents, Toni tried to understand their Korean without asking them to restate what they said because he knew that his grandparents spoke in Korean only. Thus, we believe that the grandparents' visits had played a significant role in Toni's Korean language learning and use.

Toni's mother further stated that having a regular conversation with his grandparents during phone calls or via Skype had helped Toni to acquire Korean words and expressions. She stated:

> When Toni heard Korean words or expressions that he did not know from his grandparents over the phone or via Skype, he often asked me the equivalent words in English or the meaning of those unfamiliar expressions. I believe that because of this practice, Toni was able to acquire many Korean words and expressions that are not commonly used in the U.S. context.

The mother's journal entries also showed how Toni worked as a language broker (Orellana & García, 2014; Dorner, Orellana, & Li-Grining, 2007) for his grandparents. When Toni's family went out for dinner with his grandparents, the mother observed that Toni explained the food menu to his grandparents in Korean since he was aware that they did not read the English menu. One day, after having a meal in a Chinese restaurant, the family was given fortune cookies. Toni looked at his grandparents' fortunes and translated what they said in English into Korean for his grandparents. Toni's mother stated that Toni appeared to understand that he should take responsibility for translating English into Korean for his grandparents:

> Toni had seen that we (she and her husband) usually explained or translated what was happening in English into Korean for his grandmother when he was young. Toni recently tried to explain the context or situation that occurred in English by using Korean to his grandparents. From my perspective, Toni seemed to understand that he was the one who can deliver the information that was given in English into Korean as a speaker of both English and Korean.

Similarly, the journal entries by Julie's mother also showed the influence of Korean relatives on Julie's language use and learning. During the data collection of this study, Julie's aunt, who lived in Korea and barely spoke English, visited Julie's house. Julie's mother observed that Julie spoke Korean exclusively when she talked to her aunt. The mother once recorded Julie's language use when the family played the board game "monopoly." Julie, who was familiar with the game's instructions, tried to explain to her aunt how to play it using Korean exclusively, which was different from her normal language use with her parents. Julie's mother believed that the presence of Julie's aunt provided a good opportunity for Julie to be immersed in Korean as she tried to use Korean all the time with her aunt who only spoke Korean:

> I noticed that when Julie explained the instructions to her aunt, her speech was a little bit clumsy and awkward since she explained everything only in Korean. I know that she could have explained more fluently if she used English, but I saw that she stayed in Korean because Julie knew that her aunt would not understand if she used English. Also, since her aunt knew Julie's language use and proficiency as a Korean-American, her aunt did not concern about or criticize Julie's somewhat limited Korean expressions or awkward pronunciations. I think this led Julie to freely use her Korean without hesitation or reluctance.

Both Toni and Julie's language use with their relatives promoted their Korean language use and learning. Their language use examples above illustrate that they considered their different interlocutors' language preferences and proficiencies and then chose their languages accordingly.

Media influence

Korean media also seemed to play an important role in Toni and Julie's Korean language learning. The journal entries kept by Toni's mother reported that Toni watched one of his favorite Korean television programs, *Running Man*, on every Sunday evening with his father. In this program, there were many Korean entertainers, and they were engaged in diverse activities that included funny episodes. According to the mother's journal, Toni knew the entertainers' names, the nicknames that they used in the program, and each of their hilarious characteristics. However, because many of the conversations among the entertainers were not always straightforward (e.g., using exaggerated expressions to make jokes, adding humorous language with jargon), it was difficult for Toni to understand the conversation completely. His mother observed that Toni sometimes asked his father about words or expressions that the characters used in certain situations. The mother believed that, although Toni did not know the meanings of every single word, he mostly appeared to grasp the intended messages in certain situations because he knew the overall context and circumstances. Toni's mother stated:

> Although Toni could not get all the dialogues among the entertainers, he seemed to understand what was going on in certain situations. I think Toni's incomplete Korean communicative skills did not hinder him from understanding or enjoying watching the program; rather, the exposure to the Korean program accelerated Toni's Korean communicative skills.

The journal entries by Julie's mother also showed how Korean media positively influenced Julie's Korean learning. According to the mother's journal, Julie watched a Korean program in which many famous Korean singers appeared in a competition to select a top singer. The mother often recorded when Julie repeated the Korean songs as she listened to them. During the mother's interview, it was revealed that Julie knew many Korean singers and memorized their songs by listening to them repeatedly. The mother shared that Julie occasionally asked her mother to print out the lyrics of her favorite Korean songs so that she could sing them by looking at the lyrics, which eventually led her to memorize the lyrics, although sometimes she did not know all the meanings of the phrases. The mother believed that listening to Korean songs and reading the Korean lyrics had assisted Julie to gain Korean vocabulary and to improve her Korean pronunciation:

> I have seen Julie singing Korean songs many times at home. I think that singing Korean songs helped Julie learn Korean easily since it provided Julie a good opportunity to learn about Korean vocabulary in context and to acquire more native-like pronunciation.

Developed courtesy manners appropriate for their heritage culture

During the data collection of this study, Toni's and Julie's behavioral performances were observed, which demonstrated their understanding of Korean courtesy and manners. Comparison of Toni's and Julie's nonverbal behaviors between 1st and 3rd grade showed that they have developed Korean courtesy manners when speaking Korean. Toni and Julie were able to use required body gestures when greeting (e.g., bowing) appropriately in their 3rd grade.

Bowing when greeting

When Koreans greet older people, they use not only honorifics (Brown, 2011, 2015) but also a specified body gesture (i.e., bowing). Bowing is the act of lowering the torso and head as a social gesture toward older people (Brown & Winter, 2018). Since I was not the 3rd-grade teacher at the Korean HL school during the data collection, the students did not see me in the classroom regularly. However, I met Toni and Julie occasionally in the hallway in the school building during the semester of data collection. Whenever the students greeted me, they bowed to me while using honorifics (the formal form of "hi" in Korean). Their actions indicated that they had learned about how to bow and use honorifics when addressing an adult.

During the interview with Toni's mother, the mother revealed that she and her husband had taught Toni how to greet his grandparents politely by bowing. The mother stated that since Toni regularly saw his grandparents, he often practiced bowing when greeting them, which led him to use the body gesture when he met other Korean adults. In Julie's case, her mother stated that when Julie visited Korea once a year, she and her husband showed Julie how others bowed when they greeted adults and taught her the proper way to greet older people. After that, the mother observed that Julie began to bow when she greeted older Korean people.

Appropriate use of honorifics

Using honorifics is a required practice in the Korean language, which is a formal and humble form in Korean that indicates the hierarchical social status of speakers and plays an essential role in social interaction as it conveys esteem, courtesy, or respect when addressing or referring to a person (Brown, 2011; Kim-Renaud, 2001; Lee, 2005). According to Toni's mother, when he became a 2nd-grader, his father constantly asked him to use honorifics to address his parents. The mother also said that Toni had more opportunity to practice Korean honorifics when his family visited Korea every summer.

Julie's mother also explained that Julie learned about when and how to use Korean honorifics when speaking in Korean. According to Julie's mother, her parents had not asked her to use honorifics when she talked to them. But when Julie was in 2nd grade, there was an occasion when her mother saw Julie not using honorifics when she met a Korean adult neighbor. Since then, the mother had tried to teach Julie how to use honorifics to other Korean adults in a proper manner.

Summary

This chapter presented two focal 3rd-grade Korean bilingual students' language use over time by examining different patterns between their 1st- and 3rd-grade oral and written language use (Spring 2014 vs. Spring 2016). The comparison of findings indicated that there was an increase in Korean and a decrease in English in the students' oral and written language use over the 2 years. It was further revealed that the patterns and functions of their translanguaging when speaking and writing in the two grades were different. As 1st-graders, Toni and Julie frequently employed oral translanguaging into English because they did not know the corresponding words in Korean. That is, their translanguaging in 1st grade was often found when they borrowed their language repertoires from English for the unknown or unsure Korean words, which consequently helped them complete their talk.

In 3rd grade, however, it displays that they had learned about most of the Korean words that they had not known in 1st grade. In other words, Toni and Julie's translanguaging in 3rd grade occurred not because they did not know the correspondences in Korean, but because they were flexibly employing their bilingual resources from both languages. Their translanguaging in 3rd grade implies that they were sociolinguistic competent in both languages. In other words, although Toni and Julie engaged in translanguaging as a bilingual's natural practice in both 1st and 3rd grades, their translanguaging practices in 3rd grade appeared to be more strategic and purposeful (e.g., to highlight) than in 1st grade. In the same sense, analysis of their language use in 3rd grade displayed that they decisively and intuitively translanguaged (e.g., bilingual re-voicing; Gort & Sembiante, 2015), which suggests that their translanguaging met a metalinguistic function. However, their use of translanguaging in 1st grade rarely showed much evidence of metalinguistic awareness.

Regarding their written translanguaging, when Toni and Julie were in 1st grade, they most frequently translanguaged into English for common nouns even though the equivalences exist in Korean as they did not know them. On the other hand, their translanguaging in 3rd grade mainly occurred when they incorporated English proper nouns in their Korean sentences. Toni and Julie seemed to understand that they were supposed to use Korean as much as possible for their Korean HL school writing, and writing is a more formal practice than speaking. The comparison of Toni's and Julie's language use between 1st and 3rd grade showed that they were able to improve their oral communication and writing skills in Korean. They did not appear to experience HL shift or loss despite their minimum exposure to Korean as well as their rapid increase in English usage. Instead, they had developed a certain degree of oral proficiency, including vocabulary knowledge, and writing skills (such as sentence structure, spelling) in their HL.

The 3rd-grade Korean teacher's (Mrs. Joen's) expectation that her students use Korean during class might have influenced their increased use of Korean both in speaking and writing in the 3rd-grade classroom. In addition, the parents' Korean-language-only rule at home played a pivotal role in the focal 3rd-graders' longitudinal language use between 1st and 3rd grade. It was discovered that the parents focused on their children's literacy learning in Korean at home by providing Korean book reading time and Korean dictation tests, which assisted their children to improve their Korean literacy skills. Frequent communication with Korean relatives and exposure to Korean media (television programs and songs) also seemed to influence their increased Korean language use over the years. Overall, the findings showed that the focal 3rd-graders did not experience HL shift or loss; rather, they were able to improve their communicative skills in becoming competent Korean speakers both sociolinguistically and socioculturally as they have developed Korean courtesy manners in their heritage culture, such as appropriate use of formal Korean (i.e., honorifics) and required body gestures (e.g., bowing).

References

Brown, L. (2011). *Korean honorifics and politeness in second language learning.* Amsterdam: John Benjamins.

Brown, L. (2015). Revisiting "polite"-*yo* and "deferential"-*supnita* speech style shifting in Korean from the viewpoint of indexicality. *Journal of Pragmatics, 79*, 43–59.

Brown, L., & Winter, B. (2018). Multimodal indexicality in Korean: "Doing deference" and "performing intimacy" through nonverbal behavior. *Journal of Politeness Research, 15*(1), 25–54.

Dorner, L. M., Orellana, M. F., & Li-Grining, C. P. (2007). "I helped my mom," and it helped me: Translating the skills of language brokers into improved standardized test scores. *American Journal of Education, 113*(3), 451–478.

Gort, M., & Sembiante, S. (2015). Navigating hybridized language learning spaces through translanguaging pedagogy: Dual language preschool teachers' languaging practices in support of emergent bilingual children's performance of academic discourse. *International Multilingual Research Journal, 9*, 7–25.

Kim-Renaud, Y. (2001). Change in Korean honorifics reflecting social change. In Thomas E. McAuley (ed.), *Language Change in East Asia* (pp. 27–46). London: Curzon.

Lee, J. B. (2005). On the study of Korean honorifics from the sociolinguistic standpoint. *Journal of Korean Linguistics, 47*, 407–448.

Orellana, M. F., & García, O. (2014). Conversation currents: Language brokering and translanguaging in school. *Language Arts, 91*(5), 386–392.

Wang, M., Park, Y., & Lee, K. (2006). Korean-English biliteracy acquisition: Cross language phonological and orthographic transfer. *Journal of Educational Psychology, 98*(1), 148–158.

7 Summary, discussions, and implications

Overview of the study

This study employed qualitative discourse analysis methods to investigate how eight 1st- and 3rd-grade Korean emergent bilingual students (4 in each grade) used Korean and English in their oral speech and writing over 14 weeks at a Korean HL School in the U.S. The participating students attended all-English schools during the week, were exposed to Korean at home and attended a Korean HL School on Saturdays. A qualitative discourse analysis was employed to document the students' oral and written language uses in the HL classrooms. Based on their use of Korean and English, the patterns and functions of their translanguaging practices were further analyzed. By utilizing case studies, the mothers' responses from two semi-structured interviews presented the parents' perspectives and attitudes toward their children's bilingualism. In addition, two of the focal mothers' journals about their children's (Joon and Nari) daily language use displayed the parents' practices at home for their children's language use and learning.

As a longitudinal study, two focal 3rd-graders' (Spring 2016) spoken and written language performance were compared to their 1st-grade (Spring 2014) language use data to identify whether the 3rd-graders had undergone any HL regression, or they were able to develop their HL over the years. The mothers of the focal 3rd-graders' responses from the interviews and their journal reports were analyzed to learn about how the parents and other sociocultural factors had influenced their children's language use and development as they got older.

Discussion of the findings

This chapter discusses the major findings by addressing the research questions posed at the beginning of the book. In the discussion below, I combine Research Question 1 (What characterized the Korean bilingual 1st-graders' oral and written language use and translanguaging practices at a Korean HL School?) and Research Question 3 (What characterized the Korean bilingual third-graders' oral and written usage use and translanguaging practices at a Korean HL School?) to provide the bilingual students' language use and translanguaging performance findings. I further discuss different patterns and functions of oral and written translanguaging practices observed between the 1st- and 3rd-graders. Then, I discuss Research Question 4 from the longitudinal study (How did the two focal 3rd-graders' oral and written language use differ compare to their earlier use as 1st-graders?). I then have combined Research Question 2 (What were the parents of 1st-graders' attitudes toward bilingualism and their home practices to support their children's HL learning?) and Research Question 5 (What were the sociocultural and family influences on the focal 3rd-graders' longitudinal language use?) to discuss the immigrant parents' roles and other sociocultural factors that influence on their bilingual children' language use and learning.

First- and 3rd-grade bilingual Korean students' oral and written language use

The three 1st-grade English-proficient students' (Joon, Yuri, and Rena) oral language use showed that they used more English (34%, 29%, 31%, respectively) than Korean (15%, 21%, 21%) when speaking. They also employed more Korean (76%, 74%, 58%) than English (2%, 5%, 11%) while writing. The three 1st-graders often engaged in translanguaging practices when they spoke (51%, 50%, 48%) and wrote (22%, 21%, 31%). Meanwhile, Nari (the 1st-grade Korean-proficient student) predominantly used Korean while speaking (93%) and writing (97%), and she did not engage in much translanguaging practices (5% in speaking and 3% in writing).

In terms of the 3rd-grade students, the three English-proficient students' (Toni, Julie, and Suji) language use showed that they spoke more Korean (51%, 49%, 50%, respectively) than English (9%, 8%, 9%). The three 3rd-graders' writing also showed that they composed mostly in Korean (91%, 88%, 85%). Their translanguaging practices were discovered throughout their spoken language (40%, 43%, 42%), and a few cases of their written translanguaging were detected at the word level as they incorporated English words in their Korean sentences (9%, 12%, 13%). Yet, unlike the 1st-grade English-proficient students, the 3rd-graders did not engage in sentence-level translanguaging when writing (except for three English sentences by Suji). Meanwhile, Mina, the 3rd-grade Korean-proficient student, used Korean 90% of the time when speaking and 93% of the time when writing. Her translanguaging performance was rarely observed from her spoken and written language use (6% and 7%, respectively).

Although the English-proficient students in both grades reported during the interviews that English was the more comfortable language for them, close analysis of their language use both in speaking and writing displayed that the 3rd-graders engaged in less translanguaging than the 1st-graders did. The older-grade students seemed to be more cognizant of their language use, and they appeared to meet their teacher's (Mrs. Joen's) expectation by using Korean in the Korean HL classroom. In addition, the translanguaging practices by both grades were less observed in their writing than their spoken language. Both the 1st- and 3rd-graders understood that writing was a more formal activity than speaking that involves more spontaneous practice. Especially for the 1st-grade English-proficient students, although they frequently engaged in translanguaging when they spoke, their written translanguaging was much decreased when writing in the Korean HL classroom.

Oral translanguaging practices by the English-proficient students

Both the 1st- and 3rd-grade bilingual students' language use revealed that the English proficient students (Joon, Yuri, and Rena as 1st-graders and Toni, Julie, and Suji as 3rd-graders) engaged in translanguaging practices when they engaged in oral communication and compositions. The following four different functions—sociolinguistic knowledge, metalinguistic awareness, metacognitive insight, and sociocultural understanding—were discovered in both grades of students' oral and written language use.

The majority of the 1st- and 3rd-grade English-proficient students' oral translanguaging functioned as sociolinguistic knowledge (49%, 48%, 57% for Joon, Yuri, and Rena, and 63%, 61%, 60% for Toni, Julie, and Suji, respectively) (see Appendices A and C). Both grades' translanguaging for sociolinguistic knowledge (Canale & Swain, 1980) was commonly exhibited when they flexibly chose the lexical items from their two languages and varied their language use according to the interlocutors. For instance, both the 1st- and 3rd-graders translanguaged by moving across their languages when considering their interlocutors; they often chose Korean to talk to their Korean teachers but mainly employed English when communicating with their English-proficient peers. The students in both grades conformed to a principle of *code alignment* (Sayer, 2013). According to Sayer, bilingual speakers tend to follow the language that their interlocutors use. Both groups' translanguaging into Korean to speak to their Korean teachers indicate that their translanguaging practices naturally occurred, depending on their interlocutors' language use. These findings corroborate Jørgensen and Holmen's (1997) argument that people who speak two languages "employ their full linguistic competence in two (or more) different languages at any given time adjusted to the needs and the possibilities of the conversation, including the linguistic skills of the interlocutors" (p. 13). The English-proficient students' language use demonstrated that English and Korean were part of their language repertoires, which they could freely employ.

The 1st- and 3rd-grade English-proficient students' oral translanguaging sometimes demonstrated their metalinguistic awareness (32%, 36%, 27% for Joon, Yuri, and Rena, and 31%, 33%, 32% for Toni, Julie, and Suji, respectively; see Appendices A and C). Both grades' translanguaging for metalinguistic awareness was commonly discovered when they demonstrated their comparative linguistic knowledge of Korean and English and regulated their own language use to make jokes. For example, both grades played with humor by telling jokes through translanguaging, which suggests that they regulated their two languages as metalinguistically cognizant bilinguals. Previously, Jonsson (2013) showed that adolescent Spanish bilingual students purposefully translanguaged when they made jokes so that they could emphasize their ideas and further express their feelings. Similar to the older students in Jonsson's study, the younger students in this study showed that they were also able to convey meanings, deliver messages, and express themselves extensively by employing translanguaging.

The findings further revealed that the English-proficient students in both grades engaged in oral translanguaging when they used their metacognitive insight through inner speech. The 1st-grade English-proficient students' uses of translanguaging for metacognitive insight were occasionally observed (10%, 7%, 10% for Joon, Yuri, and Rena, respectively), but only one example for this function was found from the 3rd-grader's (Toni's) speech (1%; see Appendices A and C). The three 1st-graders and Toni were involved in a private speech during their cognitive tasks, and their self-directed dialogues indicated that they engaged in the process of internalization (Vygotsky, 1978) by translanguaging from Korean to English. This example of translanguaging behavior is similar to the finding presented by Martínez-Roldán (2015). One of the Spanish-English bilingual students in her study used Spanish when reading and discussing a book with the teacher but used English when talking and making comments to himself. The student's translanguaging practice for self-directed dialogue was similar to what the students did in the present study. As Vygotsky (1978) argued in his internalization theory, the students appeared to be moving from interpersonal dialogues in Korean with their Korean teachers to an intrapersonal speech by using English to talk to themselves.

The findings revealed that the 1st- and 3rd-grade English-proficient students' oral translanguaging also functioned as their sociocultural understanding when they used culturally familiar or relevant referents (e.g., family members, traditional or cultural practices). Although their use of translanguaging for sociocultural knowledge was rarely observed (9%, 9%, 6% for Joon, Yuri, and Rena, and 5%, 6%, 8% for Toni, Julie, and Suji, respectively; see Appendices A and C), when their translanguaging occurred for this function, the use of Korean added cultural meanings to their English discourses. In Gort's (2008) study, young children who were learning two languages often added lexical items from a more proficient language when they spoke in their less proficient language, whereas, when they spoke in their proficient language, their use of translanguaging was rarely observed because they were more likely to stay in their proficient language. However, the English-proficient students in this study incorporated their language repertoires from Korean (which was regarded as their less proficient language) when they spoke in English to deliver meanings that were culturally unique and distinctive. This is a unique finding because it implies that the emergent bilinguals in this study were able to utilize their vocabulary knowledge regardless of the level of their Korean proficiency. Overall, the English-proficient students' oral translanguaging indicates their bilingualism since the findings showed that the bilingual students' translanguaging leveraged their communication and meaning-making.

Different functions of oral translanguaging between 1st- and 3rd-graders

Both the English proficient 1st- and 3rd-graders' translanguaging functioned for the same four categories: sociolinguistic knowledge, metalinguistic awareness, metacognitive insight, and sociocultural understanding. Yet, a close analysis revealed that there were differences in translanguaging functions between the 1st- and 3rd-graders' spoken language use.

In terms of the sociolinguistic function of the students' translanguaging, both the 1st- and 3rd-graders utilized their dual lexicon by incorporating English words in their Korean discourses. However, the 3rd-graders demonstrated that they knew the translanguaged words in Korean as their speech often included the translanguaged words in both languages in their former or subsequent utterances. Whereas, the 1st-grade English-proficient students often borrowed lexical items from English for their unknown Korean words. In other words, the 3rd-graders flexibly utilized their dual lexicon from their two languages, and there was no finding of lexical item borrowing from English as they knew the words in Korean. In addition, although the students in both grades varied their language use according to the interlocutors, close analysis revealed that the 1st-graders translanguaged following their interlocutors' lead, while the 3rd-graders initiated translanguaging by considering their interlocutors' language preference and proficiency. The findings indicate that the 3rd-graders' translanguaging for the sociolinguistic function seemed to be more purposeful and sophisticated than that of the 1st-graders.

The English-proficient 1st- and 3rd-graders' translanguaging for metalinguistic awareness was commonly discovered when both grades utilized a strategy as they encountered the unknown Korean words. When they were not able to derive the Korean word while speaking in

Korean, one of the 1st-graders (Yuri), for example, utilized her meta-linguistic awareness by providing examples of the word categories using English. On the other hand, the 3rd-grade students (Julie and Toni) utilized their metalinguistic awareness by providing synonyms in Korean instead of borrowing the words from English directly. In other words, when the students did not know the words in Korean, 1st-graders employed English to ensure their understanding of unknown Korean words. While, the 3rd-graders solved their problems by providing the synonyms in Korean, which allowed them to maintain their speech in Korean. Although both graders demonstrated their metalinguistic awareness through translanguaging, the examples by the 3rd-graders appeared that they were more metalinguistically competent than the 1st-graders because the 3rd-graders demonstrated that they were more cognizant about their language use and manipulated their languages according to the purpose (speaking in Korean) and setting (at the Korean language school).

Written translanguaging practices by the English-proficient students

The 1st- and 3rd-grade English-proficient students' translanguaging from their writing samples also demonstrated their sociolinguistic knowledge, metalinguistic awareness, metacognitive insight, and sociocultural under-standing. For example, the majority of their translanguaging in writing was for a sociolinguistic function (52%, 64%, 70% for Joon, Yuri, and Rena, and 50%, 51%, 54% for Toni, Julie, and Suji, respectively; see Appendices B and D). Two of Yuri's (1st-grader) writing samples, for instance, displayed that she repeated her sentences in English after writing them in Korean, which was an example of "bilingual echoing" (Gibbons, 1987, p. 80). Similarly, in Gort's (2012) study, 1st-grade bilingual students engaged in bilingual echoing by repeating words and sentences in another language during their thoughts. Yet, the students' bilingual echoing was discovered when they spoke, and they were less likely to repeat words or sentences in another language in their actual writing. In contrast, Yuri used this bilingual echoing strategy while writing to ensure the reader's understanding of her written work, demonstrating that she utilized her sociolinguistic knowledge through translanguaging.

Similarly, another 1st-grader, Joon, also presented his sociolinguistic knowledge through translanguaging during composition when he did not come up with the word (*baby*; see Excerpt 4.18 in Chapter 4) in Korean. Velasco and García (2014) showed a similar writing strategy used by a Korean emergent bilingual kindergartener in their study. The student in their study also wrote down several English words in his Korean writing so that he could revisit the text and switch them into Korean later. Velasco and García explained it as a "bilingual's postponing strategy" (p. 18), which assisted bilingual writers to self-regulate their translanguaging practice. Similar to their finding, Joon was using a bilingual's postponing strategy by writing down the word ("baby") in English first, switching the word into Korean when he revisited his writing. The findings imply that emergent bilingual writers are able to find corresponding words in another language if they do not know the word in the target language or do not come up with it at that moment, which should be considered a unique bilingual writing strategy.

The translanguaging examples for metalinguistic function were sometimes found in the English-proficient students' writing (41%, 30%, 25% for Joon, Yuri, and Rena, 42%, 40%, 37% for Toni, Julie, and Suji, respectively; see Appendices B and D). They presented their metalinguistic awareness in writing by distinguishing the spaces for composing in Korean and English. They used Korean when they composed the bodies of the texts but often chose English when providing text labels in drawing spaces. In their research, Velasco and García (2014) showed that a Korean bilingual kindergartner wrote his diary entry using Korean but used English for the text labels to describe his drawing. Velasco and García explained that the student's translanguaging performance was related to the idea of continua of biliteracy—"communication occurs in two (or more) languages in or around writing" (Hornberger, 1990, p. 213) because the student used all the semiotic repertoires/multimodalities available in both writing and drawing. Similar to their finding, the students in this study employed their full linguistic resources available to them by regulating their language choices for different areas in their compositions. The students distinguished the places for writing in Korean and drawing in English. This finding corroborates Velasco's and García's finding that emergent bilingual writers composed in the target language for the final draft, although they might have used their entire language repertoires during the process of thinking (e.g., organizing ideas), indicating their metalinguistic awareness.

There were only two examples of the 1st-grade students engaging in an inner speech during the process of writing, which demonstrated the metacognitive function of translanguaging (2% for both Joon and Yuri; see Appendix B). One of the 1st-grader's (Yuri) writing samples showed that she borrowed her linguistic resources from English (*twin*; see Figure 4.25 in Chapter 4) because she did not know the correct spelling of the word in Korean. In order to utilize her linguistic resources, she engaged in self-directed dialogue or metatalk (Swain, 1998), which involved translanguaging, to resolve her writing problem. A student in Gort's (2012) study made a metacognitive statement when she was rereading and reviewing an English draft that she previously had written in Spanish. When the student found errors in her writing, she verbally articulated through self-talk what and how she would revise her writing in English. Similar to the student in Gort's study, the 1st-graders in this study were also engaged in self-talk through translanguaging when they monitored their first draft through metacognitive statements in English. The findings imply that when bilingual writers engage in translanguaging during their self-talk, they are able to reflect and evaluate on what they wrote using their metacognitive insight.

Similar to their oral translanguaging use, the 1st- and 3rd-grade English-proficient students' uses of translanguaging for sociocultural function were occasionally found in their writing (5%, 4%, 5% for Joon, Yuri, and Rena, and 4%, 9%, 9% for Toni, Julie, and Suji, respectively; see Appendices B and D). The sociocultural function of translanguaging was discovered when the students chose to write certain words in Korean within their English sentences or when they inserted culturally relevant Korean words among other English text labels (e.g., family members, Korean food items). The students' employment of Korean delivered and enriched the cultural meanings in their written work, which reflects their appropriate sociocultural knowledge.

Researchers in past studies (Edelsky, 1986; Lanauze & Snow, 1989) discovered that Spanish-English bilingual students utilized their knowledge and understanding from their L1 writing (such as writing skills and writing strategies in Spanish) during the process of writing in their L2 (English). Yet, their written products for the school tasks were in one language (English) only, and they did not directly include the words or phrases from their L1 (Spanish). Unlike the previous findings, the students in this study directly used linguistic repertoires from English when they wrote in Korean to plan, think, and complete their compositions (Canagarajah, 2013; Velasco & García, 2014). Although switching languages in writing was considered a rare behavior in the past (Edelsky, 1986), researchers recently viewed bi-linguals' translanguaging while writing as a bilingual writer's unique strategy (Canagarajah, 2013; Velasco & García, 2014). Overall, the English-proficient students' written translanguaging indicates their bilingu-alism since the students demonstrated that they utilized their full linguistic resources to deliver their thoughts and ideas through writing. This fluid and natural way that both grades translanguaged while writing indicated that they were drawing from their integrated linguistic resources (Wei, 2018), not employing their languages individually.

Different functions of written translanguaging between 1st- and 3rd-graders

As discussed previously, both the English proficient first and third graders' translanguaging in their writing also demonstrated their socio-linguistic knowledge, metalinguistic awareness, metacognitive insight, and sociocultural understanding. Similar to their oral translanguaging practices, analysis of the students' written translanguaging also revealed that there were differences in translanguaging functions between the 1st- and 3rd-graders' written performance.

In terms of the sociolinguistic function, one 1st-grader (Joon) wrote in English first, demonstrating quicker lexical access to English because he could not think of the Korean word at the time he was writing. Another 1st-grade student (Rena) utilized her dual lexicon by borrowing the words from English because she was unsure about the correct Korean spelling of the words. The other 1st-grader (Yuri) repeated her sentences in English after writing them in Korean because she wanted to ensure that the reader understood her writing. That is, there was evidence of written translanguaging into English by the 1st-graders because they were either not confident in their Korean writing or did not know the correct spellings of certain Korean words. In contrast, the 3rd-graders did not show any evidence that they borrowed linguistic resources from English in their Korean writing samples; instead, the 3rd-graders identified different linguistic features from the two languages by applying their sociolinguistic knowledge. The 3rd-graders demonstrated that they purposefully utilized their linguistic resources both from English and Korean as needed. The findings indicate that the 1st-graders' translanguaging for the sociolinguistic function might have been prompted unconsciously or instinctively, whereas the 3rd-graders' written translanguaging appeared to involve their self-awareness as they had different purposes for employing English in their Korean writing.

The 1st- and 3rd-grade English-proficient students presented their metalinguistic awareness in writing by distinguishing the spaces for writing in Korean versus in English. Most of the students' writing samples showed that they used Korean when they composed the bodies of the texts but wrote in English to describe their drawings using text labels. The students in both grades appeared to differentiate official from unofficial writing. However, the 1st-graders usually copied what they had written in English from their drawing spaces when composing their main texts in Korean; thus, their Korean writing repeatedly included English words. In contrast, the 3rd-graders did not copy or directly reproduce what they had written in English; rather, they rewrote the words in Korean for their main texts. In other words, although the 3rd-graders utilized their linguistic resources from English when providing text labels in the drawing spaces, they were more likely to stay in Korean when writing the bodies of the texts. The findings suggest that the 3rd-graders were becoming metalinguisitcally competent bilinguals as they were more cognizant about their language use in writing and able to distinguish different linguistic features from both languages.

Overall, the students' translanguaging findings in both grades imply that older students have developed a greater sociolinguistic understanding and metalinguistic awareness than younger students. It is, however, true that people develop sociolinguistic competence and metalinguistic awareness as they age (Palmer, David, & Fleming, 2014), which might inform the outcome that the students showed more sociolinguistic and metalinguistic advantages in 3rd grade.

Translanguaging practices by the Korean-proficient students

The Korean-proficient students (Nari, 1st-grader, and Mina, 3rd-grader) mainly uttered their responses in Korean when participating in the class discussions. For instance, Nari always spoke in Korean in the classroom except for the two cases—when repeating others' words that were delivered in English and when there were no corresponding words in Korean. However, both Nari and Mina chose to use English during recess to interact with their English-proficient peers. Their use of Korean and English suggests that they were able to move across the languages, considering the different settings (during in-class vs. recess) and inter-locutors (Korean language teacher vs. English-proficient bilingual peers). These findings demonstrate that Nari and Mina were using their meta-linguistic awareness to choose their languages accordingly and also present their sociolinguistic knowledge as they successfully communicated in both languages.

Analysis of Nari and Mina's writing samples revealed that they composed their writing primarily in Korean. Nari's writing samples presented only one incidence (for her English name) of translanguaging throughout all her writing pieces. When she introduced her English name in her diary entry, she employed transliteration (García, Johnson, & Seltzer, 2017) by applying her knowledge of English phonetics to write it using Korean letters. Although Nari included English proper nouns (e.g., her foreign friends' names, names of the places in the U.S. context) in her Korean writing, she transliterated all the English proper nouns into Korean. Thus, her writing samples exhibit only one case of direct translanguaging using English. This finding demonstrates that Nari was able to utilize her English phonological awareness and Korean ortho-graphical processing skills—learners' ability to form and access ortho-graphic representations, which are linked to print exposure (Stanovich & West, 1989)—when transliterating English words into Korean. Several researchers contend that bilingual individuals also translanguage when they employ their bilingualism to compose a monolingual text (García et al., 2017). Nari's transliteration examples substantiate García et al.'s (2017) claim as she translanguaged when she employed her bilingualism to compose monolingual texts.

Mina's (the 3rd-grader) writing samples displayed the occasional use of translanguaging. Mina's use of written translanguaging also displayed when she incorporated English proper nouns (e.g., her foreign friends' names, English book, or movie titles). However, unlike Nari, who employed transliterations for English proper nouns using Korean letters,

Mina directly included English words in her Korean sentences. Although Mina appeared to be a more Korean-dominant speaker than Nari (Mina had been in the U.S. for 2 years, while Nari was born in the U.S.), she was more likely to engage in translanguaging practices than Nari. From this finding, it appears that Nari seemed to be more conscious about her language use and understood that she should write in Korean as much as possible for the Korean school task; thus, she tried to put on her efforts to write all the words using Korean letters. Whereas Mina, the older student, might not have been advanced metalinguistic and cognitive processing skills (Bialystok, 2018; Palmer et al., 2014) than the younger student; thus, she might have been able to recognize when to use the particular language for different purposes and showed the ability to manipulate her languages accordingly through translanguaging. It is also plausible to imply that Mina's use of English and translanguaging might have been greatly influenced by her classmates in the classroom where English was prevalent by the English-proficient peers.

Longitudinal findings related to the focal 3rd-graders' language use

As a longitudinal study, the two focal 3rd-graders' (Toni and Julie) language use (Spring 2016) was compared to their previous language use when they were 1st-graders (Spring 2014). The comparison findings showed the patterns of their language use in 1st and 3rd grade and helped to understand whether and to what extent the 3rd-graders had developed their HL over the years. Close examination of Toni's and Julie's spoken and written language use in their 1st- and 3rd-grade classes revealed that there had been a decrease in their use of English but an increase in Korean. The different patterns and functions of their oral and written language use between their 1st and 3rd grade are discussed below.

Focal 3rd-grade Korean bilinguals' oral language use

In terms of their oral language use, both Toni and Julie often engaged in translanguaging (47% and 55%, respectively) and spoke more in English than in Korean in 1st grade (41% in English vs. 12% in Korean for Toni; 32% in English vs. 13% in Korean for Julie). Although their 3rd-grade language use revealed that they still engaged in translanguaging (40% and 43%, respectively), they spoke more in Korean than in English (51% in Korean vs. 9% in English for Toni; 49% in Korean vs. 8% in English for Julie). There was increased use of Korean and a decrease in their use of English in terms of their oral language use in the classroom (three times increase when using Korean and three times decrease when using English). The focal students' improved vocabulary knowledge in Korean is considered to be a factor in determining their increased use of their HL in 3rd grade. When both Toni and Julie were 1st-graders, they often translanguaged into English for unknown Korean words, but they demonstrated in 3rd grade that they had acquired the equivalent Korean words that they had not known as 1st-graders. Schmitt (2000) pointed out that vocabulary knowledge is considered as a critical tool for L2 learners because a limited vocabulary in L2 hinders successful communication. Emphasizing the importance of vocabulary acquisition, Schmitt argued, "lexical knowledge is central to communicative competence and to the acquisition of a second language" (p. 55). Similarly, Nation (2001) further explained the close relationship between vocabulary knowledge and language use by stating that vocabulary knowledge enables language use, and at the same time, language use leads to an increase in vocabulary knowledge. As the previous researchers proved, the focal 3rd-graders' increased vocabulary knowledge in HL appeared to be a significant factor for them to be able to maintain their conversation in Korean.

Beyond the frequency of their language use, the function of the focal third graders' translanguaging appeared to be different from their 1st-grade findings. The students' translanguaging in 1st grade often occurred when they borrowed lexical items from English for their unknown Korean words; thus, it functioned as an extension of their limited Korean vocabulary for the communicative purpose. On the other hand, their translanguaging in 3rd grade indicates that they used English purposefully for different purposes (e.g., to emphasize the meaning of their speech, to present their bilingual identity). Particularly, Julie's translanguaging was close to the concept of bilingual re-voicing (Gort & Sembiante, 2015) as she repeated the word ("nervous") in English that she had used in Korean. It was discussed that Julie restated her language through translanguaging to affirm and emphasize her intended meaning. Similarly, Toni's translanguaging also presented his bilingual identity since he intuitively chose the word ("meaning") in English in his Korean discourses. These findings indicate that both Julie and Toni utilized their metalinguistic awareness and metacognitive thinking as they purposefully selected the words in another language through translanguaging strategically for different purposes.

Focal 3rd-grade Korean bilinguals' written language use

Similar to the comparison findings in the focal 3rd-graders' oral language use, there was an increase of Korean and a decrease of English in their written language use. When Toni and Julie were 1st-graders, they often translanguaged while writing in Korean, and their translanguaging practices were observed both at word and sentence levels. It was revealed that more than half of their 1st-grade writing included English sentences (21% and 26% in Toni's and Julie's writing samples) in addition to their use of translanguaging at the word level (36% and 28%, respectively). On the other hand, both Toni and Julie as 3rd-graders predominantly wrote in Korean (91% and 92%, respectively). Although they occasionally incorporated English words into their Korean sentences (9% and 8% of word-level translanguaging, respectively), they did not entirely translanguaged into English sentences.

Comparison of their word-level translanguaging between the grades showed that when Toni and Julie were in 1st grade, they most frequently translanguaged into English for common nouns, verbs, and adjectives (e.g., cartoon, pretty, invite for each word category) that exist both in Korean and English. Whereas, their 3rd-grade findings showed that they translanguaged when there were no equivalent words in Korean (e.g., proper nouns in English such as their foreign friends' names). Similar to their oral language use findings, vocabulary knowledge appeared to play an important role in their writing performance in Korean. It is interesting to find that both Toni and Julie engaged in translanguaging practices between their receptive and productive skills of language as they read the text in Korean but provided their written retellings in English. When it comes to bilinguals' oral communication, it is considered as a common pattern that they orally provide their responses in their stronger language after listening to others in their weaker language. Although the language alternations between receptive and productive skills of languages are regarded as unique and rare practices regarding bilingual's literacy performance, the two focal students in this study engaged in translanguaging by moving across their languages for reading versus writing, and their written work in English demonstrated their Korean reading comprehension.

Analysis of their presentation of text labels in drawing spaces revealed the frequent use of translanguaging in both grades. Although Toni and Julie had developed their Korean writing skills by 3rd grade, they still employed English to describe their drawings, as they believed that providing text labels in drawing spaces was a less formal activity than writing the main text. Velasco and García (2014) reported a similar finding in their study that elementary-grade bilingual students delivered their written thoughts by using their two languages with drawings in their writing samples. Both findings indicate that emergent bilingual writers are able to use all the linguistic and semiotic repertoires (writing in both languages and drawing) by engaging in multimodal translanguaging practices (Busch, 2012; Durán, 2017).

In addition to the shift in the focal students' written language use and the development in their writing skills in Korean, Toni's and Julie's language preference when writing appeared to have shifted from English to Korean. Whenever they had an option to choose their language to write in their 1st-grade classroom, they always chose English first to initiate their composition. However, when they were in 3rd grade, they were able to deliver their thoughts and ideas using Korean consistently for their in-class writing and diary entries. These findings indicate that Toni and Julie as 1st-graders used to feel more comfortable writing in English than Korean, which might have led them to use more English than Korean during their writing in the 1st-grade classroom. However, their 3rd-grade written language use indicates that they were more likely to use Korean in the Korean HL school as they became older. This finding does not assure that they became more confident in writing in Korean than in English; however, it is predictable that they understood that they were supposed to write in Korean for their Korean HL school tasks. The shift in their writing performance could imply that they were able to develop their confidence in writing in Korean as they had expanded their Korean vocabulary and gradually increased their writing practices in Korean over the years.

Focal 3rd-grade Korean bilinguals' HL development over time

For the Korean students in the U.S., like Toni and Julie, there has been a pervasive hypothesis that their Korean might be jeopardized due to their minimum exposure to Korean and its reduced status in the U.S. as well as their rapid increase in English usage (Cha & Goldenberg, 2015; Murphy, 2014; Ro & Cheatham, 2009). Indeed, previous literature revealed that when emergent bilinguals attended all-English schools taught only in English, the students tended to experience HL shift or loss because they did not have much exposure and opportunity to develop their HL (Hinton, 2008; Montrul, 2018; Polinsky, 2018; Shin, 2010, 2014). However, the present study showed that the focal 3rd-graders who were attending all-English schools during the week did not lose their HL since they continued to use their HL at home and were able to improve Korean proficiency by interacting with other Korean speakers at the Korean HL school. The findings showed that Toni and Julie had improved their Korean (e.g., vocabulary development, oral proficiency, writing skills) between 1st and 3rd grade thanks to their family's and relatives' involvement and the influence of Korean media. The Korean teacher's (Mrs. Joen's) emphasis on using Korean in the 3rd-grade classroom also appeared to influence their increased use of Korean. In addition, both Toni and Julie had developed Korean courtesy manners as they appropriately used formal Korean (i.e., honorifics) and customary body gestures (e.g., bowing). Accordingly, their 3rd-grade Korean language further demonstrates their understanding and knowledge of cultural values and manners beyond their sociolinguistic competence in their HL.

Sociocultural influences on the Korean bilingual students' language use

Interviews with the 1st- and 3rd-grade students and their mothers as well as the journals reports by the focal mothers suggested that there were sociocultural influences on the students' language use and learning. The findings showed that there was a close relationship between the parents' attitudes toward HL education and the children's actual language use and literacy development. Among the parents of the four 1st-graders, Rena's parents were the most supportive of their child's English use and learning. For Rena's parents, learning English was obligatory, but Korean was an extra language for their children; thus, it was not mandatory for Rena to acquire perfect Korean proficiency. In contrast, Nari's parents believed that teaching HL to their children was of the greatest significance. Since the parents had positive perspectives towards raising Nari as a balanced bilingual, they not only greatly valued teaching Korean to Nari but also took their responsibility to teach her Korean as much as possible.

Indeed, from the 1st-graders' classroom language use, Nari was the student who rarely translanguaged into English but stayed predominantly in Korean when speaking (93%) and writing (99.5%) in the Korean HL classroom. On the other hand, Rena presented her oral and written responses most often in English. The parents' liberal views on Rena's English use and their common use of English at home might have influenced Rena to habitually translanguage into English when she spoke in the classroom. Researchers reported that supporting HL did not directly influence Korean children's school performance in the U.S.; thus, Korean immigrant parents showed more interest in developing their children's English than Korean (Shin, 2010, 2014). The findings from Rena's parents substantiate the previous research finding as the parents' emphasis on English was to assist Rena to adapt to the mainstream school and society (Hinton, 2008). However, as Nari's family revealed, Korean immigrant parents' positive attitudes often led their children to learn and develop Korean because these attitudes were more likely to influence the children's motivation to learn Korean at home (Lü & Koda, 2011; Shin, 2014; Song, 2016). The parents' perspectives and attitudes towards their children's HL education coincide with the analysis of the 1st-graders' language use in the HL classroom.

Similar to the 1st-graders' findings, parents' attitudes and practices played a pivotal role in the focal 3rd-graders' longitudinal language use between 1st and 3rd grade. Based on the parents' requests, both Toni's and Julie's home language use had shifted from English to Korean, and their HL language use and practices at home appear to result in their increased use of Korean when participating in the Korean HL classroom. The focal 3rd-graders' mothers had engaged in their children's language and literacy learning on a regular basis at home; they held Korean book reading time and Korean writing dictation tasks with their children on a regular base. The mothers believed that Korean book reading time had helped their children to develop their reading fluency and comprehension, and Korean dictation tests had assisted their children to improve their Korean vocabulary and spelling for writing. Aligned with Wong-Fillmore's earlier (1991) recommendation that immigrant parents provide adequate support in HL in the home setting for their children to learn and develop their HL, the home literacy practices that the focal 3rd-grade parents provided in this study played a vital role in scaffolding their children's HL development.

Beyond the parents' home practices and endeavors for their children's HL learning, there were other sociocultural factors that influenced both the 1st- and 3rd-grade students' language use. For example, for Joon's parents, the family's future residency, which would depend on the father's job prospects (either in U.S. or Korea) was an important factor for the parents to decide which language they need to put greater emphasis for their children's future success. In Rena's case, the parents' age of immigration (during their teenage years) as well as their fluency in English seemed to impact their home language use. Although the mother regarded their fluent English as an advantage and a beneficial tool for communication in her family, the parents' frequent use of English at home might have led Rena to use less Korean in her oral discourse.

Furthermore, the amount of interaction with other Korean relatives (e.g., grandparents) appeared to be another sociocultural factor that influenced the students' language use and learning. For instance, Nari often communicated with her grandparents who resided back in Korea using Skype, and the frequent amount of time that Nari talked to her grandparents seemed to provide her with opportunities to use and practice Korean. Similarly, the focal 3rd-graders, Toni and Julie, whose relatives (grandparents and aunt, respectively) from Korea had regularly visited their homes; thus, they continued to have opportunities to communicate with them by using Korean exclusively. This finding substantiates previous research findings that maintaining family ties with relatives (i.e., grandparents) motivated immigrant children to learn and maintain their HLs (Melo-Pfeifer, 2015; Park & Sarkar, 2007). For both Toni and Julie, their exposure to Korean media (television programs and songs) also appeared to impact their increased Korean language use over time. Researchers argued that immigrant children can be exposed to heritage culture through media, and their understanding of heritage culture can help them accelerate their HL learning (Hua & Wei, 2016). In addition, since both Toni and Julie voluntarily exposed themselves to Korean media, it is assumed that they had positive attitudes towards Korean culture, and this positive attitude might have encouraged them to foster their HL learning.

The existence of siblings and the age of siblings (older vs. younger) also appeared to be the factor that affected the bilingual children's language use and learning. All of the 1st-graders except Nari (who had a younger brother) had older siblings, while all of the 3rd-graders except Toni had younger siblings (Toni was an only child). The 1st-graders who had older siblings used more English with their older siblings because their older siblings tended to use more English when interacting with them. Past studies found that younger children who have older school-aged siblings often hear English because English is the language of peer interaction among school-aged children, and the older siblings bring English into bilingual homes (Bridges & Hoff, 2014; Fogle, 2013; Shin, 2014). Thus, older siblings might be the primary source of the social language (English) exposure and input for later-born children in bilingual homes, the existence and influence of older siblings could consequently lead to the diminution of HL use for younger siblings. Indeed, although all the 1st-graders in this study were second-generation Korean-Americans and were born in the U.S., the difference between their language use and proficiency (English proficient vs. Korean proficient) might have been influenced by the existence and age of their siblings as the three English-proficient students—Joon, Yuri, and Rena—had older siblings, but the Korean-proficient student, Nari, had a younger sibling.

Yet, research demonstrated that the rate of HL development is not as rapid in later-born children as in first-born children because parents who speak the HL are the main language input for older children, whereas younger children can often receive English input from their older siblings (Lee, 2013; Shin & Lee, 2013). Indeed, one of the 1st-graders (Nari) and all other 3rd-graders, who were first-born children in their homes, displayed that they used more Korean than the other later-born 1st-graders in this study. As discussed, there were a variety of sociocultural factors, including parents' supports and involvement, interaction with Korean relatives, exposure to Korean media, and the existence of and age of the siblings, in the bilingual students' language use and development.

Implications of the study

The findings of this study display how 1st- and 3rd-grade Korean emergent bilingual students used both Korean and English when they spoke and wrote in HL classrooms, where the language of instruction was in Korean. The findings revealed that the emergent bilingual students were able to use their entire language repertoires through translanguaging to successfully participate in verbal interactions and writing tasks. It was discovered that the amount of and functions of the students' translanguaging emerged differently in terms of the diverse contexts (e.g., age/grade level, immigration status, the influence of the teachers and parents). Considering these findings, I provide implications for researchers by addressing directions for future research in the fields of bilingual and biliteracy education. I then provide implications for educators and parents of emergent bilingual learners to better support their dual language and literacy learning.

Implications for researchers in bilingual/biliteracy education

Researchers have to understand that although the school provides instruction in one language, if the classroom teachers allow students to translanguage, the classroom can become a vibrant bilingual space where the students and teachers can display dynamic bilingualism that allows the students to use their entire language repertoires flexibly. The translanguaging findings in this study corroborate previous findings (e.g., Martínez-Roldán, 2015) that showed translanguaging is not solely a teacher's pedagogical approach or strategy to enhance bilingual children's instruction; rather, it is also the way that emergent bilingual students actually mediate their understanding and advance their learning. Thus, researchers should be aware that translanguaging practices can operate naturally and effortlessly in settings when bilinguals interact with one another.

Acknowledging the argument that translanguaging practices include how bilinguals utilize their language resources in their everyday interactions (García & Leiva, 2014), this research demonstrated how translanguaging occurs in homes and families (Dorner, Orellana, & Li-Grining, 2007; Song, 2016) beyond its presence in the classroom. It is important to keep in mind that translanguaging practices work as a vehicle for emergent bilingual children to expand their understanding and enrich their learning in both academic and non-academic settings (Hornberger, 2003). When researchers pay close attention to bilingual children's complex and rich linguistic experiences and resources at home as well as bilingual families' efforts to support their children's HL development, they can advocate and empower bilingual families' and their children's linguistic and cultural resources as valuable assets (Cummins & Persad, 2014; Gregory, Long, & Volk, 2004).

Despite a growing body of research on bilingual students' translanguaging practices, additional researchers need to examine how translanguaging is used by different types of emergent bilinguals (e.g., children in various grade levels whose languages are other than Spanish-English). By doing so, researchers can understand whether and how bilingual students from other language minority groups utilize their entire language and linguistic resources. Similarly, more research is needed to examine how translanguaging practices are presented in other instructional settings other than dual-language classrooms (López-Velásquez & García, 2017) to comprehend how teachers employ translanguaging practices in diverse classroom settings to enhance their bilingual students' understanding while learning. For instance, researchers need to investigate how HL teachers can use translanguaging as pedagogical strategies to improve their instruction for bilingual students' language and literacy learning (Jiang, García, & Willis, 2014). The findings will help researchers to better understand how to support translanguaging practices in HL classrooms without jeopardizing students' access to their HL. In this way, researchers can inform teachers of HL learners about how their translanguaging practices can provide the hybrid learning space and time for their students to use all their available language and linguistic resources in the classroom.

Researchers in bilingual education have contributed to this field of study by providing findings of bilingual children's use of their entire language repertoires to enhance their learning in academic settings (Durán & Palmer, 2014; Worthy, Durán, Hikida, Pruitt, & Peterson, 2013). Further study of bilingual children's translanguaging practices when writing beyond their use of oral translanguaging can provide much more understanding about what emergent bilingual writers do with their linguistic repertoires (Canagarajah, 2013; Durán, 2017; Velasco & García, 2014). In addition, it is worthwhile to investigate how teachers' translingual modeling (Durán, 2017) can scaffold emergent bilingual students' literacy practices and facilitate the dynamic practice of translanguaging in writing in classrooms. By focusing on the ways in which bilingual children participate in home- and community-based discourses through translanguaging, researchers can contribute to constructing the practices and pedagogies to expand emergent bilingual children's language and literacy repertoires and to develop bilingual instructional strategies for HL speakers to mediate learning ecologies. These directions for future research will help us to understand how to support bilingual children's overall language and literacy learning and development.

Given the sociopolitical contexts that surround HL and bilingual education (Melo-Pfeifer, 2015), teachers of bilingual students need to realize that pedagogies based on language separation could easily marginalize students' HLs. When teachers welcome what bilingual students already know about their language use and value them as competent bilinguals, then they can create instructional spaces that assist students to draw on their bilingual resources. Teachers of language minority students should motivate their students to use their HLs strategically in the classroom so that the students can maintain and further develop their HLs instead of losing theirs. HL teachers need to understand that one way to advance bilingual students' HL learning is to provide them with positive HL learning experiences (Song, 2016) by strategically employing and facilitating their own and their students' translanguaging. As shown in this study, although the 3rd-grade teacher did not encourage translanguaging, the 3rd-graders utilized their full language resources as much as they needed to engage in class discussions and literacy activities. This finding suggests that HL teachers should encourage their HL bilingual students to engage in translanguaging practices when they verbally communicate and participate in writing tasks. Educators should also know that they can scaffold bilingual students' translanguaging and translingual practices by modeling so that the students can naturally engage in the dynamic practice of translanguaging in the classroom.

It is imperative for teachers of bi/multilingual students to not emphasize English only in the classroom but to be open towards multilingualism (Piccardo, 2013). By doing so, teachers can appreciate and value the students' diverse linguistic and cultural assets, which would help them accept bilingual students' hybrid and dynamic language practices. In addition, teachers must move beyond the mere acceptance of translanguaging to create a supportive classroom environment in which students can be comfortable using their language(s) as they participate in collaborative discussions. By providing spaces and times in the classroom in which bilingualism is modeled and encouraged, teachers can also purposefully promote dynamic bilingualism (Flores & Schissel, 2014). As García and Sylvan (2011) defined translanguaging as "the process by which bilingual students and teachers engage in complex discursive practices to make sense of, and communicate in, multilingual classrooms" (p. 389), teachers of bilingual students have to keep in mind that bilingualism occurs when teachers and students negotiate and mediate their learning together.

Because the use of translanguaging in the HL and bilingual classrooms is a relatively new concept, it is recommended that HL instructors, bilingual teachers, and researchers collaborate on how to model, encourage, and teach students to employ translanguaging as they further develop their home and school languages.

Implications for immigrant parents of emergent bilinguals

Immigrant parents whose children are emergent bilinguals of HL learners should acknowledge that they play a vital role in their children's HL maintenance and development. This study showed that when the parents had positive attitudes towards their children's HL language, the children were more likely to use Korean at home and develop it over the years. The findings indicated that the emergent bilingual students were more or less exposed to and practiced their HL depending on their parents' attitude and perspective toward their children's language use and learning. Hence, parents of emergent bilingual children should encourage the use of HL at home and provide diverse opportunities for their children to make use of it if they want their children to improve their HL.

In terms of oral proficiency development, parents should encourage their children to use their HL at the conversational level with their family members at home. As this study showed, immigrant parents should understand that communicating with other family relatives from the origin of the country can provide an opportunity for their children to learn and practice their HL. Parents can also promote their children's literacy skills in HL by providing a variety of reading materials and spending reading and writing time with their children together. In addition, as this study exhibited the positive impact of media in HL learning, parents can provide songs, television programs, or video resources in HL so that their children are more likely to be motivated in developing HL from their positive learning experiences.

References

Bialystok, E. (2018). Bilingual education for young children: Review of the effects and consequences. *International Journal of Bilingual Education and Bilingualism, 21*(6), 666–679.

Bridges, K., & Hoff, E. (2014). Older sibling influences on the language environment and language development of toddlers in bilingual homes. *Applied Psycholinguist, 35*(2), 225–241.

Busch, B. (2012). The linguistic repertoire revisited. *Applied Linguistics, 33*(5), 503–523.

Canagarajah, A. S. (Ed.). (2013). *Literacy as translingual practice: Between communities and schools.* New York, NY: Routledge.

Canale, M., & Swain, M. (1980). Theoretical bases of communicative approaches to second language teaching and testing. *Applied Linguistics, 1*, 1–47.

Cha, K., & Goldenberg, C. (2015). The complex relationship between home language proficiency and kindergarten children's Spanish and English oral proficiencies. *Journal of Educational Psychology, 107*(4), 935–953.

Cummins, J., & Persad, R. (2014). Teaching through a multilingual lens: The evolution of EAL Policy and Practice in Canada. *Education Matters, 2*, 3–40.

Dorner, L. M., Orellana, M. F., & Li-Grining, C. P. (2007). "I helped my mom," and it helped me: Translating the skills of language brokers into improved standardized test scores. *American Journal of Education, 113*(3), 451–478.

Durán, L. (2017). Audience and young bilingual writers: Building on strengths. *Journal of Literacy Research, 49*(1), 92–114.

Durán, L., & Palmer, D. (2014). Pluralist discourses of bilingualism and translanguaging talk in classrooms. *Journal of Early Childhood Literacy, 14*, 367–388.

Edelsky, C. (1986). *Writing in a bilingual program: Había una vez.* Norwood, NJ: Ablex.

Flores, N., & Schissel, J. L. (2014). Dynamic bilingualism as the norm: Envisioning a heteroglossic approach to standards-based reform. *TESOL Quarterly, 48*(3), 454–479.

Fogle, L. W. (2013). Parental ethnotheories and family language policy in transnational adoptive families. *Language Policy, 12*(1), 83–102.

García, O., & Sylvan, C. (2011). Pedagogies and practices in multilingual classrooms: Singularities in pluralities. *The Modern Language Journal, 95*(3), 385–400.

García, O., & Leiva, L. (2014). Theorizing and enacting translanguaging for social justice. In A. Blackledge & A. Creese (Eds.), *Heteroglossia as practice and pedagogy* (Vol. 20, pp. 199–216). Heidelberg, Germany: Springer.

García, O., Johnson, S., & Seltzer, K. (2017). *The translanguaging classroom. Leveraging student bilingualism for learning.* Philadelphia, PA: Caslon.

Gibbons, J. (1987). *Code-mixing and code-choice: A Hong Kong case study.* Clevedon, UK: Multilingual Matters.

Gort, M. (2008). "You give me idea!": Collaborative strides toward bilingualism and biliteracy in a two-way partial immersion program. *Multicultural Perspectives, 10*(4), 192–200.

Gort, M. (2012). Evaluation and revision processes of young bilinguals in a dual language program. In E. B. Bauer & M. Gort (Eds.), *Early biliteracy development: Exploring young learners' use of their linguistic resources* (pp. 90–110). New York, NY: Routledge.

Gort, M., & Sembiante, S. (2015). Navigating hybridized language learning spaces through translanguaging pedagogy: Dual language preschool teachers' languaging practices in support of emergent bilingual children's performance of academic discourse. *International Multilingual Research Journal, 9*(1), 7–25.

Gregory, E., Long, S., & Volk, D. (2004). *Many pathways to literacy: Learning with siblings, peers, grandparents, and in community settings.* London, UK: Routledge.

Hinton, L. (2008). Trading tongues: Loss of heritage languages in the United States. In A. Reyes & A. Lo (Eds.). *Beyond Yellow English: Toward a linguistic anthropology of Asian Pacific America* (pp. 331–346). Oxford University Press.

Hornberger, N. H. (Ed.) (2003). *Continua of biliteracy: An ecological framework for educational policy, research and practice in multilingual settings.* Clevedon, UK: Multilingual Matters.

Hua, Z., & Wei, L. (2016). Transnational experience, aspiration and family language policy. *Journal of Multilingual and Multicultural Development, 37*(7), 655–666.

Jiang, Y. B., García, G. E., & Willis, A. I. (2014). Code-mixing as a bilingual instructional strategy. *Bilingual Research Journal, 37*(3), 311–326.

Jonsson, K. (2013). Translanguaging and multilingual literacies: Diary-based case studies of adolescents in an international school. *International Journal of the Sociology of Language, 224*, 85–117.

Lanauze, M., & Snow, C. E. (1989). The relation between first and second language writing skills: Evidence from Puerto Rican elementary school children in bilingual programs. *Linguistics and Education, 1*(4), 323–339.

Lee, B. Y. (2013). Heritage language maintenance and cultural identity formation: The case of Korean immigrant parents and their children in the USA. *Early Child Development and Care, 183*(11), 1576–1588.

López-Velásquez, A. M., & García, G. E. (2017). The bilingual reading practices and performance of two Hispanic 1st-graders. *Bilingual Research Journal, 40*(3), 246–261.

Lü, C., & Koda, K. (2011). The impact of home language and literacy support on English- Chinese biliteracy acquisition among Chinese heritage language learners. *Heritage Language Journal, 8*, 119–231.

Martínez, R. A., Hikida, M., & Durán, L. (2015). Unpacking ideologies of linguistic purism: How dual language teachers make sense of everyday translanguaging. *International Multilingual Research Journal, 9*(1), 26–42.

Martínez-Roldán, C. M. (2015). Translanguaging practices as mobilization of linguistic resources in a Spanish/English bilingual after-school program: An analysis of contradictions. *International Multilingual Research Journal*, 9(1), 43–58.

Melo-Pfeifer, S. (2015). The role of the family in heritage language use and learning: Impact on heritage language policies. *International Journal of Bilingual Education and Bilingualism*, 18(1), 26–44.

Montrul, S. A. (2018). Heritage language development: Connecting the dots. *International Journal of Bilingualism*, 22(5), 530–546.

Murphy, V. (2014). *Second language learning in the early school years: Trends and contexts*. Oxford: Oxford University Press.

Nation, I. S. P. (2001). *Learning vocabulary in another language*. Cambridge: Cambridge University Press.

Palmer, E., David, A., & Fleming, S. (2014). Effects of age on metacognitive efficiency. *Consciousness and Cognition*, 28, 151–160.

Park, S. M., & Sarkar, M. (2007). Parents' attitudes toward heritage language maintenance for their children and their efforts to help their children maintain the heritage language: A case study of Korean-Canadian immigrants. *Language, Culture and Curriculum*, 20(3), 223–235.

Piccardo, E. (2013). Plurilingualism and curriculum design: Toward a synergic vision. *TESOL Quarterly*, 47(3), 600–614.

Polinsky, M., (2018). Bilingual children and adult heritage speakers: The range of comparison. *International Journal of Bilingualism*, 22(5) 547–563.

Jørgensen, J. N., & Holmen, A. (Eds.). (1997). *The development of successive bilingualism in school-age children. Copenhagen Studies in Bilingualism*, 27. Copenhagen: Royal Danish School of Educational Studies.

Ro, Y. E., & Cheatham, G. A. (2009). Biliteracy and bilingual development in a second- generation Korean child: A case study. *Journal of Research in Childhood Education*, 23, 290–308.

Sayer, P. (2013). Translanguaging, TexMex, and bilingual pedagogy: Emergent bilinguals learning through the vernacular. *TESOL Quarterly*, 47(1), 63–88.

Schmitt, N. (2000). *Vocabulary in language teaching*. Cambridge: Cambridge University Press.

Shin, S. J. (2010). "What about me? I'm not like Chinese but I'm not like American.": Heritage language learning and identity of mixed heritage adults. *The Journal of Language, Identity, and Education*, 9(3), 203–219.

Shin, S. J. (2014). Language learning as culture keeping: Family language policies of transnational adoptive parents. *International Multilingual Research Journal*, 8(3), 189–207.

Shin, S. J., & Lee, J. S. (2013). Expanding capacity, opportunity, and desire to learn Korean as a heritage language. *Heritage Language Journal*, 10(3), 64–73.

Song, K. (2016). "Okay, I will say in Korean and then in American": Translanguaging practices in bilingual homes. *Journal of Early Childhood Literacy*, 16(1), 84–106.

Stanovich, K. E., & West, R. F. (1989). Exposure to print and orthographic processing. *Reading Research Quarterly*, 24(4), 402–433.

Swain, M. (1998). Focus on form through conscious reflection. In C. Doughty & J. Williams (Eds.), *Focus on form in classroom second language acquisition* (pp. 64–81). Cambridge: Cambridge University Press.

Velasco, P., & García, O. (2014). Translanguaging and the writing of bilingual learners. *Bilingual Research Journal*, *37*(1), 6–23.

Vygotsky, L. S. (1978). *Mind in society: The development of higher psychological processes*. Cambridge, MA: Harvard University Press.

Wei, L. (2018). Translanguaging as a practical theory of language. *Applied Linguistics*, *39*(1), 9–30.

Wong-Fillmore, L. W. (1991). When learning a second language means losing the first. *Early Childhood Research Quarterly*, *6*(3), 323–347.

Worthy, J., Durán, L., Hikida, M., Pruitt, A., & Peterson, K. (2013). Spaces for dynamic bilingualism in read-aloud discussions: Developing and strengthening bilingual and academic skills. *Bilingual Research Journal*, *36*(3), 311–328.

Appendices

Appendix A Frequency of 1st-graders' oral translanguaging for each function

	Word-level translanguaging (English words in Korean speech)	Word-level translanguaging (Korean words in English speech)	Translanguaging at sentence level (from Korean to English)	Translanguaging at sentence level (from English to Korean)	Total
Sociolinguistic knowledge					
Joon	177		11	6	194 (49%)
Yuri	157		12	4	173 (48%)
Rena	124		21	3	148 (57%)
Nari	22		0	3	25 (50%)
Metalinguistic awareness					
Joon	115		9		124 (32%)
Yuri	123		8		131 (36%)
Rena	67		2		69 (27%)
Nari	10		4		14 (28%)
Metacognitive insight					
Joon			25	16	41 (10%)
Yuri			11	13	24 (7%)
Rena			14	11	25 (10%)
Nari			4	3	7 (14%)
Sociocultural knowledge					
Joon		32		2	34 (9%)
Yuri		29		2	31 (9%)
Rena		13		3	16 (6%)
Nari		4		0	4 (8%)

Appendix B Frequency of 1st-graders' written translanguaging for each function

	Word-level translanguaging (English words in Korean sentences)	Word-level translanguaging (Korean words in English sentences)	Translanguaging at sentence level (from Korean to English)	Translanguaging at sentence level (from English to Korean)	Total
Sociolinguistic knowledge					
Joon	22		0	0	22 (50%)
Yuri	30		4	0	34 (64%)
Rena	28		9	4	41 (70%)
Nari	1		0	0	1 (50%)
Metalinguistic awareness					
Joon	17		0		17 (41%)
Yuri	13		3		16 (30%)
Rena	12		3		15 (25%)
Nari	1		0		1 (50%)
Metacognitive insight					
Joon	0	1			1 (2%)
Yuri	1	0			1 (2%)
Rena	0	0			0
Nari	0	0			0
Sociocultural knowledge					
Joon	2				2 (7%)
Yuri	2				2 (4%)
Rena	3				3 (5%)
Nari	0				0

Appendix C Frequency of 3rd-graders' oral translanguaging for each function

	Word-level translanguaging (English words in Korean speech)	Word-level translanguaging (Korean words in English speech)	Translanguaging at sentence level (from Korean to English)	Translanguaging at sentence level (from English to Korean)	Total
Sociolinguistic knowledge					
Toni	89		12	10	111 (63%)
Julie	106		9	11	126 (61%)
Suji	83		14	7	104 (60%)
Mina	17		2	5	24 (73%)
Metalinguistic awareness					
Toni	49		6		55 (31%)
Julie	64		4		68 (33%)
Suji	48		7		55 (32%)
Mina	5		3		8 (24%)
Metacognitive insight					
Toni			1		1 (1%)
Julie			0		0
Suji			0		0
Mina			0		0
Sociocultural knowledge					
Toni		8		1	9 (5%)
Julie		9		2	11 (6%)
Suji		11		2	13 (8%)
Mina		0		1	1 (3%)

Appendix D Frequency of 3rd-graders' written translanguaging for each function

	Word-level translanguaging (English words in Korean sentences)	Word-level translanguaging (Korean words in English sentences)	Translanguaging at sentence level (from Korean to English)	Translanguaging at sentence level (from English to Korean)	Total
Sociolinguistic knowledge					
Toni	13				13 (50%)
Julie	21				21 (51%)
Suji	29				29 (54%)
Mina	10				10 (32%)
Metalinguistic awareness					
Toni	11		0		11 (42%)
Julie	17		0		17 (40%)
Suji	17		3		20 (37%)
Mina	21		0		21 (68%)
Metacognitive insight					
Toni	1				1 (4%)
Julie	0				0
Suji	0				0
Mina	0				0
Sociocultural knowledge					
Toni		1			1 (4%)
Julie		4			4 (9%)
Suji		5			5 (9%)
Mina		0			0

Index